POLITICAL SATIRE
IN THE
AMERICAN REVOLUTION,
1763-1783

Political Satire

IN THE

American Revolution,

1763-1783

By Bruce Ingham Granger

Department of English, University of Oklahoma

Cornell University Press

ITHACA, NEW YORK

PRINTED IN THE UNITED STATES OF AMERICA
BY THE VAIL-BALLOU PRESS, INC.

To Rosemary

PREFACE

In the period of the American Revolution the colonies as a whole awakened to literary self-consciousness for the first time. Although native drama was still in its infancy and fiction not yet born, the literature of these years, surveyed by Moses Coit Tyler in his still valuable *Literary History of the American Revolution*, reveals vigor and excellence throughout a wide range of genres familiar to the eighteenth century. An essential branch of this literature, scarcely better known today than when Tyler blazed the way long ago, is political satire. While literary and social historians have long recognized that personalities, issues, and events of the Revolution were held up to ridicule at the time, the present study is the first to explore this satirical record in detail. The focus throughout is on American aspects of the period 1763–1783, both intercolonial and international; so it is that most of the satires herein considered were written by Americans for Americans, so also that those treating of matters largely provincial or European in their implications are excluded. I have let the satires themselves tell this not-so-familiar story of the Revolution, providing only as much history as seemed necessary to make their meaning clear and give continuity to the narrative. Because satire is first and always a literary mode, the opening chapter defines it, sets these satires in the proper literary environment, and examines their generic range. Thereafter, brief evaluations of some of the pieces that possess distinct literary merit are introduced into the story that unfolds.

The 530 satires of the period 1763–1783 which form the basis of this study are to be found in the files of American newspapers and magazines, in broadsides, pamphlets, and manuscripts, and also in the *Scots Magazine* and the *Gentleman's Magazine*, which were searched at the Brown, Cornell, Harvard, William and Mary, and Yale libraries; the historical societies of Maryland, Massachusetts, New York, Pennsylvania, Rhode Island, and Wisconsin; the public libraries of Baltimore, Boston, New York, and Philadelphia; and the American Antiquarian Society, Boston Athenaeum, John Carter Brown Library, Charleston Library Society, Library Company of Philadelphia, Library of Congress, Newberry Library, and Virginia State Library. Although I cannot, of course, claim to have discovered every satire printed (or written) in America during these twenty years, those located seem broadly representative. Fewer than half of these satires actually appear in the course of this story. Many are inferior as literature, others are redundant, still others would have required a disproportionate amount of history to explain. Generally speaking, each satire is introduced at the appropriate point in its entirety rather than several times and fragmented. In order to convey the flavor of the original as faithfully as possible, quotations have not been altered even when orthography, punctuation, and syntax are questionable.

The terms "patriot" and "loyalist" describe the major division within the American community; since the line separating patriot from loyalist was not sharply drawn until 1774, the phrase "government party" designates those forces in America that cooperated with the Ministry before that date. "Ministerial" and "antiministerial" characterize those within the British community who supported and opposed the Ministry.

Of the many who have given assistance I owe a special debt to Professors John R. Alden, Merrill Jensen, and Harold W. Thompson for their helpful criticism as the manuscript took shape; to the American Antiquarian Society for a grant-in-aid in the summer of 1955; to the Faculty Research Committee of the University of Oklahoma for largely defraying travel and clerical expenses; and to the staffs of the libraries named above for their unfailing courtesy. Finally, I am grateful to the editors of *American Literature* and *American Quarterly* for permission to use the material which appeared in my articles, "Hudibras in the American Revolution" (*Am. Lit.*, XXVII [1956], 499–508) and "The Stamp Act in Satire" (*Am. Quar.*, VIII [1956], 368–384).

BRUCE INGHAM GRANGER

Norman, Oklahoma
December 1959

CONTENTS

POLITICAL SATIRE

IN THE

AMERICAN REVOLUTION,

1763-1783

CHAPTER I

The Literary Scene

"THE true end of satire," says Dryden, "is the amendment
of vices by correction." "The poet is bound, and that *ex officio*,
to give his reader some one precept of moral virtue, and to caution him against some one particular vice or folly." [1] This conviction, that the satirist should attack vice and promote virtue,
was voiced no less insistently in Revolutionary America than in
Augustan England. "A satirist of true genius, who is warmed by
a generous indignation against vice, and whose censures are conducted by candor and truth," writes one American, "merits the
applause of every friend of virtue." [2] It is safe to say that in the
eighteenth century the Anglo-American community regarded
the satirist as *Censor Morum*.

This community, moreover, regarded as most successful that
satire which served the cause of virtue by ridiculing irrationality
and error. In what might stand as an apologia for the satires that
comprise the present study the loyalist author of "The American
Times" (1779) sounds this Juvenalian note: "The Masters of
reason have decided, that when doctrines and practices have been

[1] *The Poetical Works of Dryden*, ed. G. R. Noyes (Boston, 1909), pp.
109, 318.
[2] From a commonplace book of "The Occasional Writer," *New American Magazine* (Woodbridge, N.J.), I (1759), 430, quoted in Agnes
Sibley, *Alexander Pope's Prestige in America, 1752–1835* (New York,
1949), p. 87.

fairly examined, and proved to be contrary to truth, and injurious to society, then and not before may ridicule be lawfully employed in the service of virtue. This is exactly the case of the grand American rebellion: it has been weighed in the balance and found wanting; able writers have exposed its principles, its conduct, and its final aim. Reason has done her part, and therefore this is the legitimate moment for satire." From such a statement it may be concluded that, as amendment is the aim of satire, ridicule is the general method. William Hazlitt observes that the ridiculous "is that which is contrary not only to custom but to sense and reason, or is a voluntary departure from what we have a right to expect from those who are conscious of absurdity and propriety in words, looks, and actions," and that as such it "is properly the province of satire." [3] In ridiculing his object, however, the writer should, in the words of Swift, "beware of letting the pathetic part swallow up the rational," for unless he strives to disguise the nature and extent of his emotional involvement his work will fall short of satire.[4]

Satire itself is here defined as an indirect, a disguised verbal attack on persons or things. This indirection the satirist achieves by conforming to one of three basic rhetorical patterns—invective, burlesque, or irony—or, what is sometimes the case, by a combination of these.[5] Indirection ensures a delayed response on the part of the reader, and as satire progresses from invective to burlesque to irony this delay is ever greater. Invective, precisely because it denotes abuse, depends heavily on metaphor, simile, and other tropes to achieve indirection. Freneau's *British Prison Ship* (1780), though often called a satire, attacks its object too directly to be invective even. In the lines,

> Weak as I am, I'll try my strength to-day
> And my best arrows at these hell-hounds play,

[3] *The Complete Works of William Hazlitt* (London and Toronto, 1930–1934), VI, 8.

[4] *The Works of Jonathan Swift* (London, 1883), VIII, 206.

[5] David Worcester sets up this general classification in *The Art of Satire* (Cambridge, Mass., 1940).

> To future years one scene of death prolong,
> And hang them up to infamy, in song,

the author admits what all but a few passages in this long poem confirm, that he is too involved in his recent experiences aboard the "Scorpion" and the "Hunter" to stand off and disguise his attack.[6] In view of the fact that most of the writers in Revolutionary America were long on indignation and some of them short on talent, it should not be surprising that three political satires out of four are predominantly invective. Burlesque and irony, on the other hand, require not merely that the writer employ tropes but that he keep a tight rein on the whole composition. Burlesque distorts its object by creating an incongruity between matter and manner. Irony inverts its object through verbal and situational paradox.

I

Political satire is addressed to the "great public," social satire to the "little." The high-church, monarchial argument of *Hudibras,* coming in the backwash of the English Civil War, was listened to by all sorts and conditions of men throughout the kingdom, whereas the varieties of pride exposed in *The Rape of the Lock* amused a knowing London audience. Not only does the political satirist seek a national hearing, his rhetoric is often cruder and of greater reach than that of the social satirist. Among the most successful of the handful of political satires published in pre-Revolutionary America are John Wise's *The Churches Quarrel Espoused* (1710), a reply to the growing Presbyterian community in New England; *Androboros, a Biographical Farce in Three Acts* (1714), attributed to Governor Robert Hunter (and Lewis Morris?) of New York, an attack on the Council and lieutenant-governor; *The History of Colonel Nathaniel Bacon's Rebellion in Virginia* (1731), a Hudibrastic poem at-

[6] *The Poems of Philip Freneau,* ed. F. L. Pattee (Princeton, 1902), II, 25. Hereafter referred to as Pattee.

tributed to Ebenezer Cook, written in ridicule of Bacon and praise of Governor Berkeley; *A True and Historical Narrative of Georgia* (1741), a tirade by Patrick Tailfer and others against Governor Oglethorpe; Joseph Green's *Entertainment for a Winter's Evening* (1750), an account in Hudibrastics of a Masonic meeting in Boston; and Nicholas Scull's *Kawanio Che Keeteru* (1756), a Hudibrastic attack on those Pennsylvania Quakers who opposed putting the province in a posture of defense at the time of the French and Indian War. Down to this time the record is indeed scant, but the furor over stamped paper which arose shortly heralded an age of satire.

In the January, 1779, issue of the *United States Magazine* young Hugh Henry Brackenridge addressed his subscribers with a rush of patriotic enthusiasm:

The British officers who are, some of them, men of understanding, on perusal of our pamphlets in the course of the debate, and the essays and dissertations in the news-papers, have been forced to acknowledge, not without chagrin, that the rebels, as they are pleased to call us, had some *d–mn'd* good writers on their side of the question, and that we had fought them no less successfully with the pen than with the sword. We hope to convince them yet more fully, that we are able to cultivate the *belles-lettres*, even disconnected with Great-Britain; and that liberty is of so noble and energetic a quality, as even from the bosom of a war to call forth the powers of human genius, in every course of literary fame and improvement.

Although it, too, was deserving of praise, partisanship required that Brackenridge keep silent about loyalist literature. Granted that the sustained growth of a vigorous national literature lay half a century ahead, the literary record of the Revolution is nonetheless impressive. This time of upheaval afforded men of ability an opportunity to declare their literary as well as political independence. From the first years of the century Americans had been exposed to current English literature, on the bookstalls and in the almanacs, newspapers, and magazines. Michael Kraus has observed that while "it was a sign of good taste to choose the best literature available on which to model their own, . . . [what] was deplorable was the slavish adherence of American writers even in the matter of materials, for they seemed utterly oblivious to their native wealth." [7] Writers of the Revolutionary period explored new forms and indigenous material more courageously than their immediate predecessors. As it happened, though, this literary self-consciousness proved abortive; the postwar generation showed itself too respectful once again of English models and, what was worse, oversensitive to English critical opinion.

The colonial press moved gradually toward freedom from censorship. Livingston R. Schuyler observes that while greater freedom existed in New England than in the South, "in no colony would the Governor, as representing the Crown, permit a criticism of its actions to pass without censure, and, if possible, punishment." [8] Toward a freer press the Zenger case of 1735 settled "the right of juries to find a general verdict in libel cases." [9] So it was that when Governor Bernard tried to get a libel indictment against Edes and Gill's *Boston Gazette* in 1768 for attacks on himself and Chief Justice Hutchinson, the grand jury refused and the Massachusetts Assembly declared that "the Liberty of the Press is a great Bulwark of the Liberty of the People: It is therefore the incumbent Duty of those who are constituted the Guardians of the People's Rights to defend and maintain it." [10]

The year 1765 found the American press, unanimous in its opposition to the Stamp Act, aware for the first time how greatly it might help shape political opinion at home and abroad. In the years ahead editors like Brackenridge, Freneau, Gaine, Mein, Paine, Rivington, and Towne, less respectful of governor and

[7] *Wm. & Mary Quar.*, ser. 3, I (1944), 233.

[8] *Magazine of History* (Tarrytown, N.Y.), II (1905), 325.

[9] *Ibid.*, p. 380.

[10] Quoted in Clyde A. Duniway, *The Development of Freedom of the Press in Massachusetts* (New York, 1906), p. 127.

Crown than their predecessors had been, possessing a "continent-wide view of affairs," would assume this responsibility as the flood of periodical, broadside, and pamphlet literature mounted.[11] Coincident with this change in policy, even though "only about half the men and only one quarter of the women" in America could read, the people, as distinct from the professional and mercantile classes who had long been subscribers, began to give the press greater support.[12]

The newspaper in America, that "general source throughout the nation, / Of every modern conversation," exerted an influence second only to the Bible and the almanac.[13] Seven Revolutionary satires out of ten appeared originally in the newspapers. Frequently these were reprinted from London papers; occasionally the converse took place. The remaining satires were first printed as broadsides or pamphlets or appeared in contemporary magazines. None of these other media, however, reached nearly so wide an audience.

The authorship of only one-third of these satires can be ascertained. The most important of the patriot satirists are Benjamin Franklin, Philip Freneau, Francis Hopkinson, William Livingston, John Trumbull, Mercy Warren, and John Witherspoon; of the loyalist, Jacob Bailey, Jonathan Odell, and Joseph Stansbury; and of English satirists in America, John André and Charles Lee. It goes almost without saying that loyalist and English satirists were generally men of property and standing. What may not be so well known, many of the patriot satirists were similarly prominent.[14] Thus it happens that Robert Munford and John Trumbull attack radical patriots as vigorously as they do

[11] Arthur M. Schlesinger, *Prelude to Independence: The Newspaper War on Britain, 1764–1776* (New York, 1958), pp. 57–58.

[12] Philip Davidson, *Propaganda and the American Revolution* (Chapel Hill, 1941), p. 209; Schuyler, *Magazine of History*, II, 379–380.

[13] "The News-Paper," *New-York Gazette*, Apr. 16, 1770, p. 2.

[14] Davidson, *Propaganda*, p. 3, describes patriot propagandists as in the main "substantial, propertied people, people of standing in their communities," a generalization that is valid for the satirists in particular.

loyalists and Britons. Confronted with an ever-shifting civil and
military scene, most of the satirists composed in haste and found
little time to revise; the notable exception is Trumbull, whose
M'Fingal was written at intervals over a seven-year period. From
the Juvenalian verse of Freneau and Odell through Trumbull's
and Bailey's Rabelaisian caricatures to the seeming geniality of
Hopkinson and the Swiftian bite of Franklin, this body of satire
runs the rhetorical spectrum.

One cannot measure the accomplishment of these satirists
justly unless he keeps steadily in view the neoclassical environment in which they lived and wrote. Fundamental to the theory,
if not always the practice, of neoclassicism is an insistence on
what Arthur Lovejoy calls aesthetic uniformitarianism. "The
artist is simply the spokesman of the reason, and it is exclusively
to the reason in other men that he must appeal; and 'reason' here
is not chiefly synonymous with intellect and antithetic to feeling—which, indeed, it may include—but is a name for that which
is fundamental and constant in the generic constitution of man." [15]
That is to say, the neoclassical point of view is social in its
orientation, holding that literature should strive first of all to
be decorous. What is important here, this concern for decorum
gave rise to the concept of genres, according to which literature
in general, and poetry in particular, readily subdivides into certain acceptable classical and nonclassical traditions. This concept underlies Addison's famous discussion of true and false wit.
Whereas false wit admits such bastard species as the acrostic,
rebus, anagram, and pun, true wit fathers only the traditional.
"The Genius of *Heroic Poetry*," writes Addison, surveying
those that follow in the train of Truth and Wit, "appeared with
a Sword in her Hand, and a Lawrel on her Head. *Tragedy* was
crowned with a Cypress, and covered with Robes dipped in
Blood. *Satyr* had Smiles in her Look, and a Dagger under her
Garment. *Rhetorick* was known by her Thunderbolt; and
Comedy by her Mask" (*Spectator*, No. 63). Even in Addison's

[15] *Mod. Phil.*, XXIX (1932), 291–292.

day, though, the satiric spirit in England and America had become so diffuse as to burst out of such formal confines, and as the century advanced forms evolved that lay beyond the pale. The political turmoil in Revolutionary America seems to have encouraged more and varied experimentation than occurred in England during the same period, this even though most Americans honored neoclassical precepts.

Although eighteenth-century American literature was powerfully influenced by current English practice, the number of works which are neoclassic in both form and thought is relatively small. The Revolutionary generation, as it happened, came of age at a time when English neoclassicism was making its heaviest impact on the American mind; yet even Bailey, Brackenridge, Franklin, Freneau, Hopkinson, Odell, Paine, and Trumbull, whose work during these years is heavily neoclassic, sometimes found their ideas yeasting over and the traditional molds which would have contained them earlier in need of modification. Thus Franklin made the letter to the press into a more flexible vehicle for satire than his English contemporary "Junius," and Freneau in his Hudibrastic verse tapped the potentialities of the anapest to an extent that would have surprised even Jonathan Swift. Still, the work of these Revolutionary satirists can be described as neoclassic in the main.

II

While the concept of genres continued to influence the range of American literature well into the nineteenth century, the proliferation of forms as early as the Revolutionary period would have bewildered Addison. Nevertheless, a sizable majority of the satires in the present work are cast in traditional forms: heroic and Hudibrastic couplets, songs and ballads, farce and melodrama, the periodical essay, and the letter to the press.

No form was more highly honored at this time and none more frequently practised than the heroic couplet, the conventional measure for the heroic play, epistle, verse essay, and verse satire. Fashioned into an efficient literary instrument by Dryden, it was further refined by Pope, who practically discarded the Alexandrine and the triplet and tightened the closed couplet by making extensive use of such rhetorical devices as balance and antithesis. Both poets were much admired and their example often emulated by writers of the Revolution, but a more immediate model was Charles Churchill, whose works were soon reprinted in America.[16] By employing such devices as repetition and apostrophe more frequently than his predecessors had done, Churchill achieved the effect of enjambment, making his expression more highly rhetorical; as Wallace Brown puts it, "his mature style makes every possible use of qualifications, interruptions, and elaborations of the main thought." [17] Fifty-six of the satires are cast in heroic couplets. It is the characteristic measure of the early Freneau. Freneau's bludgeoning invective resembles more nearly the manner of Churchill than that of his early master, Pope; and into poems like *General Gage's Confession* he introduces repetition, parenthesis, and apostrophe in order to enlarge the limits of the couplet and heighten the rhetorical effect.

These satires in heroic measure are both Popean and Churchillian. The great majority of them adhere uncompromisingly to the closed couplet and rarely admit Alexandrines and triplets. Balance is frequent, within the line: "Wild as the soil, and as the heav'ns severe"; and within the couplet: "Ye lawyers, who for law confusion teach, / Ye preachers, who for gospel discord preach." [18] Likewise antithesis: "It pleas'd Saint Anthony to preach to brutes; / To preach to Devils best with Duffield

---

[16] Carl and Jessica Bridenbaugh note that "Bradford's 1769 [Philadelphia] edition of the poetical works of Charles Churchill, issued with the co-operation of Rivington of New York, had over 2,200 advanced subscribers," *Rebels and Gentlemen* (New York, 1942), p. 80.

[17] *Charles Churchill: Poet, Rake, and Rebel* (Lawrence, Kansas, 1953), p. 131.

[18] *The Times* (Boston, 1765), p. 51; *The American Times* (New York, 1780), p. 57.

suits." [19] On the other hand, some of the poems make liberal use of parenthesis, apostrophe, internal punctuation, and repetition. In the following passage, for example, enjambment is achieved through repetition:

> We *for dominion* over *others* fight,
> To conquer *others* we exhaust our might;
> *For self dominion* they in war engage,
> The *noblest* battle that a *man* can wage;
> *For self dominion* they unite in plan,
> The *noblest* effort of enlighten'd *man*.[20]

And the following rhetorical question is set down in the highly qualified manner characteristic of Churchill's later style:

> *Must he*, whose tongue,
> Such able peals of elocution rung,
> Whose tow'ring genius seem'd at times to rise,
> And mix a kindred fervour with the skies,
> Whose pointed judgment, and connected sense,
> Gave weight to wit, and worth to eloquence;
> *Must he*, Oh shame to genius! *be the first*
> *To practice arts himself so loudly curst?* [21]

The tradition of English high burlesque, developed at the end of the seventeenth century, gave rise to the mock-heroic poem, which usually employs heroic measure. "Conventionally," writes David Worcester,

high burlesque treats a trivial subject in an elevated manner, and low burlesque treats an elevated subject in a trivial manner. . . . Parody and mock-heroic belong to the family of high burlesque. Both use the grand manner for trifling themes, but parody adopts the manner of a specific work, while mock-heroic copies a whole

[19] "The Word of Congress," *Royal Gazette* (New York), Sept. 18, 1779.
[20] "A Bon Mot of Dr. Price versified," *Connecticut Gazette* (New London), Sept. 13, 1776, p. 4. Italics mine.
[21] "To Governor Johnstone," *Pennsylvania Packet*, July 28, 1778. Italics mine. A. O. Aldridge, *Penn. Mag. Hist. & Biog.*, LXXIX (1955), 87, assigns this poem to Thomas Paine.

class of writing. Conversely, travesty and the Hudibrastic poem are branches of low burlesque. Travesty imitates a particular model, the Hudibrastic a general type.[22]

There is no clear example of the mock-heroic poem in the present study; indeed, this variety of high burlesque is generally social, not political, in intent. Examples of parody, on the other hand, are numerous. "The Gentle Shepherd," for example, parodies Pope's pastoral, "Summer; or, Alexis," substituting George Grenville and Lord Sandwich for Pope and Dr. Garth. In place of Pope's closing lines,

> But soon the sun with milder rays descends
> To the cool ocean, where his journey ends.
> On me Love's fiercer flames for ever prey,
> By night he scorches, as he burns by day,

the anonymous parodist writes,

> But soon the sun with milder rays descends
> To western climes, where my stamp duty ends:
> On my poor effigy their furies prey,
> By night they burn me, as they hang by day.[23]

Revolutionary writers parodied forms other than the heroic couplet, inevitably Hamlet's soliloquy, "To be or not to be," and songs and ballads like John Tait's "Banks of the Dee" (1775), "The Liberty Song" (1768), and "Chevy Chase." [24] Thus, John

[22] *The Art of Satire*, pp. 47–48. See also Richmond P. Bond, *English Burlesque Poetry, 1700–1750* (Cambridge, Mass., 1932), pp. 3–5, 14–15.
[23] *London Chronicle*, Apr. 26, 1776, p. 396; reprinted in *Songs and Ballads of the American Revolution*, ed. Frank Moore (New York, 1856), p. 31.
[24] Parodies on "To be or not to be" appear in the *South-Carolina Gazette*, Mar. 16, 1769, p. 2; *Middlesex Journal* (London), Jan. 30, 1776, p. 4; *Columbian Magazine* (Philadelphia), II (Feb., 1788), 112; *Independent Ledger* (Boston), Sept. 6, 1779, p. 4; *Pennsylvania Gazette*, Mar. 27, 1776, p. 1; *New-Jersey Journal* (Chatham), Nov. 5, 1783, p. 2; and *Maryland Journal* (Baltimore), July 5, 1775, p. 4. Examples of parodies on songs and ballads include one on "The Banks of the Dee," printed in Moore's *Songs*, pp. 81–82, where it is attributed to Oliver Arnold; "A Parody upon a well-known Liberty Song," *Boston Gazette*, Sept. 26, 1768,

André's "Cow-Chace" parodies an eighteenth-century version of "Chevy Chase." One quatrain in the English original,

> For Witherington needs must I wayle,
>   As one in doleful dumpes;
> For when his legges were smitten off,
>   He fought upon his stumpes, [lines 209–212]

is rendered thus:

> But lest their chieftain Washington,
>   Should mourn them in the mumps,
> The fate of Withrington to shun,
>   They fought behind the stumps.

The Hudibrastic tradition in America, given its initial impetus by *Hudibras* (1663–1678), enjoyed continuity from the turn of the century. The continuum was preserved during Revolutionary times when no fewer than seventy-five Hudibrastic poems treating of matters political appeared in America. The term "Hudibrastic," as Edward Ames Richards cautions, "may refer to the nature of the thing attacked, to the content of the story or fable, to the point of view of the satirist, to the form of the verse, or to a mixture of two or more of these elements." [25] The great majority of these poems attack personalities, patriot, loyalist, and English; occasionally, however, the satirists seize on issues and events. It is perhaps significant that fully a third of the poems are travesties of speeches and proclamations.

The fabulous elements present in Hudibrastic poetry partake of low burlesque. The Hudibrastic hero, for all that he abuses his talents, is conceived as not a mere caricature but one who, we feel, remains potentially heroic to the end. Invent for such a character episodes that border on the epic or romantic, and situations arise which the satirist can exploit. But in keeping

---

Supplement Extraordinary; "The Parody Parodized; Or, the Massachusetts Song of Liberty," *St. James Chronicle* (London), Nov. 8, 1768, p. 4; and "The Cow-Chace," *Royal Gazette*, Aug. 16, 30, Sept. 23, 1780, written by John André.

[25] *Hudibras in the Burlesque Tradition* (New York, 1937), p. 31.

with the changed texture of the tradition in the eighteenth century, very few of these poems are strongly narrative. In only
four does the hero emerge a recognizable figure, and only
M'Fingal is accompanied by the traditional man-at-arms. Only
Jacob Bailey's Jack Ramble has love adventures, in the midst
of which he is as discomfited as Butler's knight courting the
widow. These poems exploit low-burlesque situations to good
advantage. Thus, it is absurd that a sergeant's company should
creep forth at dead of night to spike the guns of a children's fort,
whose magazine "Bore deathful stores, for years to come, / Of
oyster-shells, long pikes and grubs, / Promiscuous heap'd with
staves and clubs," and that they, finding the children still defiant
on the morrow, should advance "With baynets fix't" and demolish "all the works of fort— / To spite the little childrens
sport." [26] The Hudibrastic tradition, unlike the mock-heroic,
never takes seriously the epic and romantic conventions it employs, such as invocation and description, and invariably it
travesties heroic allusions.

The loss of a clearly defined point of view, which marked the
tradition increasingly after 1700, attenuated the satirical matter
and in time debilitated the tradition itself. In the case of these
poems there were substituted for the earlier whipping boys—
Presbyterianism, Dissent, Catholicism—certain less tangible revolutionary and imperialistic principles which had burgeoned during the eighteenth century.

More prominent than the thing attacked, the fable, or the
point of view are the prosodical and other verse features, such as
simile, extravagance of language, and epigram, which these poems
exhibit. Two-thirds of them are cast in iambic measure (almost
half of these contain hypermetric lines), one-third in anapestic.[27] Feminine rhymes are everywhere present and, less often,

[26] *Charleston Gazette*, Jan. 18, 1780, p. 2.
[27] The habit of crowding extra syllables into a foot had led to the
emergence of this measure early in the century; Swift, for example,
employed it in several of his travesties. In Revolutionary America it was
Freneau who saw its potentialities and developed it.

double feminine rhymes like *"in limbo patrum . . .* go a'ter
'em" and "ham-eater . . . diameter." [28] Broken rhyme is frequent. Usually this is accomplished by composing half of the
rhyme of two or three words: "Amanuensis . . . whence is";
"hobble, you . . . Don A. W."; "Lake Eri, or . . . Superior";
"Med'cines . . . dead since"; "a few setts (Of books) . . .
Massachusetts"; "many paraded . . . Jack Cade, did." [29] Rarely,
half of the rhyme is composed from the first part of the word,
the remainder carrying over to the next line:

> You've push'd and turn'd the whole world up-
> Side down, and got yourselves at top.[30]

Pronunciation is wrenched by slurring syllables, shifting the accent, and treating vowel and consonant quality casually: "doodle
dances . . . rebel Yankees"; *"sub-pone . . .* thereupon"; "pan-
cake . . . Atlantic"; "atrabilious . . . peccadilloes"; "discover
. . . philosopher"; "impunity . . . *procul a fulmine"*; "Antip-
odes . . . forbodes." [31]

The incongruity present in a low-burlesque simile arises from
the absurdity of comparing the human victim to something
smaller, often an animal. Thus, the political trimmer keeps himself concealed at home like a mouse in the "belly of a cheese";
and General Clinton, according to a young lady at New York,
hasn't budged beyond the British lines these two years past,
"But, perhaps, th' poor man could not get on his legs, / After

[28] *Providence Gazette*, Feb. 3, 1776, p. 2; Pattee, II, 131.

[29] *Newport Mercury*, Sept. 20, 1765, p. 2; *Connecticut Courant* (Hartford), Aug. 7, 1775, p. 4; *The Poetical Works of John Trumbull* (Hartford, 1820), I, 173 (hereafter referred to as Trumbull or by volume and
page in the body of the text); "Loyalist Rhapsodies," Library of Congress MSS, Dec. 10, 1777, p. 63; Pattee, II, 235; "A Card To my Cousin
Tom, the Patriot," Historical Society of Pennsylvania MS, Feb. 4, 1774.

[30] Trumbull, I, 92.

[31] *Pennsylvania Journal*, June 28, 1775, p. 1; *Illustrated Ballad History
of the American Revolution*, ed. Frank Moore (New York, 1876), p.
359; Pattee, II, 132; Trumbull, I, 38; *New Eng. Quar.*, II (1929), 83;
New York Journal, Sept. 8, 1777; *New-York Packet*, Oct. 3, 1782, p. 1.

sitting so long—like a hen o'er spoiled eggs." [32] Studied extravagance of word and phrase is a conspicuous feature of these poems; often it results in periphrasis. Gage, early in the siege of Boston, threatens "That whosoe'er keeps gun or pistol, / I'll spoil the motion of his systole." [33] Epigram, a rhetorical device with which Butler had so crowded his cantos as to make *Hudibras* heavy slogging, ceased in time to be a common feature of the tradition, for most of his successors did not command powers of detachment and rhetoric equal to constructing epigrams of adequate concentration. *M'Fingal* contains the most successful epigrams of the period: concerning M'Fingal's reputed power of second-sight, Trumbull says, "But optics sharp it needs, I ween, / To see what is not to be seen" (I, 6); and as the tar and feathers are being made ready for him, M'Fingal wryly observes, "No man e'er felt the halter draw, / With good opinion of the law" (I, 111).

Two of these poems, *M'Fingal* and Freneau's "The Political Balance," permanently enriched the tradition. Both explore low-burlesque situations with commendable invention, wit, and objectivity, though they might have succeeded still farther had the architectonics been firmer. Of all the Hudibrastic poems here considered *M'Fingal* possesses the firmest narrative line. In the traditional iambic measure and with Butlerian vigor Trumbull relates how Squire M'Fingal, a New England Tory double dyed, is twice bested by the Whigs, first in extended debate with Honorius and later in battle before the Liberty Pole. He blurs the focus somewhat by attacking radicals on the American side as well as loyalists and the British. Nevertheless, his poem towers above all the rest as to largeness of design, artistic control, and invention. Only the tediousness of the vision which consumes most of the last canto taxes the reader's patience. Indeed, this poem approaches more nearly than *Hudibras* the eighteenth-

---

[32] *New Eng. Quar.*, II, 75; *New-York Packet*, Nov. 9, 1780, p. 1.
[33] *Pennsylvania Journal*, June 28, 1775, p. 1.

century ideal of "one, entire, ridiculous Action," for Trumbull never disengages our attention from the fable so completely as Butler, who devotes an entire canto (III. ii) to theological debate.[34]

Still more numerous than these Hudibrastic poems are the satires written to the tunes of songs and ballads. While the majority of the tunes are contemporary with the eighteenth century, several date from the seventeenth or even earlier: "A Begging We Will Go," "The British Grenadiers," "Chevy Chase," "The Cut-Purse," "Derry Down," and "The Old Courtier of the Queen." [35] The tunes to which the satirists wrote most often were "Derry Down," "Yankee Doodle," "Chevy Chase," "Hearts of Oak," and "The Vicar of Bray." [36]

"The Vicar of Bray" relates how between the reigns of Charles II and George I the vicar thrice turned coat, accommodating his religious and political principles to the times. The liveliest of three imitations pictures a trimmer in the time of George III with principles just as flexible as the vicar's.[37] The first stanza of the original ballad reads:

> In good King Charles's golden day,
>   When loyalty no harm meant,
> A zealous High-Churchman was I,
>   And so I got preferment,
> To teach my flock I never miss'd,

[34] *Grub-street Journal*, Oct. 1, 1730, quoted in Bond, *English Burlesque Poetry*, p. 46. For a more detailed analysis of these Hudibrastic poems see my article in *Am. Lit.*, XXVII (1956), 499–508.

[35] William Chappell, *Popular Music of the Olden Time* (London, 1855–1859), pp. 345, 772, 198, 350, 299; Cyrus L. Day and Eleanore B. Murrie, *English Song-Books, 1651–1702* (London, 1940), p. 121.

[36] The tune "Hearts of Oak" was composed by the English organist William Boyce, the words ("Come cheer up, my lads, 'tis to glory we steer") were written by David Garrick, and the song was sung in *Harlequin's Invasion* (1759) (Chappell, *Popular Music*, p. 715). The present satires, however, were prompted by John Dickinson and Arthur Lee's "Liberty Song" ("Come join hand in hand, brave Americans all"), written in 1768 to the tune "Hearts of Oak."

[37] "The American Vicar of Bray," *Royal Gazette*, June 30, 1779.

> Kings were by God appointed,
> And lost are those that dare resist,
> Or touch the Lord's annointed.
> And this is law I will maintain,
> Until my dying day, Sir,
> That whatsoever King shall reign,
> I'll still be the vicar of Bray, Sir.

The imitation begins:

> When Royal George rul'd o'er the land,
> And loyalty no harm meant,
> For Church and King I made a stand
> And so I got preferment.
> I still oppos'd all party tricks
> For reasons I thought clear ones;
> And swore it was their politics,
> To make us Presbyterians.
> And this is law, etc.

Aspiring playwrights in the period of the American Revolution were well aware that during the early part of the century farce had helped drive legitimate comedy from the English stage and that by the mid-century melodrama, characterized by spectacular settings, gloom and mystery, artificial sentimentalism, unnatural poetic justice, pathetic morality, and the hero-villain antithesis, had displaced the heroic play. So it happened that the closet drama, as distinct from the stage play, came into vogue in the second half of the century.[38] The immediate tradition available to the playwright, therefore, was far thinner than that to the writer, say, of Hudibrastics. During the Revolution there appeared a dozen satirical plays, neither better nor worse than run-of-the-mill English farces and melodramas of the day. In the farcical subplot of *The Blockheads: or, The Affrighted Officers* Tabitha, a Boston girl, elopes with a British officer Lord Dapper, who "looks like a baboon upon stilts"; although skeptical

[38] Allardyce Nicoll, *A History of English Drama, 1660–1800* (Cambridge, Eng., 1952), II, 216–217; III, 98, 223.

of his abilities, she will have him ("he will serve for a cully to fleece for my indulgencies in dress and fashion"). Her father complains to his wife that he was unable to prevent the elopement: "My daughter I am afraid, is debauch'd by a painted monkey, who I saw with her at the gate—the villain drew his sword upon me, but like a true British general, I thought fit to run away." Mercy Warren's closet drama, *The Adulateur*, on the other hand, is unrelieved melodrama, complete with patriotic hero and ministerial villain. In one scene "a GHOST with naked breast exposing his wounds" enters the hall where the patriots have gathered to discuss ministerial tyranny. More difficult to classify are plays like *The Fall of British Tyranny*, which mingles farcical and melodramatic ingredients, and the comic opera, *The Blockheads; or, Fortunate Contractor*. Allied to such traditional dramatic forms as farce and melodrama is the dialogue, both in prose and in verse; the liveliest of these, *A Dialogue between a Southern Delegate and his Spouse*.[39]

The vitality of these plays derives largely from the civilian and military types depicted. In the opening scene of *The Battle of Brooklyn* Joe King tells his master, Lord Sterling, "Yes, by heavens! you drank stinkabus enough last night, to split the head of an Indian!" and continues in this familiar and insolent vein to the end of the play. The antipatriot *Americans Roused in a Cure for the Spleen* finds a parson, justice, innkeeper, deacon, barber, Quaker, and Congressman in converse. Barber Trim, the most memorable of these characters, declares, "If I was deny'd the privilege of my shop to canvass politicks, . . . you may e'en take my razors, soap, combs and all, and set fire to my shop"; falling under the spell of the smooth-tongued parson,

[39] The dramatic dialogue derived in part from the popular college exercise. John Smith, for example, wrote two such dialogues during the war, both produced at Dartmouth College: "A Dialogue between an Englishman and an Indian" (written Mar. 4, 1779), on the position of the underprivileged, and "A Little Tea Table Chitchat" (June, 1781), on the problem of inflation. These pieces are reproduced in facsimile and discussed by Harold G. Rugg, *Theatre Annual*, I (1942), 55–69.

though, he determines at the end to drop his "shop preachments, or else, for the future, to take the right side of the question." In Munford's *The Patriots* there appear the braggart recruiting captain, Flash, and his sergeant, Trim, types popularized in George Farquhar's *Recruiting Officer* (1706), a long-time favorite on the American stage. Trim has his own plan for encouraging enlistments: "I have the recruiting jugs full to the brim. Peach brandy, the best liquor in the world." [40]

The two prose forms in which satirists of the Revolution most frequently worked were the periodical essay and, what is loosely allied to it, the letter to the press. If it had not in fact already taken place, the tradition of the periodical essay in America was certainly launched with the founding of the *New-England Courant* (1721). The appearance of the *Maryland Gazette* (1727) and other newspapers with Addisonian overtones merely confirmed the presence of the tradition. In Revolutionary times Samuel Johnson wrote of Addison, whose style was still much admired after half a century and emulated in America: "His prose is the model of the middle style; on grave subjects not formal, on light occasions not groveling; pure without scrupulosity, and exact without apparent elaboration; always equable, and always easy, without glowing words or pointed sentences. . . . His sentences have neither studied amplitude, nor affected brevity; his periods, though not diligently rounded, are voluble and easy." [41] Hugh Blair, in his influential *Lectures on Rhetoric and Belles Lettres* (1760), advised those who wished to acquire "a proper style" to possess fully the thoughts on "a page of one of Mr. Addison's papers," rewrite the passage from memory,

[40] Courtlandt Canby, having pointed out some close parallels between Munford's play and Farquhar's, concludes, "The bother, of course, about naming any single play as *the* prototype of Munford's *Patriots* is that most of these elements are the stock in trade of many comedies—and represent standard, eighteenth-century theatrical cliches," *Wm. & Mary Quar.*, ser. 3, VI (1949), 446n.

[41] *The Lives of the Most Eminent English Poets* (London, 1896), II, 103–104.

and then compare the two (Lecture XIX). It was about this time that the periodical essay came back into vogue in England, only now it frequently assumed a partisan and censorious tone such as Addison and Steele had not allowed themselves to adopt.[42] In Revolutionary America so insistent a rhetorical appeal was made in the essay as to blur the line between it and the letter to the press. Most of the forty-three essays included in the present study, however, are cast in one of several traditional species: moral dialogue (or soliloquy), beast fable, dream vision or one of its allied forms, prose allegory, the adventures of a coin. Especially significant are the last three.

Building on ancient tradition, eighteenth-century essayists refined and altered the dream vision in a manner that secured it a place in the periodicals. In *The Spectator* alone there are at least six clear examples of the species.[43] The medieval convention of experiencing the vision in a pleasant outdoor setting persisted. One Revolutionary essay opens, "This morning about six o'clock being in a gentle slumber, I dreamed and in my cogitations I found myself in a fertile garden that gradually descended to a beautiful meadow, surrounded with little hills[,] a pleasant grove, and a fruitful plain." [44] One of the refinements on the tradition, reflecting contemporary interest in *Arabian Nights* literature, was the metamorphosis. In one antipatriot satire the narrator dreams of being in a court of justice where he sees Chief Justice McKean metamorphosed into a blood-hound, Silas Deane into a French marquis, Charles Lee into an adder, William Livingston into a wolf, John Jay into a snake, the Continental Army into a timid hare, and Washington into

[42] Thomas Wright, *Caricature History of the Georges* (London, 1898), p. 217.

[43] Nos. 3 (Public Credit), 63 (True, Mixed, and False Wit), 83 (Gallery of Living and Dead Painters), 514 (Journey to Parnassus), 524 (Waters of Heavenly and Worldly Wisdom), and 558 (Mountain of Miseries). Four other visions do not include the dream: Nos. 159 (Mirzah), 460 (Paradise of Fools), 463 (Golden Scales), and 501 (Grotto of Grief).

[44] *Royal American Magazine* (Boston), I (Dec., 1774), 471.

a gamecock; the oddity of this last transformation "excited in me such a disposition to laugh, that I immediately awakened, and was forced reluctantly to resign the character of A DREAMER." [45] In what is certainly the most fully realized of these dream visions the narrator and a friend sit up late discussing the proposed Stamp Act, "but parted no wiser than we met; and going to bed full of the matter, I had a very odd dream. . . ." The setting is not the conventional one but an enclosure near a town whither horses and asses are brought to be branded. The asses tamely submit to the master brander; not so the horses. When a venerable native defends their insubordination, the people start huzzaing, "in which I joined so heartily, that the good woman at my side gave me a hunch with her elbow, and asked me if I had the cholic or gripes, and so ended my vision." [46]

Prose allegory, as distinguished from both beast fable and dream vision, was a well-established species of essay by the eighteenth century. Two Revolutionary satires resemble one of the most popular English political allegories of the century, John Arbuthnot's *History of John Bull* (1712). In the first the narrator tells what happened to the seven natural children "which John Bull had in his younger Days by Doll Secretary, his Mother's Maid."

How the old Lady [Parliament] would suffer no Bastards in her Family; and how the poor Infants were turned adrift on the Fish Ponds as soon as born; how they landed on the Western Shore, and were there nursed by a wild Bear all under the green Wood Tree. . . . And how, as soon as they had cut their Eye Teeth, and were able to walk alone, John claimed them for his own. . . .

Of two Children more, which John had afterwards in lawful Wedlock, viz. a Boy which he called Georgey, after his great Patron, and a Girl, which he called Peg [Nova Scotia], after his Sister Margaret. . . .

How young Master Baboon, old Lewis's only Son, fell in Love

[45] *Royal Gazette*, Jan. 23, 1779, p. 2; written by John André. A sequel appeared in the same paper a week later.
[46] *Providence Gazette*, Nov. 10, 1764, pp. 2-3.

with Miss Virgey; and how he came behind with Intent to ravish her; how she squealed and alarmed her Dad.

It is further related how John Bull and old Lewis Baboon, who carried Lord Strutt (Spain) along, "had a long Tussle; how John's Children saved their old Dad from a broken Head, and helped to seize young Lewis and tie him; how the old Folks agreed to leave young Lewis in Custody, and drink Friends themselves; and how John made his Children pay a Share of the Reckoning without giving them any of the Drink." The allegory concludes with the history of the Stamp Act and its repeal.[47] In constructing *A Pretty Story* Hopkinson was shrewd enough to select homely ingredients and place them in a familiar context. The nobleman of a great estate (King of England) takes a wife (Parliament). In time some of their children leave home and settle on a distant tract; the wife views these children avariciously and plots with the steward (chief minister), after he has debauched her, hoodwinking the nobleman and working her will against the children until at last they rebel. Of such simple but rhetorically effective materials is this allegorical history, which resembles Arbuthnot's at many points, built.[48]

The adventures of a coin is a species of essay which appeared occasionally in the eighteenth century.[49] A temporary vogue followed the success of George Johnstone's *Chrysal, or the Adventures of a Guinea* (1760–1765), in which novel a guinea passes through the hands of many, rich and poor alike, and re-

[47] "The PROEM," *London Chronicle*, Apr. 5, 1766, p. 324; reprinted in the *Newport Mercury*, Aug. 4, 1766, p. 1, where it is entitled "The History of John Bull's Children."

[48] In both, as George Hastings points out, countries are called estates, the English king is a landowner, Parliament is his wife, the prime minister carries on an affair with her, Parliament holds the purse strings, and England's quarrel arises out of her efforts to hold her trade (*Am. Lit.*, I [1929], 41–44).

[49] Thus *The Tatler*, No. 249, relates the adventures of a shilling, and *The Adventurer*, No. 43 (Apr. 3, 1753), those of a halfpenny.

lates its adventures to an alchemist. In a series of four adventure essays published in the *United States Magazine*, Hard Money and Continental Currency debate on the subject of inflation. Brackenridge, the editor, led off with the "Representation and Remonstrance of HARD MONEY"; after reciting the customary vital statistics, Hard Money accuses Continental Currency of lack of breeding ("he is as aukward and as stiff as a piece of pasted paper").[50] At one point in the debate Continental Currency, who comes off the winner, remarks that at the outset of the war "this *Hard-money* was apparently a warm and decided Whig," who "became of my acquaintance. . . . But now our pretensions begin to prevail, and his fears are up that he will be ranked with the failing party." [51]

There is little doubt that Francis Hopkinson, who described himself as "a great admirer of the *Spectators, Tatlers*, and *Guardians*," was the foremost essayist of the Revolution, as the skill with which he uses the foreign-visitor device, ironic mask, and hoax helps testify.[52] Abroad, the pseudo letter by a pretended foreigner reached its finest elaboration in Montesquieu's *Lettres persanes* (1721) and Goldsmith's *Citizen of the World* (1762). In Hopkinson's "Translation of a Letter, Written by a Foreigner," a distinguished Continental gentleman, writing from London to one whom he addresses simply as "Count," proposes to give "some account of the character and politics of this strange people," the English. Most of what follows is a comparison of the political literacy of Englishmen and Americans, in which the former come off a poor second.[53] Unhappily, the nationality

[50] *United States Magazine* (Philadelphia), I (Jan., 1779), 28–31. The February issue carried the "Reply of CONTINENTAL CURRENCY, to the Representation and Remonstrance of Hard Money" (pp. 72–81).

[51] *United States Magazine*, I (Mar., 1779), 110–121; written by William Livingston. The debate came to an end with the publication of "*The* ADVENTURES of a CONTINENTAL DOLLAR" in the June and September issues (pp. 264–268, 365–367).

[52] *Pennsylvania Magazine*, II (Apr., 1776), 186.

[53] *Pennsylvania Packet*, Feb. 4, 1777, p. 2.

Hopkinson the patriot sometimes donned an ironic mask. The
more effectively to attack the loyalist press at Philadelphia late
in 1776, especially the person of James Humphreys, he addressed
two letters to the *Pennsylvania Evening Post,* signing himself
"A Tory." "I am *a Tory,*" he explains, "the son of a Tory, born
and bred in the pure principles of unconditional submission, and
a true friend to the Hanoverian family." "Now, it is the indis-
pensable duty of all those who would be called the friends of
arbitrary government and of the said George III. to render all
the assistance in their power to the aforesaid fleets and armies,
and to the worthy Lords and Generals, whom this just and
benign monarch hath commissioned to direct and manage them."
Turning then to his personal target, the Tory continues:

"I have anxiously desired to see a printing press in this city
subservient to the purposes of Lord and General Howe." Mr.
Humphreys is just the man. You can imagine my shock, therefore, on boasting of Humphreys' *Ledger* to one whom I supposed to be a Tory like myself, to hear him say, "Would not
our council of safety be very justifiable in silencing a press,
whose weekly productions insult the feelings of the people, and
are so openly inimical to the American cause?" It is true we
must take precautions. "You can hardly imagine what regularity prevails in our board of tories. We are all formed into committees of various denominations, and appointed to various du-

[54] Freneau, on the other hand, succeeded admirably. The *Freeman's
Journal* between Nov. 21, 1781, and Aug. 14, 1782, carried his nineteen
"Pilgrim" papers, wherein the foreign visitor, a middle-aged Swiss descended from William Tell, then living in a cave near Philadelphia, tells
how early in life he embraced "the profession of travelling *pilgrim,* or
religious and philosophical wanderer" and has spent the last thirty years
making "observations upon men and manners." In revised and expanded
form these essays, more heavily social than political in nature, reappeared
as "The Philosopher of the Forest" in *The Miscellaneous Works of Mr.
Philip Freneau* (New York, 1788).

ties." We have efficient committees of wiles and stratagems, false reports, true intelligence, lies, extortion, and depreciation. "Some narrow minded people say, that we are doing all we can to ruin our country, and entail a miserable slavery on our unborn posterity. We believe we are doing the best we can for ourselves —and pray what has posterity done for us, that we should run the risk of confiscation and a halter for them?" [55]

Late in the war Hopkinson perpetrated a hoax, a literary fact not clearly recognized by his biographer.[56] In the *Pennsylvania Packet* for November 10, 1781, he has the loyalist printer James Rivington give notice that he

will dispose of his remaining stock in trade by public auction. The sales to begin at his store on Monday, the 19th instant, and will be continued from day to day (Sundays excepted) from the hours of ten to one in the forenoon, until the whole shall be disposed of. . . . The scanty limits of an advertisement are by far insufficient to admit of an adequate display of his extraordinary and miscellaneous collection.

There follows a partial list of books, plays, maps and prints, philosophical apparatus, and patent medicines. Then a concluding note: "To every Purchaser to the value of five Pounds, will be delivered *gratis*, One Quire of counterfeit Continental Currency. Also two Quires of Proclamations, offering Pardon to *Rebels*." Ten days later Hopkinson has Rivington address the printer of the *Packet* as though from New York:

Your paper of the 10th instant, No. 805, reached this city, and an Advertisement therein inserted, and signed with my signature, hath attracted universal notice and particular attention, and hath, moreover, rendered me the subject of much satyrical stricture.

The author of this most wicked forgery, whoever he is, hath most nefariously, and with malice aforethought, made use of my name as a vehicle to impose on the judicious public the nugatory produc-

[55] *Pennsylvania Evening Post*, Nov. 16, 26, 1776.
[56] See George E. Hastings' discussion of these two letters in *The Life and Works of Francis Hopkinson* (Chicago, 1926), pp. 313-314.

tions of his own flimsy brain, as the genuine offspring of my prolific pen.

This spirited apology concludes, "I have only to request that you will not admit into your paper any more of the false and wicked insinuations of the author of the aforesaid advertisement."

In the journalistic practice of the later eighteenth century the letter to the press, or editorial, enjoyed great prestige as a literary form. Internationally famous, of course, were the antiministerial letters of "Junius," first printed in the London *Public Advertiser* (1769–1772). No fewer than seventy-four satirical letters, treating of the Revolution, appeared in the contemporary Anglo-American press. When not drafted as conventional letters to the editor, the letter to the press took the form of anecdote, annotations, "we hears," a list of queries, or, as was frequently Franklin's habit, a more belletristic form like parody, imitation, fable, colloquy, hoax, or fictitious controversy. Other than Franklin, Charles Lee, William Livingston, and John Witherspoon made significant contributions in this form. Lee and Livingston both employed the ironic mask, Lee appearing on one occasion as a quasi apologist for the illiteracy of James Rivington, and Livingston, in order to expose Hugh Gaine, innocently giving out what purports to be a series of foreign and New York dispatches "Printed and sold by Hugo Lucre." [57] Witherspoon, who remarked that in his political pieces Swift is "a pattern of style which has scarcely been exceeded since his time," adopts the manner of the Dean in letting the printers Rivington and Benjamin Towne make an ironic defense of their behavior.[58]

[57] "A Breakfast for R********," probably written in 1775, printed in the *Memoirs of the Life of the Late Charles Lee* (New York, 1792), pp. 84–87; "The Impartial Chronicle," *Pennsylvania Packet*, Feb. 18, 1777, p. 1.

[58] Varnum L. Collins, *President Witherspoon: a Biography* (Princeton, 1925), II, 213. "The Humble Representation and earnest Supplication of James Rivington," *United States Magazine*, I (Jan., 1779), 34–40; "The humble Confession, Recantation, and Apology of Benjamin Towne," *New York Packet*, Oct. 1, 1778, p. 2.

In the half century which separates his youthful essays in the *New-England Courant* from his letters to the English press, Franklin's satirical manner took on a deeper and more elusive coloring. Not that he ever abandoned completely the urbanity he early acquired from Addison, in underlying irony and rhetorical organization his later satires resemble more nearly the manner and matter of Swift and Defoe. In these letters he brings rhetoric into play with varying success. The comparison of an empire to a cake, introduced at the beginning of "Rules for Reducing a Great Empire to a Small One," is not so happily chosen as the *reductio ad absurdum* which informs "An Edict by the King of Prussia." [59] While the analogy serves Franklin well for a time, by the third rule (there are twenty all told) he is chafing under its restrictions and breaks beyond its confines, never to return. On the other hand, the ironical formula: England is to Prussia as America is to England: embraces Franklin's aim with ease and ensures unity.

As journalists from the turn of the century had so conclusively shown, a persona, or mask, can be made to serve the cause of satire well. None excelled Swift in the use of this device.[60] Without arguing for direct influence, it can be demonstrated that Franklin's ironic masks, like those of Swift, are of two major kinds: that of the spectator or detached observer; and the situational, in which the satirist relinquishes the role of observer and the "self-developing irony of the situation" speaks for itself directly to the reader.[61] In "An Edict by the King of Prussia" he assumes the spectator mask. On September 5, 1773, a well-meaning, impartial correspondent writes from Danzig, "We have

[59] *Public Advertiser* (London), Sept. 11, 22, 1773.

[60] In addition to Swift, Roger L'Estrange, John Tutchin, G. P. Marana, Ned Ward, Addison, Steele, and Defoe made extensive use of the persona. See William Ewald, *The Masks of Jonathan Swift* (Oxford, 1954), pp. 4–7.

[61] John M. Bullitt, *Jonathan Swift and the Anatomy of Satire* (Cambridge, Mass., 1953), pp. 57, 60–61; Ricardo Quintana, *Univ. Tor. Quar.*, XVII (1948), 135.

long wondered here at the supineness of the English nation, under
the Prussian impositions upon its trade entering our port," and
encloses Frederick's edict "Given at Potsdam, this twenty-fifth
day of the month of August, one thousand seven hundred and
seventy-three, and in the thirty-third year of our reign." Like
Defoe's *Shortest Way with the Dissenters* this edict deceived
Londoners when it first appeared. Illustrative of the situational
mask, wherein personae are created "who embody and illustrate
the ironic contradictions between what *seems* to them and what,
as the reader knows, actually *is*," is "The Sale of the Hessians." [62]
The irony present in the many euphemisms, the epigram "Glory
is true wealth," and the mock-heroic allusion to Thermopylae
spring from the situation itself; after all, Schaumbergh's reason
for commending Hohendorf on so careful a reckoning of the
Hessians killed in the American war is purely mercenary.

In view of the rhetorical power displayed in these letters I
cannot concur in Verner Crane's judgment that "for all his verbal
charm and facility, Franklin was not a literary artist of the first
order." [63] Within the province of satire at least, Franklin stands
high. His unerring eye for an opening and relentless pressing
of each advantage; the ingenuity and invention he exhibits in
exploring and exploiting the historical situation; his skill in con-
trolling irony, that subtlest of satiric patterns—these stamp him
as an extraordinarily gifted satirist.

[62] Bullitt, *Swift*, p. 61. "The Sale of the Hessians," dated Feb. 18, 1777,
is printed in *The Writings of Benjamin Franklin*, ed. A. H. Smyth
(New York, 1905–1907), VII, 25–27. Hereafter referred to as Smyth.

[63] *Benjamin Franklin's Letters to the Press, 1758–1775*, ed. Verner W.
Crane (Chapel Hill, 1950), p. xxv. Hereafter referred to simply as Crane.

CHAPTER II

The Stamp Act

On April 10, 1763, George Grenville succeeded John Stuart, third Earl of Bute, as chief minister of state. At once he launched a program designed to ensure adequate defenses for the newly enlarged North American empire and stabilize post-war economy at home. One English satirist, who was aware of Grenville's considerable talent for finance, related how John Bull "made Choice of fair George, the Gentle Shepherd, for his House Steward, because he could tell, without the Book, that two and three made Five and the Multiplication Table by Heart." [1] Responding to the widely held view that America was largely to blame for the increase in the national debt as a result of the Seven Years' War, the Grenville Ministry determined to help meet expenditures by raising revenue in America.[2] Among the resolutions constituting the Sugar Act of 1764, the fifteenth, which did not call for immediate action, provided that "towards further defraying the said Expences, it may be proper to charge certain Stamp Duties in the said Colonies and Plantations." [3] The

---

[1] "The Proem," *London Chronicle*, Apr. 5, 1766; reprinted in the *Newport Mercury*, Aug. 4, 1766, p. 1. Grenville had gained the sobriquet "Gentle Shepherd" during the debate on the Cider Act.

[2] Fred J. Hinkhouse, *The Preliminaries of the American Revolution as Seen in the English Press* (New York, 1926), p. 52.

[3] *Journals of the House of Commons*, XXIX, 935, quoted in Edmund S. and Helen M. Morgan, *The Stamp Act Crisis* (Chapel Hill, 1953), p. 26.

revenue from the proposed stamp tax—a tax marking a departure from ancient custom in the administration of the colonies —was to be used solely for colonial defense, even though many Americans supposed it otherwise. During the year of grace which was allowed before this proposal was presented, several of the colonies protested in assembly and in the press that Parliament did not possess the right to levy such a tax; but Grenville, not realizing apparently how outmoded the old colonial system had become during several decades of salutary neglect, refused to let this right be called into question.[4]

Several months before the stamp proposal was to be introduced, there appeared in the American press a dream allegory, in which the narrator, thinking on the proposed "stamping law," falls asleep and dreams that all the horses of the town, amongst them "half a dozen asses," are herded into a pasture.

Soon after, the master-brander with his retinue approached the pasture in great pomp, one carrying a large silver brand in the form of the letter S—— and upon entering the field, they began with the asses, and branded them without the least interruption: They then drew near to the horses, and would have laid hold on a stately BAY horse, but taking fright at the glittering of the brand, he snorted, kicked up his heels, and went off; I was sorry to see him fling the dirt in the gentleman's face; and the whole drove being struck with the same panic, they leapt the fence and ran off snorting and flinging up their heels, so that I saw them no more.

A gentleman explains that the horses are all of the English breed, most of them having had Old Noll (Cromwell) for a sire, a horse that had bucked when ridden with French spurs. When a venerable native asks the chief man of the branding company to explain this business if he can, he is reminded of the great expense his master incurred in "freeing your pastures from robbers, and fencing them anew." The old man replies that even though it was his own people who subdued the wild soil and spilled their blood in its defense, "we would gladly have excused the fenc

[4] Morgan, *Stamp Act*, pp. 59–60.

ing" except that "we were never visited by our friends 'till there was something to be got by us." He warns an arrogant young man in the retinue that "wiser heads may consider whether the sport may be worth the money it will cost; the beasts are wild and numerous, and their range very extensive." "You allow, Sir," says the branding master interrupting, "that a shilling taken for the brand or for furniture is but the same; —pray why then is there any difference?" The old man answers:

It is the same Sir, to our master, but not to us. Have you never heard that branding is a mark of property; if the brand was once put on, I should not wonder if your next errand here was for the beasts, or their hides.—Mutual confidence will give our master a better and more durable property in what we have than any branding; but where distrust and diffidence comes in it's stead, no good can ensue; opportunities will never be long wanting for masters to oppress their servants, or for servants to —— their masters.

At the loud huzzas which greet this vehement speech the narrator wakes up.[5] The effectiveness of this allegory derives in large measure from the direct and unaffected diction, sparse but apt detail, and a homely setting that would have been familiar to most contemporary readers.

I

During the debate on the Stamp Act no member of the Opposition questioned Parliament's right to tax the colonies, and on March 22, 1765, it became law. Accordingly, all legal and commercial documents, pamphlets, newspapers, almanacs, cards, and dice would be dutiable after the first of November. While the Act bore directly against lawyers, merchants, printers, and tavern owners, in the long run all classes would feel its force.

[5] *Providence Gazette*, Nov. 10, 1764, pp. 2–3. Moses Coit Tyler suggests that this essay may have been written by Stephen Hopkins of Rhode Island, the only colonial governor as it happened who refused to take the oath to support the Stamp Act (*The Literary History of the American Revolution* [New York, 1897], I, 61n.).

In the interim an allegorist told how John Bull married his daughter *"Lady N--th Am---can Liberty"* to Toleration and "gave her in Dower a certain Tract of uncultivated Land, which she called after her Name." When Commerce, who had won Mrs. Bull's esteem, paid court to the daughter as well, Mrs. Bull

determined to make a bold Push; at once to destroy her Daughter, disavow her Son-in-Law, make Slaves of all their Children and Servants, and take the Estate into her own Hands.— She accordingly issued out Orders that her Servants should take her and *Stamp* her in so barbarous a Manner that she should not survive the Wounds; . . . honest John was never forward in the Ruin of his Daughter, but was made to acquiesce, thro' the tyrannical Disposition of his Wife, and the Mildness of his own natural Temper. . . . Thus died the most amiable of Women, the best Wife, the most dutiful Child, and the tenderest Mother.— Happy for her family, she has left one Son, . . . prophetically named *I–d–p––d––ce*, and on him the Hopes of all her disconsolate Servants are placed for relief under their Afflictions. . . . Her Remains will not be interred till the First Day of November, 1765.[6]

The earliest and most radical of the many colonial protests that followed the passage of the Stamp Act were the Virginia Resolves of May 30. The fifth resolution, which reserved to the Assembly "the only and sole exclusive right and power to lay taxes and impositions upon the inhabitants of this Colony," was a forceful statement of the colonial position.[7] Although this resolution was rescinded by the conservatives before the session ended, because it was widely published with the other six the public supposed that it too had passed. The Massachusetts Assembly, for one, threw caution to the winds and quickly endorsed the Resolves. "The People of *Virginia*," according to one Bostonian, "have spoke very sensibly, and the frozen Politi-

[6] *New-York Gazette; or, the Weekly Post-Boy*, Sept. 5, 1765, p. 5.
[7] *Documents of American History*, ed. H. S. Commager (New York, 1958), p. 56.

cians of a more Northern Government say, They have spoke
Treason." Recollecting with what timidity the Assembly had
let Lieutenant-Governor Hutchinson and the Council tone down
an earlier petition addressed to the King,[8] he further observed
that the "spirited RESOLVES" of the Virginians "do indeed serve
as a perfect Contrast for a certain tame, pusilanimous, daub'd,
insipid Thing, delicately touch'd up, and call'd an *Address;*
which was lately sent from this Side the Water, to please the
Taste of the Tools of Corruption on the other." He inveighed
against the motives which prompted Hutchinson and the Council on that occasion:

Curs'd Prudence of interested designing Politicians! who have done
their utmost to have the Liberties of Millions of honest and loyal,
and let me add, brave and free-born *American* Subjects,—brave
because free-born,—sacrificed to their own Ambition and Lust of
Dominion and Wealth. . . . These dirty Sycophants, these ministerial Hacks, would fain have us believe that his Sacred Majesty,
ever lov'd by his *American* Subjects, would be displeased to hear
their Murmurs at the Sight of Chains! [9]

The symbol of British authority in Massachusetts at this time
was Governor Francis Bernard, who considered the Stamp Act
ill timed and even ill advised but vowed to see it enforced. It
was Bernard who hurried the stamped paper to Castle William
upon its arrival at Boston late in September, declaring "that he
had no authority to open any of the packages" and that the
paper had been deposited in the strengthened garrison "to prevent imprudent people from offering an insult to the king." [10]
One Hudibrastic writer was quick to travesty this declaration:
Lest any think that I plan to distribute the stamps, I, Francis
Bernard, now declare

[8] Morgan, *Stamp Act,* p. 35.

[9] *Boston Gazette,* July 8, 1765, p. 2. The Morgans think that the author
may have been the Massachusetts lawyer, Oxenbridge Thacher (*Stamp
Act,* p. 100).

[10] Thomas Hutchinson, *The History of the Colony and Province of
Massachusetts-Bay,* ed. L. S. Mayo (Cambridge, Mass., 1936), III, 92.

That I've no order, warrant, might,
Or whatsoever power, or right,
To deal about th' aforesaid papers,
Or peep into th' inclosing wrappers,
T' untie the cords, or ope the locks,
Of trunk, or case, or tierce or box.

. . . . .

Each single trunk, and pack, and bale,
To be put up like bottled ale;
And well defended in the castle
With pike, & musket, sword, & pistol;
There to remain entire and whole
Each pack unpack't, unroll'd each roll,
And every nail, and hinge and chest,
Secure from violence to rest,
Undrawn, unbroken, and unpry'd,
Unfelt, unsmelt, untasted, & uney'd,
Unboil'd, unbak'd, unroasted, and unfry'd;
Protecting them from all abuse,
And keeping them unus'd, for use.[11]

On September 25, Bernard addressed the Assembly. Admitting
that the expediency of a particular tax might be denied, he up-
held Parliament's right to tax the colonies. He asked whether
the province could bear "a cessation of law and justice, and of
trade and navigation" at this time in the year, and, thinking
of the August riots in Boston, urged that compensation be made
"to the sufferers by the late dreadful disturbances." A month
later the Assembly answered that it had the sole right to legislate and determine taxes for the province and refused to order
compensation.[12] In the course of a Biblical imitation which reviews the history of the Stamp Act, Francis the Ruler addresses
the wise men in the Sanhedrim:

20. I say not that the tribute is well or ill placed, but the decree
hath gone forth, and we must submit.

[11] *Connecticut Gazette* (New Haven), Sept. 27, 1765, p. 4.
[12] Hutchinson, *History*, Appendices C and D, III, 334–343 *passim*.

21. For, alas! what availeth opposition to the will of the decree when those who made it have power to establish the right thereof.

22. Now if you should deny that right, what do you but bring down the heavy vengeance of the rulers of Britain upon you? And how can you abide in the day of their wrath?

23. Neither will your petition to our Lord the King avail, if you deny the power of his great council over you.

24. But while you refuse this tribute, the calamities that will fall upon you will be great; for without the marked papers and skins of lambs, your ships cannot come in nor go out of your cities, and the courts of justice will be shut, that if a man smiteth you or taketh your garment from you, you cannot make him come before the judge in the gates.

25. And now behold I advise you to restore unto those whose habitations have been torn down, and whose things have been destroyed, that which they have suffered from the violences of the men of Belial.

26. And strive ye to quiet the minds of the people, that they may be obedient unto the tribute until such times as it should be taken off.

To all this the wise men answer that their forefathers came to America "under the faith of certain decrees which the Kings of the children of England granted unto them," the chief of these being that "they should have their own Sanhedrim, in which they should be taxed." How then, they ask, "can we give up the rights of our forefathers?" [13]

Bernard's authority challenged by a resolute legislature, one satirist represented him as replying, "So differently from your usual Way you have answer'd my Speech, / That nothing could offend me more, save a Kick in my Breech." [14] Even at this early date Bernard realized that the "Question will not be whether there shall be a Stamp Act or not; but whether America shall

[13] "The Book of AMERICA," *Newport Mercury*, May 19, 1766, pp. 1-2 (from the London *Gazetteer*).

[14] "*His Excellency* BERNARDUS FRANCISCO's *Speech versify'd*," *Weyman's New York Gazette*, Dec. 9, 1765, p. 2.

or shall not be Subject to the Legislature of Great Britain." [15] His popularity in Massachusetts declined steadily from this time, and there was a mutual feeling of relief when he embarked for England in 1769, never to return.

Cadwallader Colden, acting governor of New York at the time of the Stamp Act, behaved with less discretion than Bernard and suffered accordingly. Encouraged by the promise of additional troops for Fort George, he informed Sir William Johnson that he expected "to defeat all their Measures and that the Stamps shall be delivered in proper time after their arrival. I shall not be intimidated." [16] When the stamped paper arrived he took it into custody. On the night of November 1 a mob made effigies of Colden and the devil, seized his coach, and "soon reared a large Pile, to which setting Fire, it soon kindled to a great Flame, and reduced the Coach, Gallows, Man, Devil, and all to Ashes." [17] Three days later Colden was persuaded to deliver the stamped paper to the city hall, whereupon the rioting ceased.[18] Although he had labored hard to execute the Act, the aged governor was reprimanded by an unsympathetic Ministry for not having put forth still greater effort. Five years later William Livingston, defeated in a provincial election by the government party, retaliated with a political allegory that finds Colden in soliloquy. Last among his "sundry and divers and supernumery meritorious Services and Sufferings, Losses and Crosses, Writings and Fightings" in the cause of the Crown, this Colden recollects:

My Landlord once took a notion of having all the Horses and Cattle of his Tenants marked and branded, they paying so much a Head to

[15] Bernard to Barrington, Nov. 23, 1765, *The Barrington-Bernard Correspondence*, ed. E. Channing and A. C. Coolidge (Cambridge, Mass., 1912), pp. 95-96.

[16] Colden to Johnson, Aug. 31, 1765, *Colden Letter Books*, II, 27, 28, quoted in F. L. Engelman, *Wm. & Mary Quar.*, ser. 3, X (1953), 565.

[17] *New-York Gazette*, Nov. 7, 1765, quoted in Engelman, *Wm. & Mary Quar.*, X, 572.

[18] Engelman, *Wm. & Mary Quar.*, X, 576.

the Agents whom he appointed for that Purpose. But on sending the *Marking-irons,* the Tenants rose in a Body; and attempted to seize and destroy the *notarial Instruments,* stock and block. Upon this, in sheer Fidelity to his Interest (expecting however a small Gratuity in the End, if his Honor should be so minded) I took all the Irons into my own Tenement. To rescue them out of my Possession, they attacked the Messuage. Determined to repel the Assault, I threw up Trenches, fortified the Passes, covered the Fences with Brush, and furbished up every Sword, Pistol, Bayonet, and Fowling-piece in the House. I pierced the Garret for threescore Muskets. I ordered a Chauldron of boiling Water into the third Story; and disposed of my Dung-cart, ready loaded, to defend the Postern. I cast four pewter Urinals into Bullets; and converted an old Frying-pan into a Breast-plate. I turned two Spits into Spiers, and six Brass Kettles into as many Drums. Of my Mustard-grinder I made an excellent Bomb; and a very comfortable Helmet of an half worn Iron Chafing-dish. Thus fortified and accoutred, and looking like *Mars,* as one Egg is like another. I called to my Assistance a trusty Band of his Dependents; and threatened to return the Attack, by setting Fire to every Hut, Cottage, Barn, Hovel, Cow-pen, Dove-house, Hen-roost, Barrack, and Stable on the whole Estate. In short, I displayed the most heroic Conduct, and though I never had any Connection with military Affairs, save in a certain Capacity that requires neither Powder nor Ball, I exhibited both the Skill and Bravery of the most experienced General; and finally preserved all the Irons from the meditated Destruction. To revenge their Disappointment, the In-surgents carried off, and burnt my Wheel-barrow; and consigned to the same Fate two of my Family Pictures, *the Devil's* and *my own.* But effectually to prevent their renewing the Siege, I ordered a Detachment in the dead of Night, to take off the Locks, and p——s in the Barrels of every Musket in the Vicinity.[19]

[19] *A Soliloquy* (New York, 1770), pp. 13–14. Charles Evans explains that this satire was "occasioned by a suit in equity in his Majesty's name, by Lord Dunmore, against Lieutenant-Govenor Colden for a moiety of the profits of government during Colden's administration," *American Bibliography* (Chicago, 1903–1934), IV, 233. Alice Keys, after praising Colden, is forced to admit that "unfortunately the moment his mind touched on politics, . . . his sympathy, his plasticity, his humanity

Historically more significant than these demonstrations against dutiful governors like Bernard and Colden was a call to inter-colonial action. On June 8, 1765, the Massachusetts Assembly voted to send a circular letter to the other provincial assemblies, urging that a congress be held "to consider of a general and united, dutiful, loyal and humble Representation of their Condition to His Majesty and the Parliament; and to implore Relief." On October 19, twenty-seven delegates met at New York (New Hampshire, Virginia, North Carolina, and Georgia were not represented) and petitioned "His Majesty's person and Government" in language more conciliatory than that used by Virginia, asking "that no taxes be imposed on them but with their own consent, given personally or by their representatives" and urging that the Stamp Act be repealed.[20]

II

Copies of the resolutions of the Stamp Act Congress had scarcely been dispatched to England when the first of November arrived, the day on which the Act was to go into force. "Must I be thus *mark'd* or *Stamp'd?*" lamented the *New-Hampshire Gazette*, speaking for the freedom of all. "Tyranny, Popery, and arbitrary Power soon began to disappear, upon my coming on the Stage, and have by me received many a fatal Blow since; but it may be expected, that as soon as I am *extinct*, they will arise, and overspread the Land." [21] One writer dreamed he encountered a "Croud of PAPERS." "To each of them, as to the Prophet's Ass, / A Tongue was giv'n to tell his wretched Case." Before the *Bond* has finished telling his case,

---

even, dropped from him and he became a martinet, an intolerant theorist, an implacable stickler for the letter of the law, while tact and common sense became qualities to him unknown," *Cadwallader Colden* (New York, 1906), p. 365.

[20] Quoted in Morgan, *Stamp Act*, p. 103; Commager, *Documents*, p. 58.

[21] "The LAMENTATION of the NEW-HAMPSHIRE GAZETTE," *New-Hampshire Gazette* (Portsmouth), Oct. 31, 1765, pp. 1–2.

> Him interrupt the *Papers* of the *Court;*
> *Summons* and *Writ,* and all of ev'ry Sort.
> Must we be st--pt, when we so much have done
> To serve the present and the Ages gone?
> We've call'd the Debtor to discharge his Debt;
> We many Rogues at Justice' Bar have set.

The *Licence Paper* cries out,

> For Ages past I've fill'd the generous Bowl,
> And pour'd seraphick Pleasures on the Soul
> Of old and young, the Statesman and the Priest,
> And lull'd their troubled Minds to quiet rest.

King and Parliament, hearing the "wretched *Papers* dying groans," repeal the grievous laws, whereupon the narrator applauds and, waking, finds it all a dream.[22] As a matter of fact, after November 1 scarcely a sheet of stamped paper was to be obtained north of Georgia, and though many of the courts were closed, most of the printers and tavern owners did business as usual.[23]

Unable to lay hold on Bute and Grenville, whom they regarded as chief architects of the Stamp Act, the Americans dealt severely with the stamp distributors in their stead. Regarded as traitors to the land of their birth, they suffered loss of esteem as well as persecution. "Philoleutherus" boasted that distributors "have been intimidated into a resignation, by those hardy sons of liberty, and have the mortification to see all their vile schemes of enriching themselves out of the plunder of their fellow-subjects, blasted in an instant." Don't you "vile miscreants" know, he harangued, that we love liberty and abhor slavery!

Murder your fathers, rip up the bowels of your mothers, dash the infants you have begotten against the stones, and be blameless; —but

[22] "A Dream," in *A New Collection of Verses applied to the First of November* (New Haven, 1765), pp. 19–23.

[23] Mary A. M. Marks, *England and America* (London, 1907), I, 41; Morgan, *Stamp Act*, p. 188; John C. Miller, *Origins of the American Revolution* (Boston, 1943), p. 142.

enslave your country! entail vassalage, that worst of all human miseries, that sum of all wretchedness, on millions! This, this is guilt, this calls for heaven's fiercest vengeance.[24]

Andrew Oliver, a fourth-generation resident of Massachusetts and in this instance a more or less innocent victim, had vigorously opposed passage of the Stamp Act and then, to help enforce it, reluctantly accepted the job of distributor.[25] On the morning of August 14 he was hung in effigy at Boston, on an elm known thereafter as the Liberty Tree. That night the effigy was burned and a building of Oliver's, thought to have been intended for the stamp office, razed. Oliver resigned the next day. The events of the fourteenth were recounted soon after in angry doggerel.

> A stately elm appear'd before my eyes,
> Whose lofty branches seem'd to touch the skies.
> Its limbs were bent with more than common fruit,
> It bore the Devil, O[live]r and B[u]te.

At nightfall a hero orders the bodies cut down and placed on the bier.

> This done, he cries "Let ev'ry man resort
> In solemn order, with the corpse to *court*"
> March then (said he) in one united throng
> "And as you march, be this the fun'ral song:
>   *Great* Jove *decrees, and go these mortals must,*
>   *'Tis earth to earth, and* STAMP *'em in the dust.*"

As they bear the bodies toward Fort Hill, only a "stately EDIFICE" opposes their way,

> but soon they down with this
> Low in the dust they made the structure lay

---

[24] *Constitutional Courant* (Woodbridge, N.J.), Sept. 21, 1765, p. 1; reprinted in *Pub. Col. Soc. Mass.*, XI (Dec. 1907), 423–427. Only one issue of this fake journal appeared, printed by William Goddard (Schlesinger, *Prelude*, p. 73).

[25] Herbert S. Allan, *John Hancock* (New York, 1948), p. 87.

> Then STAMP the bricks, and bore the wood away.
> Now from the ruins ev'ry one retire,
> Up to the *mount*, and raise the fun'ral fire.[26]

Of all the distributors Jared Ingersoll of Connecticut gained the greatest notoriety. It surprised him mightily, upon returning from England in early August to take up his duties, to find himself under attack in the press; for though he failed to prevent the stamp tax, "he had done more than any other man to reduce the size of it." [27] On September 15 he was forced to resign. A month earlier "Cato" had inveighed:

Those who lately set themselves up for Patriots and boasted a generous Love for their Country, . . . are THEY now creeping after the Profits of collecting the Unrighteous *American* Stamp Duty! . . . Where are the Mercenary Publicans who delight in Nothing so much as the dearest Blood of their Country? Will the Cries of your despairing, dying Brethren, be Music pleasing to your Ears? If so, go on! bend the Knee to your Master Horseleach, and beg a Share in the Pillage of your Country.—*No*, you'll say, *I don't Delight in the Ruin of my Country, but, since 'tis decreed she must fall, who can blame me for taking a Part of the Plunder?* Tenderly said! Why did you not rather say,—*If my Father must die, who can accuse me as defective in filial Duty, in becoming his Executioner, that so much of the Estate, at least, as goes to the Hangman, may be retained in the Family?*

If anyone should ask, *"But had you not rather these Duties should be collected by your Brethren, than by Foreigners?"* we would reply:

No! vile Miscreant! indeed we had not. . . . A Foreigner we could more chearfully endure, because he might be supposed not to feel our Distresses; but for one of our *Fellow Slaves*, who equally shares in our Pains, to rise up and beg the Favour of inflicting them, is intolerable. The only Advantage that can be hoped for from this

[26] *Liberty, Property and No Excise* (Boston, 1765); reprinted in the *Magazine of History*, XXI (1922), 135–139.
[27] Morgan, *Stamp Act*, p.232.

is, that it will rouse the most indolent of us to a Sense of our Slavery, and make us use our strongest Efforts to be free.[28]

John Hughes, the stamp distributor for Pennsylvania, a man long affiliated with the government party, began to receive suggestions early in September that he ought to resign. On October 7, the colony being unwilling to brook further delay, he promised not to execute the Act until the other colonies should do so.[29] If Hughes doesn't refuse to act, a Philadelphian had inveighed in September,

> Grant Heaven, that he may never go without,
> The Rheumatism, Itch, the Pox or Gout.
> May he be hamper'd with some ugly Witch,
> And dye at last in some curst foulsome Ditch.
> Without the Benefit of Psalms or Hymnes,
> And Crowds of Crows devour his rotten Limbs.
> May wanton Boys, to Town his Bones convey,
> To make a Bonfire on a Rejoicing Day.[30]

Early in September a mob forced the Maryland distributor Zachariah Hood to flee for his life, "over the top of a house at midnight . . . in nothing but his breeches and shirt" (according to one account). He sought refuge at New York but, when confronted by another mob on November 26, offered his resignation rather than be handed over to the Maryland Sons of Liberty.[31] In what purports to be a genuine account of the execution of "Z. H. Esq.," one writer tells how Hood

was brought from the place of confinement in a cart, . . . to the whipping post, and received Moses's law, so well and methodically

---

[28] *Connecticut Gazette*, Aug. 9, 1765, p. 3. The author was Naphtali Daggett, Professor of Divinity at Yale College, "whose enmity Ingersoll had earned ten years before," Morgan, *Stamp Act*, p. 233. "Tom Touchit," who was of a like mind with Daggett, attacked Ingersoll in the *Boston Gazette*, Sept. 9, 1765, p. 2.

[29] Morgan, *Stamp Act*, pp. 247–252 *passim*.

[30] "The LAMENTATION, OF PENNSYLVANIA, On Account of the Stamp-Act," Philadelphia broadside, Sept. 6, 1765.

[31] Morgan, *Stamp Act*, pp. 153–154; Moore's *Ballad History*, p. 41; Miller, *Origins*, p. 132.

laid on, that he was rendered almost incapable of speaking any more, so as to be heard at the least distance. He exhibited some faint symptoms of penitence, and would willingly have suffered any corporal punishment to have lived. . . . The sons of liberty would not hear of it, but cried, *Hang him, burn him, &c. &c.* He hinted and made signs that the St– –ps lay heavy at his stomach, and took a vomit, which operated well, and gave some little relief. He was put in the pillory, then [hiatus] and afterwards burnt: He bore it with great patience, and it was observed by all, that his countenance never once changed until he was burning.

At the last Hood confesses to the executioner:

I was indulged too much in my younger years by my tutors. I never was instructed in the true and virtuous principles of religion, viz. such as to fear my God and love my neighbours. Nor did I ever regard honour, honesty, or liberty, but said, What's my country to me, I'LL GET MONEY. . . . I once more acknowledge my villainy to my country; nor have any consolation in my last moments to afford myself, as having always, when in my power, defrauded my King, the proprietor, and my countrymen.[32]

Several years later another satirist, aware apparently that according to law any person persecuted in pursuance of the Stamp Act might plead for indemnification, recalled that

On death-bed, despairing, as George Grenville lay,
And the devil stood waiting to take him away,
In rush'd Doctor Moffat and Zachary Hood,
And urged, he, their loss, ere he died would make good.
"Since our country's resentment upon us we drew
By supporting the schemes of the devil and you,
And for striving to make them a nation of slaves,
Have been treated and deemed as vile traitors and knaves,

. . . . .

'Tis but just that yourself should those losses repay,
Before you go hence with devil away;"

[32] *New-York Gazette*, Nov. 21, 1765, p. 4. In the *Maryland Gazette* (Annapolis), Aug. 29, 1765, p. 2, a London gentleman expressed similar views about Hood in a letter to a friend at Annapolis.

"Oh," faintly says Grenville, "in peace let me lie,
And the devil will pay you your due when I die:"
"No, no," they both cried, "we will not be so shamm'd,
First pay us, and then you may die and be ------." [33]

III

On October 31, 1765, some two hundred New York merchants resolved not to import any more goods from Britain nor
to sell to her after January 1 until the Stamp Act was repealed.
Within six weeks merchants at Philadelphia and Boston to the
number of 650 had reached similar agreements.[34] A "Bard of
the Woods" asked Bostonians:

> Abroad for rich Dress,
> For Silks or for Lace,
>   Why foolishly thus do we roam?
> Their Raiment and Food
> Sure do Us no good,
>   When enough of our own we've at home.
>
>   . . . . .
>
> And e're to such Acts
> As impose a new Tax,
>   That Might and not Right must sustain,
> Let us hive with the Bee,
> Eat the Crust of the Tree,
>   And away to the Fig-Leaf again.[35]

[33] Broadside, Aug., 1773, n.p.; reprinted in Moore's *Ballad History*,
pp. 38–39. On Sept. 2 the Maryland Sons of Liberty had pulled down
Hood's house (Morgan, *Stamp Act*, pp. 153–154). Thomas Moffat of
Newport, Rhode Island, was in sympathy with the Crown.

[34] Carl Becker, *The History of Political Parties in the Province of
New York, 1760–1776* (Madison, 1909), p. 30; Arthur M. Schlesinger, *The
Colonial Merchants and the American Revolution* (New York, 1918),
pp. 78–80.

[35] "*Advice from the* COUNTRY," *Massachusetts Gazette, and Boston
News-Letter*, Oct. 31, 1765, Extraordinary, p. 1; reprinted in the *Gentleman's Magazine*, XXXV (Dec., 1765), 575. Bernard confessed that "the
country people were even more violent in their opposition to the Stamp
Act than the Bostonians," Morgan, *Stamp Act*, p. 130.

British merchants realized that when these nonimportation agreements went into effect they faced probable bankruptcy, and at once resolved to work for repeal. That winter merchants from London and a score of other towns, a new Ministry headed by Rockingham organizing their discontent, sent Parliament no fewer than thirty-five petitions.[36]

Parliament convened on January 14, and debate on the question of repeal was mounted shortly. In Commons, William Pitt drew a distinction between the power to tax and the power to legislate, one which most members found novel and dangerous, and recommended

that the Stamp Act be repealed absolutely, totally, and immediately. That the reason for the repeal be assigned, viz., because it was founded on an erroneous principle. At the same time, let the sovereign authority of this country over the colonies be asserted in as strong terms as can be devised, and be made to extend to every point of legislation whatsoever; that we may bind their trade, confine their manufactures, and exercise every power whatsoever, except that of taking their money out of their pockets without their consent.[37]

In one of the ablest speeches he ever delivered, George Grenville, more concerned with what was constitutional than with what was expedient, argued that the Stamp Act should be continued in force; but, in the words of an English satirist, his tongue "was as the tongue of the wicked, and he made no great weight with the Clacking thereof." [38] According to another, in a "Dialogue on Education, between Fair George and Lame Will" the latter "proved it to be both cruel and impolitic to pinch Children till they Cry, and then pinch them for Crying." [39] This

[36] Dora Mae Clark, *British Opinion and the American Revolution* (New Haven, 1930), pp. 39, 42; Morgan, *Stamp Act*, pp. 264–265; Charles R. Ritcheson, *British Politics and the American Revolution* (Norman, Okla., 1954), p. 48.

[37] Morgan, *Stamp Act*, p. 273; *Great Debates in American History*, ed. M. M. Miller (New York, 1913), I, 49.

[38] "The first book of MARKS," *London Chronicle*, Mar. 22, 1766, p. 277; reprinted in the *Virginia Gazette* (Williamsburg), July 11, 1766, p. 2.

[39] "The PROEM," *London Chronicle*, Apr. 5, 1766.

Parliamentary debate was further celebrated in a spirited song.

> Quoth the Devil to Gr.nv.ll. I've drawn up a plan,
> And think in my conscience that thou art the MAN;
> When e're I intend any evil to do,
> You may always be sure I will pitch upon you.
>
> O'er-joy'd at the news like a courtier polite,
> He thanked the Devil, and thought all was right;
> Expecting large share, of the profits in fact,
> Arising by virtue of the *Noble Stamp-Act.*
>
> . . . . .
>
> But behold! *one* arises, unrival'd in MERIT!
> With *eloquence* fitted to his noble spirit:
> With the sound of *cheek music,* this politick *Messiah,*
> Knock'd Gr.nn.v.ll. quite stiff, as did *David, Goliah.*[40]

Benjamin Franklin chose this moment to send an ironical letter to the English press over the signature "Pacificus," arguing for repeal more bluntly than he would in an examination before Commons a fortnight hence: "There are some Persons besides the Americans so amazingly stupid, as to distinguish in this Dispute between *Power* and *Right,* as tho' the former did not always imply the latter." Force must therefore be made use of, and the "American Plea of *Right,* their Appeal to Magna Charta," set aside. I have a plan for coercing America which cannot fail, one so cheap that even Mr. George Grenville, "that great Oeconomist," can "have no reasonable Objection to it." It is to transport

Two Thousand Highlanders . . . [if] Roman Catholics, the better . . . early in the Spring to Quebec: They with the Canadians, natural Enemies to our Colonists, who would voluntarily engage, might make a Body of Five or Six Thousand Men; and I doubt not, by artful Management, and the Value of two or three Thousand Pounds in Presents, with the Hopes of Plunder, as likewise a Gratuity for every Scalp, the Savages on the Frontiers might be engaged to join,

---

[40] "A New Song, On the Repeal of the Stamp-Act," Philadelphia broadside, 1766.

at least they would make a Diversion, which could not fail of being useful.

From Canada this expedition might fall upon the Americans when they least expected it, burn their capitals, cut the throats of men, women, and children and scalp them, and destroy all their shipping. "The Business might be done without employing any of the Regular Troops quartered in the Country, and I think it would be best they should remain neuter, as it is to be feared they would be rather backward in embruing their Hands in the Blood of their Brethren and Fellow Subjects." As for the Stamp Act, "No Man in his Wits, after such terrible Military Execution, will refuse to purchase stamp'd Paper. If any one should hesitate, five or six Hundred Lashes in a cold frosty Morning would soon bring him to Reason." Pacificus concludes:

If the Massacre should be objected to, as it would too much depopulate the Country, it may be replied, that the Interruption this Method would occasion to Commerce, would cause so many Bankruptcies, such Numbers of Manufacturers and Labourers would be unemployed, that, together with the Felons from our Gaols, we should soon be enabled to transport such Numbers to repeople the Colonies, as to make up for any Deficiency which Example made it Necessary to sacrifice for the Public Good. Great Britain might then reign over a loyal and submissive People, and be morally certain, that no Act of Parliament would ever after be disputed.[41]

Masking as a peace-loving Briton, Franklin here innocently declares, "I shall think myself happy if I can furnish any Hints that may be of public Utility," and proceeds, with apparent good humor and impartiality, to propose a plan for the conquest of America so devastatingly thorough as (so he hoped) to prick the conscience of the most hardened minister of state. Having failed to anticipate the tempest that arose over the Stamp Act in America, he is here making amends by exercising his very considerable talent for irony.

At this juncture the Rockingham Ministry, more favorably

[41] *Public Advertiser*, Jan. 26, 1766, p. 2; reprinted in Crane, pp. 55–57.

disposed toward the Americans than Grenville's had been, was
faced with a dilemma: how to redress the grievances of the merchants and at the same time uphold the authority of Parliament.
It was finally decided that a declaratory act, asserting that Parliament had "full power and authority to make laws and statutes
of sufficient force and validity to bind the colonies and people
of *America,* . . . in all cases whatsoever," should be introduced
before the bill for repeal.[42] On March 18, 1766, both bills gained
royal assent. An allegorical ballad tells how Goody Bull's daughter took exception to her mother's assumption that she would
earn her own bread.

> She sobb'd and she blubber'd, she bluster'd and swore,
> If her mother persisted, she'd turn common whore,
> The Old Woman, thus threaten'd, fell down in a fit,
> And who in the nick should hop in but *Will. P–tt.*

Farmer Pitt rebukes the mother and demands, "Be rul'd by your
friends, kneel down and ask pardon; / You'd be sorry, I'm sure,
should she walk *Covent-Garden.*"

> Unwillingly aukward, the mother knelt down,
> While the absolute farmer went on with a frown,
> Come kiss the poor child, then, come kiss and be friends,
> There, kiss your poor daughter, and make her amends.

> No thanks to you, mother; the daughter replied:
> But thanks to my friend here, I've humbled your pride;
> Then pray leave off this nonsense, 'tis all a mere farce,
> As I have carried my point, you may now kiss my – – – –.[43]

Though the idea was finally dropped, Parliament for a time contemplated requiring the Americans to make payment for the
stamps they should have used while the Act was in force. Such
proceedings reminded Franklin of the anecdote about

[42] Morgan, *Stamp Act,* p. 265; Commager, *Documents,* p. 61.
[43] "*The* WORLD *turned upside down; or, The* OLD WOMAN *taught Wisdom,*" *London Chronicle,* Mar. 11, 1766, p. 236; reprinted in Moore's *Ballad History,* pp. 17–19.

1768) Lawyer Dickinson, who would play a conservative role during the struggle for independence and confederation, presented the following chain of logic:

Let these *truths* be indelibly impressed on our minds—*that we cannot be* HAPPY, *without being* FREE—that we cannot be free, *without being secure in our property*—that *we* cannot be secure in our property, *if, without our consent, others may, as by right, take it away*—that *taxes imposed on us by parliament*, do thus take it away —*that duties laid for the sole purpose of raising money*, are taxes— that *attempts* to lay such duties *should be instantly and firmly opposed*—that this opposition can never be effectual, *unless it is the united effort of these provinces*.

Here was an argument less compromising than Dulany's two years earlier; after all, Dulany had not gone so far as to deny that Parliament had the right to levy customs duties. Toward presenting a united front to the British government Massachusetts strove mightily to secure an intercolonial nonimportation agreement. And on February 11, 1768, the Assembly issued a circular letter, drawn up by Samuel Adams, informing the other colonies what it really thought of the Townshend Acts.[1] Certain in its own mind how the British Constitution should be construed, the Assembly declared that

his Majesty's American Subjects, . . . have an equitable Claim to the full enjoyment of the fundamental Rules of the British Constitution: . . . exclusive of any Consideration of Charter Rights, . . . the Acts . . . imposing Duties on the People of this province, with the sole & express purpose of raising a Revenue, are Infringements of their natural & constitutional Rights.[2]

On August 1 merchants at Boston, having failed initially to secure general nonimportation, drew up their own agreement independently. At the end of the month New York merchants

[1] There were, in addition to the Revenue Act, a bill establishing a board of customs at Boston and another suspending the New York Assembly until it complied with the Mutiny Act.

[2] Commager, *Documents*, p. 66.

and traders subscribed to an agreement more stringent than Boston's, and within a year all of the colonies except New Hampshire had joined the movement.[3] The situation of the colonies put Franklin in mind of the cows in the fable:

Forbidden to suckle their own calves, and daily drawn dry, they yet parted with their milk willingly; but when moreover a tax came to be demanded of them (and that too to be paid in grass, of which they had already too short a provision) it was no wonder they thought their masters unreasonable, and resolved, for the future, to suck one another.[4]

As a result of such nonimportation agreements British exports to America in 1769 declined by a third.[5] Early in 1770, while the government was re-examining its colonial policy, Franklin forewarned the British nation at large:

A Lion's Whelp was put on board a Guinea Ship bound to America, as a Present to a Friend in that Country: It was tame and harmless as a Kitten, and therefore not confined, but suffered to walk about the Ship at Pleasure. A stately full grown English Mastiff, belonging to the Captain, despising the Weakness of the young Lion, frequently took it's *Food* by Force, and often turned it out of its Lodging Box, when he had a Mind to repose therein himself. The young Lion nevertheless grew daily in Size and Strength, and the Voyage being long, he became at last a more equal Match for the Mastiff, who continuing his Insults, received a stunning Blow from the Lion's Paw that fetched his Skin over his Ears, and deterred him from any future Contest with such growing Strength; regretting that he had not rather secured it's Friendship than provoked it's Enmity.[6]

[3] Schlesinger, *Merchants,* pp. 120, 124; Hinkhouse, *Preliminaries,* p. 150.
[4] *Pennsylvania Chronicle,* Dec. 12, 1768, p. 397; reprinted in Crane, p. 115. A year later Franklin related the same fable in the *Public Advertiser,* Jan. 2, 1770, p. 1.
[5] Trade statistics show a decline from £2,378,000 in 1768 to £1,634,000 in 1769 (Lecky, *American Revolution,* p. 135).
[6] *Public Advertiser,* Jan. 2, 1770, p. 2; reprinted in the *New-Jersey Journal,* Dec. 27, 1780, p. 2, wherein Franklin is identified as the author. See Verner W. Crane, *New Eng. Quar.,* IX (1936), 499–504, for the text and a discussion of this and two other political fables on the Revenue Act which appeared in the same issue of the *Public Advertiser.*

In a more serious vein Franklin as the "Colonist's Advocate" argued for repeal of the Townshend Revenue Act. But neither satire nor rational argument carried much weight with an administration headed shortly by Lord North, who blustered, "The properest time to exert our right to taxation is when the right is refused." [7] The Colonist's Advocate broke off his argument when North's motion of March 5 to retain the three-pence tax on tea convinced him that total repeal would be defeated.[8] On April 12 this four-fifths repeal became law.

Americans had even less cause for rejoicing than in 1766, for here was a Ministry bent on having its cake and eating it too. When the New York merchant "Hornbloom" tells his wife the news, urging that they hold firm and not buy tea, she scolds, " 'Curse on your Heads, you nasty fumbling Crew,' / Then round his Shoulders the hard Broom-Stick flew"; whereupon he scurries off to fetch some "Shushong" for a party she is giving that night.[9] In actual fact, the colonial boycott collapsed, and trade with Britain, except for purchases of taxed tea, was resumed.[10] Next to Charleston, Boston held out longest. Even after this partial repeal patriots there continued to attack those who failed to support nonimportation. "WHAT is the difference," asks one indignant Bostonian, "betwixt an *Importer* and an *Indian?*"

1. An Indian drinks Cyder—an Importer drinks the Blood of his Country.

2. An Indian is an Enemy only to himself—an Importer is an Enemy to America.

3. An Indian will sometimes fulfil his Engagements—but the

[7] Hansard, *Parliamentary History*, XVI, 854, quoted in Van Tyne, *Causes*, p. 307.

[8] Eleven "Colonist's Advocate" letters appeared in the *Public Advertiser* between Jan. 4 and Mar. 2, 1770; Verner Crane has recently identified these as by Franklin and reprints them in his *Letters to the Press*, pp. 167–209 *passim*.

[9] "The Female Patriot, No. 1. Addressed to the Tea-Drinking Ladies of New-York," New York broadside, May 10, 1770.

[10] Miller, *Origins*, p. 307.

strongest Cords, and the most solemn Engagements will not bind an Importer.

4. An Indian not having the Means of Light, is not subject to any tormenting Reflections—an Importer is eternally haunted with Apparitions, and the Horror of a guilty Conscience.

5. An Importer, covered over with Tar, would shine with an artificial Lustre—whereas the black Colour of the Indian is natural.

6. How the Indians came into the Country is unknown—but if Importers should have their Deserts, there would be no Witchcraft in determining how they would go *out*.[11]

Intercolonial jealousies, which contributed to the collapse of nonimportation, were sometimes cause for satire. Whatever provoked the following letter to the New York press—whether the early agreement Boston merchants made not to import and their renewal of faith in the summer of 1769,[12] John Mein's enumeration of the large quantities of goods consigned to signers of the Boston agreements,[13] or feelings of guilt because the active smuggling at New York and Philadelphia made it easier for merchants and traders there to observe their agreements to the letter—its author attacks Boston merchants whose professions of nonimportation speak louder than their practice: You Gentlemen (he gibes) "can testify, That a Visage contracted to the Model of a *Spanish Mule's*,—the solemn Pace of a dispassionate *Rosinante*; and above all, a Voice modulated and attuned to the deep Drone of a Wild-Irish Bagpipe, are never failing Sources of a *Saintly Character*, however *heathenish* MORALITY may be despised or neglected." May I point out, "for the Sake of our Brethren in this City and *Philadelphia*," that "your Mode of Opposition by *professions* and *Spirited Resolutions*, had not only a wider Influence,—but at the same Time your commercial Interests were promoted, and your Trade ran on in the same equal and uninterrupted Channel."

[11] *Massachusetts Spy*, Aug. 25, 1770, p. 3.
[12] Schlesinger, *Merchants*, pp. 121–122.
[13] Published in the *Boston Chronicle*, Sept. 21–Oct. 26, 1769.

You knew that Generosity and good Nature were the distinguishing Lineaments of ENGLISHMEN—that they were easily drawn by Tenderness, but obstinate and untractable by Violence: You therefore wisely chose not to offend and make them your Enemies by discarding Commerce with them; but brib'd them to Our Interest by secret Trade; and at the same Time by severe *Denunciations* against the *Ministry*, and repeated DECLARATIONS: "That you lov'd *Liberty* better than Meat and Drink—would die for Liberty, and retire into the *howling-Wilderness* for Liberty," you closed in with the current Dispositions of the People of Great-Britain—engaged them by your *Kindness*, and a *fellow-feeling*, to espouse Our Cause—and consequently, EFFECTED A REPEAL.

I admit that some among us "have profited by your Instructions," vaporing, scolding, threatening against importation while at the same time they have *"patriotically transmited their Orders for Goods."* "Such nice and delicate Movements in Politics the Majority of us," however, "are unable to imitate." Be it resolved therefore

That any *Resolves* of the good People of BOSTON, concerning their own Wisdom, Constancy, and Patriotism, shall ever hereafter be deemed good, sufficient, and undeniable Evidence of the Wisdom, Constancy, and Patriotism of the said good Folk of BOSTON, and whoever scruples giving his *Assent*, shall, for his Obstinacy, Perverseness, and Contumacy, be sent to— the Lord deliver him.[14]

After 1770 English goods flowed into the colonies once again, and the next three years were prosperous and calm ones.[15] The collapse of the boycott crippled for a time the development of domestic manufactures, which caused "A Husbandman" to sneer, "It's not long since our oracles the merchants, made us believe it was almost an unpardonable sin to buy any English goods." "That disagreeable noise made by the rattling of the foot wheel was accounted fine music. . . . But now the case is

[14] "To the *great* FOLK, . . . of BOSTON," *New-York Gazette, and Weekly Mercury*, Sept. 3, 1770, p. 1.
[15] Miller, *Origins*, p. 315; Schlesinger, *Merchants*, p. 240.

altered—now British manufactures are far better and cheaper than can be made in America;—How disagreeable is the noise of the spinning-wheel become?" [16]

II

Most Americans had vowed in 1768 and 1769 to abstain from drinking the customed tea, a resolve more easily kept at New York and Philadelphia, where one could usually buy tea smuggled from Holland, Sweden, or Germany.[17] The expedient of four-fifths repeal in 1770 did nothing to alter their resolution. Then, on May 10, 1773, Parliament passed the East India Act. To be sure, the tax on tea was retained, but a drawback on an English import duty on tea exported from Britain to America enabled the American consumer to buy "legal" tea more cheaply than contraband.[18] Now that Americans could buy English tea at a cheaper rate, it was thought that surpluses in the East India warehouses could be reduced and at the same time Parliament's right to tax the colonies maintained. Tea-smuggling merchants at New York, taking alarm at the virtual monoply now open to the East India Company, opposed the Act. Profit, not principle, was at stake. In a letter purportedly from Amsterdam, "John Beltes Van Catch Money," Secretary of the Dutch East India Company, beseeches "Admiral Pepperpot, Commodore Mac-eat-it, Phil Blusterlong, John Bythebelt, LOWRENCE THE CLINE, Dicky the Big, Alderman Smartpole, Senator Slack, John Van Doublechin, Strophel Van Spindle, Hugo Walloon, Bobbadil Sherry, Theophanus Van Smugglemuch, and Walter Broadbrim" not to forget the services already rendered them.

Reflect how we have nursed you, think on the long credits that we have given you, and the small premium we have charged you for interest; and, beloved friends, take it not amiss when we say, some

[16] *Essex Gazette* (Salem), May 19, 1772, p. 4.
[17] Schlesinger, *Merchants*, pp. 246–248.
[18] Clark, *British Opinion*, p. 74; Schlesinger, *Merchants*, p. 263.

of you were drawn out from obscurity and indigence, through us you are placed on pinnacles, from whence you cannot look down but with surprize and giddiness: Bear in mind also, that if the people get Tea a shilling a pound less than usual, that shilling is out of your pockets; suffer it not for all our sakes. . . . Let the people be told, (aye, and convinced too) that their health and circumstances require our Tea, the poisonous quality being drawn off before we ship it.[19]

And "Isaac Van Pompkin," alarmed to think that the people here at New York now "have an opportunity of buying good English Tea, for half the price we expected to extort from them, for the trash lodged in your hands from Holland," informs the Dutch agents at St. Eustatia:

Our partner, Sawney Sedition, has wrote, published, threatened, prayed, and lied, to delude the inhabitants from buying English Tea: Duty, or no duty, he tried to make the people believe their liberties were alike affected; but all will not serve to call the people together. The consumers of Tea in this city, will no longer be blinded to their own interest; therefore, dispatch our Dutch Tea immediately, that we may get it sold before the English arrives. Oh! *Donder enblexin!* Dispatch! Dispatch! or we are undone.[20]

Early in the fall of 1773, at a time when the fateful tea ships were weighing anchor for America, a remarkable hoax was per- petrated in the English press. Written with such an air of au- thenticity that only his closest associates "smoked" it, Franklin's "Edict by the King of Prussia," one of a number of his journalis- tic tricks in which the London editor Henry S. Woodfall con- nived, was in actuality an ironic expression of colonial griev- ances against the English mercantile system dating back, some of them, to the previous century. If history chanced to play into his hands, it was not chance that Franklin could meet the

[19] "LETTER Found on board *the sloop* ILLICIT, CAPTAIN PERJURY, wrecked at OYSTER BAY," New York broadside, July 3, 1773.

[20] "To THE AGENTS Of Their HIGH MIGHTINESSES the Dutch East-India Company, at St. Eustatia," [New York] broadside, Oct. 28, 1773.

occasion with the wholly appropriate jargon of state displomacy —a language at once precise, involuted, unembellished, euphemistic. The better to insure unity Franklin constructs a *reductio ad absurdum:* England is to Prussia as America is to England. Frederick King of Prussia declares that in order to regulate commerce, improve finances, and ease taxes at home,

there shall be levied and paid to our officers of the *customs*, on all goods, wares, and merchandizes, and on all grain and other produce of the earth, exported from the said Island of Britain, and on all goods of whatever kind imported into the same, a duty of four and a half per cent *ad valorem*, for the use of us and our successors.

Moreover, iron manufacture shall henceforth be forbidden and severe restraints placed on the hat industry in said island.

To encourage, not only the manufacturing of woollen cloth, but also the raising of wool, in our ancient dominions, and to prevent both, as much as may be, in our said island, we do hereby absolutely forbid the transportation of wool from thence, even to the mother country, Prussia; and that those islanders may be farther and more effectually restrained in making any advantage of their own wool in the way of manufacture, we command that none shall be carried out of one county into another. . . . Nevertheless, our loving subjects there are hereby permitted (if they think proper) to use all their wool as manure for the improvement of their lands.

Lastly,

we do hereby also ordain and command, that all the *thieves*, highway and street robbers, housebreakers, forgerers, murderers, s—d—tes, and villains of every denomination, who have forfeited their lives to the law in Prussia; but whom we, in our great clemency, do not think fit here to hang, shall be emptied out of our gaols into the said island of Great Britain, for the better peopling of that country.

In conclusion,

all persons in the said island are hereby cautioned not to oppose in any wise the execution of this our Edict, or any part thereof, such opposition being high treason; of which all who are suspected shall be transported in fetters from Britain to Prussia, there to be tried and executed according to the Prussian law.

What renders the hoax more plausible is the impression conveyed in a postscript that the correspondent is simply an impartial witness to the matter at hand.

Some take this Edict to be merely one of the King's *Jeux d'Esprit:* others suppose it serious, and that he means a quarrel with England; but all here [at Danzig] think the assertion it concludes with, "that these regulations are copied from acts of the English parliament respecting their colonies," a very injurious one; it being impossible to believe, that a people distinguished for their love of liberty, a nation so wise, so liberal in its sentiments, so just and equitable towards its neighbours, should, from mean and injudicious views of petty immediate profit, treat its own children in a manner so arbitrary and tyrannical! [21]

The dispatching of the tea ships to America brought the controversy over tea to a head. At Philadelphia the ship was refused entry at customs and set sail at once, its cargo undisturbed.[22] Not content to let the matter rest there, on October 18 the citizens of that town resolved:

That the disposal of their own property is the inherent right of freemen; that there can be no property in that which another can, of right, take from us without our consent. . . . That the express purpose for which the tax is levied on the Americans,—namely, for the support of government, administration of justice, and defence of his Majesty's dominions in America, has a direct tendency to render assemblies useless, and to introduce arbitrary government and slavery.[23]

[21] *Public Advertiser*, Sept. 22, 1773, p. 1; reprinted in the *Pennsylvania Packet*, Dec. 13, 1773, and again in Smyth, VI, 118–124. See Smyth, VI, 146, for an anecdote concerning its reception in England. A possible source for the "Edict" is Horace Walpole's fictitious letter in French, from Frederick King of Prussia to Jean Jacques Rousseau, included in a letter of Jan. 12, 1766, to Henry Conway, *The Letters of Horace Walpole* (Oxford, 1904), VI, 396–397.

[22] Schlesinger, *Merchants*, pp. 290–291.

[23] Quoted in R. T. H. Halsey, *The Boston Port Bill as Pictured by a Contemporary London Cartoonist* (New York, 1904), pp. 70–71.

So comprehensive were these Philadelphia resolutions that the other provincial towns soon adopted them. At New York, in a salty letter that hints at an unholy alliance between sailors and tea-smuggling merchants, "Tom Bowline" advised his messmates:

As the Time is approaching, in which the Ship, with the East India Company's Tea may be expected to arrive, and be moored in our Harbour, to put the finishing Stroke to our Liberties, and ruin the Trade of our Country, by establishing a Monopoly; which will in Time (should it be effected) deprive Numbers of our worthy Merchants of their Sheet Anchor, and oblige them to quit their Moorings, and steer into the Country, to take a Trick at the Plough; and will (as sure as the Devil's in London) drive many of us to the cruel Alternative of seeking Employment in a foreign Country, to prevent starving in our own: And, as much depends upon our Steadiness, and Activity, in Regard to weathering this Storm; I must therefore, strongly recommend the Necessity of keeping a good Look out; and that we do, one and all, hold ourselves in Readiness, and heartily join our Merchants, and other worthy Citizens, in preventing this pestilential Commodity from being parbuckled on Shore.[24]

Tom got his wish, for when the tea reached New York in April it was cast into the harbor forthwith.[25]

To the northward a more memorable demonstration took place four months earlier. "Last night," wrote John Adams on December 17, 1773, "three cargoes of tea were emptied into the harbor. . . . All things were conducted with great order, decency, and *perfect submission to government*." [26] Governor Hutchinson, it seems, had refused to let one of the tea ships, whose cargo would be liable to seizure shortly for nonpayment of duty, leave Boston harbor, whereupon the local Sons of Liberty destroyed £10,000 worth of East India tea, taking care

[24] "A LETTER, From Tom Bowline, to his worthy Messmates," New York broadside, Dec. 20, 1773. Becker says that the East India Act "was disliked by all classes" in New York (*Political Parties*, p. 103).

[25] Schlesinger, *Merchants*, p. 294.

[26] *The Works of John Adams*, ed. C. F. Adams (Boston, 1850–1856), IX, 333, 334.

that no other property was damaged and no persons injured.[27] Six weeks after the Boston Tea Party a number of "the fair Daughters of Liberty" quipped, "That as hanging, drawing and quartering, are the Punishments inflicted by Law in Cases of High-Treason, we are determined, constantly to assemble at each other's Houses, to HANG the Tea-Kettles, DRAW the Tea, and QUARTER the Toast." [28] And Mercy Warren, urged by John Adams to describe this "late frolic among the Sea Nymphs and Goddesses," composed a mock-heroic poem that he in his enthusiasm was so imperceptive as to compare to *The Rape of the Lock.*[29] "The heroes of the Tuscararo tribe / . . . In order rang'd, and waited freedom's nod, / To make an offering to the wat'ry god." Amphytrite

> Was well appris'd the centaurs would conspire;
> Resolv'd to set the western world on fire,
> By scattering the weed on Indian shores;
> Or worse, to lodge it in Pygmalion's stores.

At the appearance of her rival the "fair Salacia," the heroes

> Lent their strong arm in pity to the fair,
> To aid the bright Salacia's generous care;
> Pour'd a profusion of delicious teas,
> Which, wafted by a soft favonian breeze,
> Supply'd the wat'ry deities, in spite
> Of all the rage of jealous Amphytrite.

Salacia sings a victory song and "bids defiance to the servile train, / The pimps and sycophants of George's reign." [30]

[27] Miller, *Origins*, pp. 346–347; Claude H. Van Tyne, *The Loyalists in the American Revolution* (New York, 1902), p. 15; Schlesinger, *Merchants*, p. 288; Charles M. Andrews, *The Colonial Background of the American Revolution* (New Haven, 1924), p. 158.

[28] *London Chronicle*, Mar. 31, 1774; reprinted in Halsey, *Port Bill*, pp. 308–309.

[29] *Works of John Adams*, IX, 335, 336.

[30] "Squabble among the Celestials of the Sea," *Boston Gazette*, Mar. 21, 1774, p. 1; reprinted as "The Squabble of the Sea Nymphs" in Mercy Warren, *Poems, Dramatic and Miscellaneous* (Boston, 1790), pp. 202–205.

III

Having thrown down the gauntlet, Samuel Adams and the other Boston Sons of Liberty responsible for the Tea Party bided Britain's answer. William Pitt, America's long-time friend, thought it "certainly criminal," and in Commons, Lord North thundered, "I find that resolutions of censure and warning will avail nothing; we must therefore proceed with firmness and without fear." [31] The government moved swiftly, firmly, and to the point of no return. On March 31, 1774, there was enacted the Boston Port Bill—the first of four coercive measures directed against Massachusetts—which provided that after June 1 no goods except necessaries should enter or leave Boston harbor upon pain of forfeiture, until full satisfaction had been made to the East India Company "for the damage sustained by the said company by the destruction" of the tea and "to the officers of his Majesty's revenue, and others who suffered by . . . riots and insurrections," and until the people showed themselves dutiful. It further provided that men-of-war should maintain the blockade and that the customs should be transferred to Salem.[32]

On June 5 the Boston town meeting made a Solemn League and Covenant "to suspend all commercial intercourse with Great Britain thenceforth, and neither to purchase nor use any British imports whatsoever after October 1." [33] Mercy Warren endorsed the return to nonimportation by listing ironically "the necessaries of life for a fine lady." Meeting in debate where each can "freely speak her mind," the ladies "Nobly resolve to make the sacrifice, / Quit all but the necessities of life." Clarissa's inventory, for one, is the height of modesty.

[31] Pitt to Shelburne, Mar. 20, 1774, quoted in Ritcheson, *British Politics*, p. 159; Lord North's remark is quoted in Halsey, *Port Bill*, p. 133.

[32] Commager, *Documents*, pp. 71–72. The other coercive measures passed at this session were the Massachusetts Government Act and the Administration of Justice Act (May 20) and the Quartering Act (June 2).

[33] Schlesinger, *Merchants*, p. 319.

> In finest muslins that fair India boasts,
> She sips the herbage fetch'd from China's coasts:
> For while the fragrant Hyson leaf regales,
> Who'll wear the homespun produce of the vales?

If any man refuse to applaud such moderation, let it at least be granted that "wimples, mantles, curls and crisping pins / Need not be rank'd among the modern sins." [34] The adoption of the Covenant, however, did not alter the fact that hundreds of men were thrown out of work by the closing of the port.[35] As fall lengthened into winter, the suffering became acute. Had it not been for the generosity of neighboring towns and the other colonies, the distress at Boston would have been far greater.

On June 22, 1774, Parliament enacted the Quebec Act, which provided an intelligent, long-range policy for administering that recently acquired province. Extending the boundaries of Quebec to include the territory between the Ohio and the Mississippi, north to Hudson's Bay and east to Labrador, but stipulating that no existing legal boundary was to be affected, the Act established English criminal law but wisely held that "in all Matters of Controversy relative to Property and Civil Rights, Resort shall be had to the Laws of *Canada*." What gave the greatest offense in England and America was the provision, "That His Majesty's Subjects professing the Religion of the Church of *Rome*, of, and in the said Province of *Quebec*, may have, hold and enjoy the free Exercise of the Religion of the Church of *Rome*, subject to the King's Supremacy." [36] Within the Anglo-American community there stirred the ancient fear and hatred of Roman Catholicism. It was unfortunate, if understandable, that Whigs like Pitt, Burke, Fox, and Barré did not dissociate this Act from the four Coercive Acts, which happened to be under consideration at the same time.[37] In the London press

[34] *Royal American Magazine*, I (June, 1774), 233–234; reprinted in *Poems*, pp. 208–212, as "To the Hon. J. Winthrop, Esq."

[35] Schlesinger, *Merchants*, p. 315.

[36] Commager, *Documents*, pp. 75–76.

[37] Reginald Coupland, *The Quebec Act* (Oxford, 1925), p. 94.

Goody North sang a lullaby "to the foundling brat, the Popish Quebec Bill":

> Then heigh for the penance and pardons,
>   And heigh for the faggots and fires,
> And heigh for the Popish churchwardens,
>   And heigh for the Priests and the Friars;
> And heigh for the raree-show relics
>   To follow my Canada bill-e
> With all the Pope's mountebank tricks:
>   So prithee, my baby, lie still-e.
>   Then up with the Papists, up, up,
>   And down with the Protestants, down-e:
>   Here we go backwards and forwards,
>   And all for the good of the Crown-e.[38]

In another English piece the aged narrator, troubled by thoughts of the Quebec Act, dreams that he is at court. In one apartment a foreign lady "was deputed to teach English to the succeeding monarch of England." In another the Ministry is debating the effects of the Act; "Lord North said nothing, but beat his forehead terribly, as you may have seen him in the commons house, upon one of Edmund Burk's speeches."

In the next room, I saw all the bishops seated in their mitres and pontifical dignity, excepting four, who were dancing a minuet to the bagpipe played by the Thane [Bute]; and, just as I entered, they were taking hands across, and going round the Quebec bill, which lay upon the floor. . . . The crossing of hands was to shew their approbation and countenance of the Roman religion. . . . Struck to the very soul at the apostacy of the church I awaked.[39]

Frightened by the spectre of Catholicism on their northern and western borders, Americans up and down the land spoke with a unanimity they had not evinced since the days of the

[38] "A New Song," *St. James Chronicle*, July 7, 1774, p. 4; reprinted in the *Pennsylvania Packet*, Aug. 29, 1774, p. 3, and again in Moore's *Ballad History*, pp. 331-332.

[39] "The Mitred Minuet," *London Magazine*, XLIII (July, 1774), 312; reprinted in the *Royal American Magazine*, I (Oct., 1774), 365-366. Paul Revere made an engraving for this last scene.

Stamp Act.[40] In an Address to the People of Great Britain the
First Continental Congress, echoing the more famous Suffolk
Resolves, denounced the Quebec Act as part of "the ministerial
plan for inslaving us," insofar as the Canadians, "their numbers
daily swelling with Catholic emigrants from Europe, . . . might
become formidable to us, and on occasion, be fit instruments in
the hands of power, to reduce the ancient free Protestant Colonies to the same state of slavery with themselves." [41] The following year a Massachusetts pastor fulminated, "From the
Canada bill, and some other things favourable to popery, we
have grounds to fear, that should the present schemes of arbitrary power succeed, the Scarlet Whore would soon get mounted
on her Horned beast in America, and, with the CUP OF ABOMINA-
TIONS in her hand, ride triumphant over the heads of true Prot-
estants, making multitudes DRUNK WITH THE WINE OF HER
FORNICATIONS." [42] In one satire the Devil tries to persuade General Gage, commander in chief in America, to convert the colonists to Catholicism. Even when the Devil reminds him that
"I taught you whilst you liv'd at Home, / To fear the Deity of
Rome," Gage says he has little stomach for the task:

> The POPE I've worshipp'd long, 'tis true,
> But this must be 'twixt me and you;
> With all our Zeal, we must not dare
> One Syllable of this declare;—
> For in this Place, you know, are those,
> Who fear a GOD, nor let his Foes
> Transgress all Laws divinely made,
> As if true *sinning* was a Trade.[43]

[40] Sister Mary Augustina (Ray), *American Opinion of Roman Catholicism in the Eighteenth Century* (New York, 1936), pp. 301–302.

[41] Oct. 21, 1774, *Journals of the Continental Congress*, ed. W. C. Ford
(Washington, D.C., 1904–1937), I, 87, 88 (hereafter referred to as
Journals); Ray, *Roman Catholicism*, p. 277.

[42] Henry Cumings, *A Sermon, Preached in Billerica, On the 23d of
November, 1775* (Worcester, 1776), p. 12n., quoted in Davidson, *Propaganda*, p. 126.

[43] "A DIALOGUE between two FRIENDS, viz. An unlimited COMMANDER,

The Quebec Act continued to be a topic for satire after the war
had begun. Honorius the patriot reminds M'Fingal and his tory
cohorts how "mother Britain," falling into a decline,

> "Bade North prepare his fiery furnace;
> Struck bargains with the Romish churches,
> Infallibility to purchase;
> Set wide for Popery the door,
> Made friends with Babel's scarlet whore,
> Till both the matrons join'd in clan;
> No sisters made a better span." [I, 16]

From the time of the French alliance Americans were more tol-
erant of Catholics.[44] Indeed, the moment rumors of such an alliance got abroad, loyalists began to satirize American patriots,
jeering at the spectacle of Congress attending Mass or betrayed
finally by Louis XVI.

The first Book of the American Chronicles of the Times, published serially in the Philadelphia press during the winter of
1774–1775, reviews the six months following the passage of the
Port Bill: When the men of Boston learned that the great Sanhedrim had passed "a decree that their harbours be blocked up"
and that Rehoboam the king had sent Thomas the Gageite to
enforce it, they "entered into a solemn league and covenant, that
they would obey the book of the law, and none other." The
other tribes take pity on the Bostonites.

And they got ready their camels and their asses, their mules and
their oxen, and laded them with their meat, their fine wheaten flour,
their rice, their corn, their beeves and their sheep, and their figs and
their tobacco abundantly, and six thousand shekels of silver, and
threescore talents of gold, and sent them, by the hands of the Levites,
to their brethren, and there was joy in the land.

In letters to Rehoboam, Thomas complains that the Americanites
are "giants, men of great stature, and we seemed but as cater-

now in America, and the D- - -L," *Connecticut Courant*, Oct. 17, 1774,
p. 4.
[44] Ray, *Roman Catholicism*, p. 348.

pillars in their sight." Rehoboam replies, "My Grandfather corrected them with rods, but I will chastise them with scourges." When Thomas lays siege to Boston, a man of the town declares that they do not mean to sell their birthright "for a dish of TEA." Jedediah (Samuel Adams) reads the men of Boston the letters Congress addressed to Rehoboam, in which it is charged:

Hast thou not sent forth a decree, that all the world should be taxed for the God of the TEA CHEST? . . . Would we not all to a man (were it the laws of our own land) rather sooner agree voluntarily to burn our throats with a ladle of hot mush, our own country produce and manufacture, than have the nosle of a tea pot crammed down our throats, and scalded with the abominable and baneful exotic, without our own consent?

And moreover, O king, hast thou not made a Jesuitical decree, that our half brethren the Canadians and Quebeckites fall down and worship graven images? And peradventure, we and our children be commanded to fall down and worship them also. . . . We cannot apostatise, we will not, though Belzebub himself should be belwether to his holiness, and stand at our gate with all his bald pated fryars, and imps of hell at his elbow.

Revoke these "ill advised commandments," O King!

Otherwise we do most firmly resolve, that we will have no farther dealings with thy people; and that in the space of sixty days we will not traffick with them for their TEA, their tea cups, their saucers, nor their slop bowls. . . . And whereas thou pridest thyself, our raiment will wax old, and we shall go naked and barefooted, knowest thou not, O king, the Lord our God clothed our forefathers in the wilderness, and their garments waxed not old, neither did their feet swell?

At the end Mordecai the Benjamite (Franklin) laments, "Wo unto the land whose king is a child, whose counsellors are madmen, and whose nobles are tyrants, that devise wicked counsel, for they shall be broken like potters clay." [45] The anonymous

[45] *The first Book of the American Chronicles of the Times* (Philadelphia, 1774–1775), pp. 1–70 *passim*. At Philadelphia, noted the *North-Carolina Gazette*, Mar. 24, 1775, "upwards of 3,000 copies were sold in a

author of this, the most ambitious and nearly successful of half a dozen Biblical imitations which appeared in the Revolutionary period, catches the accent of the Old Testament chronicle books, though sometimes the diction has a synthetic ring and at one point a brief passage of French dialect is jarring. The allegorical haze he casts over the entire work is less apparent than it is in *A Pretty Story*.

During the years between the Stamp Act and the outbreak of war tea was the topic of satire oftener than any other. In the course of the controversy the British government learned to its vexation that Parliament's right to legislate for the colonies, much less tax them, would not be respected, even when British regiments were quartered in their midst and warships lay offshore. The passage of the Coercive Acts made compromise by either side all but impossible. At this juncture America elected representatives to the First Continental Congress. Nine months later troops would be ordered to New England to strengthen the forces that had laid siege to Boston.

------

few days" (quoted in Schlesinger, *Prelude*, p. 45 and note). Davidson suggests that the author, whoever he was, was indebted to "The Book of AMERICA," an imitation published in the London *Gazetteer* early in 1766 (*Propaganda*, p. 243; for the satire see ch. ii, n. 13).

CHAPTER IV

The British Government before the War

On the accession of George III in 1760 the political nation of Great Britain, according to Lewis Namier, was roughly
divided into the territorial magnates, the country gentry, the
official class, the trading community, and the lower classes in
the towns. It is with the official class that this chapter and the
next have to do. "The men who did most of the work in Parliament and in the Administration," writes Namier, "can best be
described as 'the official class,' if we join under that description
professional politicians with officers in the army and navy, and
civil servants of every rank." [1] Most of these officials showed
themselves profoundly ignorant of America and seemingly indifferent to rights the colonists had long taken for granted,
and thus exposed themselves to attack by antiministerial forces.

The violence with which the colonists had opposed the Stamp
Act made it imperative that the British government approach
the American question henceforth with wisdom, moderation,
and tact, but such qualities too seldom characterized the conduct
of successive Ministries, whose membership felt increasingly that
this Act should have been enforced, not repealed.[2] The situation
was further aggravated by the fact that American jurists, who

[1] *England in the Age of the American Revolution* (London, 1930),
pp. 208–209.
[2] Lecky, *American Revolution*, p. 104; Morgan, *Stamp Act*, p. 289.

had begun to circumvent questions of constitutionality by appealing to charter and even natural rights, could not agree with the British view that the programs of Grenville, Townshend, and finally North were neither tyrannical nor unconstitutional.[3] In this state of affairs antiministerial writers, who down to 1765 had centered their attack on officials in America, now opened fire on the King and his ministers at home.[4] A minister, sneers one writer at Boston, is "a creature originally found in Turkey, but lately seen in England, infallible, absolute, uncontroulable: Of wisdom, which none dare call in question: Of power which none can resist: Of holiness such as suits his station: Of justice, goodness and truth, parallel to self-interest."[5] By the end of 1774 the attack on the home government was firmly mounted. Another Boston writer has this horrific vision of King Tyranny:

His countenance was black and horrid, his eyes were a dark yellow like a snakes, his ears were like asses, his nose like a swine's snout, his mouth like a Dragons, his teeth are covered with black rust, and his lips besmeared with clotted gore, his arms and fingers were long, and his nails like a wild cats; his body is deformed in every part, his legs are crooked, and under his feet was all the petitions of injured innocence, on his right hand stood ambition, and on his left stood flattery, his attendants were cruelty, oppression, and lunacy; his counsellors were avarice and deceit, and his prime minister was hypocrisy, his courtiers were wrath, malice, envy, hatred, injustice, intemperance, drunkenness, lewdness and lying.

An honest American farmer enters the palace, and at once his gold watch is confiscated; when he protests, Tyranny cries "traitor" and orders him hung without even the formality of a trial.[6]

[3] H. L. Osgood, *Pol. Sc. Quar.*, II (1887), 467, quoted in George L. Beer, *British Colonial Policy* (New York, 1922), pp. 309–310n.

[4] Van Tyne, *Causes*, p. 199.

[5] *A Ministerial Catechise* (Boston, 1771), p. 4.

[6] "A brief Description of the person, palace, and courtiers of King Tyranny," *Royal American Magazine*, I (Dec., 1774), 443–445.

I

At one point in the debate with Honorius, Squire M'Fingal, who frequently weakens his argument in trying to strengthen it, assures the town meeting that

> "nineteen, 'tis believ'd, in twenty
> Of modern kings for plagues are sent you;
> Nor can your cavillers pretend
> But that they answer well their end." [I, 27]

The war had started when Trumbull wrote these lines, by which time probably a majority of Americans shared his low opinion of kings in general and George III in particular. According to Namier, George never "aimed at being more than what the self-contradictory constitutional theory and practice of the time made him—the hereditary, irresponsible head of the executive in a Parliamentary State." He moved steadily toward this goal by advancing certain ministers and underministers in exchange for their unswerving devotion, and through these his "Friends," who emerged as a full-fledged party during Rockingham's Ministry, came ultimately to control Parliament. During North's Ministry (1770–1782) his ascendancy was all but complete. Americans he regarded not as foreigners to be killed or enslaved but as fellow Englishmen, who had to be reminded on occasion that they wanted more liberty than was good for them. So habitual and genuine was their affection for George that long after they had begun to criticize his ministers most Americans continued loyal to him. Had they but known, from the time of the Stamp Act controversy he was their most formidable opponent.[7]

Although George III did not figure prominently in American satire until after the war began, by the end of the sixties he was

[7] Namier, *England in American Revolution*, p. 94; Ritcheson, *British Politics*, p. 68; Sir George Otto Trevelyan, *The American Revolution* (New York, 1909), I, 226; C. Grant Robertson, *England under the Hanoverians* (New York and London, 1927), p. 241.

under attack.[8] In what purports to be a royal address to Parliament at the time of resistance to the Townshend Acts, George rages:

> My protection and care, I perceive, have been lost on
> Those friends to commotion, my subjects at Boston,
> Who deny all allegiance to me and my state,
> And publicly measures subversive create.

I shall quell disturbances, "And the mischievous schemes of those people defeat, / Who have study'd to injure myself and my state." "In all delib'rations," my Lords and Gentlemen, "let harmony reign."

> If a diff'rence in other opinions arise,
> Set contention aside, and approve yourselves wise.
> In all consultations have virtue in sight,
> And whenever your country's concerned, unite.
> Such examples will make us (in spite of this foam)
> Respected abroad, and quite happy at home.[9]

Six years later Franklin, indulging in irony, devised a speech for George to deliver before Parliament:

You must know . . . that my ministers have put me upon a project to undertake the reduction of the whole continent of North America to unconditional submission. They w^d have persuaded me to coax you into this project by representing it to you as a matter very easily to be done in a twinkling, and to make you believe that my subjects in America whom you have always hitherto considered as brave men are no better than a wretched pack of cowardly run a ways, & that 500 men with whips w^d make them all dance to the tune of Yankee Doodle; but I w^d tell you no such thing because I am very sure if you meddle with it that you will find it a very different sort of business.

---

[8] Stella F. Duff, *Wm. & Mary Quar.*, ser. 3, VI (1949), 383–397, indicates how the news from Britain in 1768–1769 about John Wilkes helped transform the colonial picture of the King into that of a tyrant.

[9] "The King's Speech, in a poetical dress," *Penny Post* (Philadelphia), Jan. 27, 1769, pp. 31–32.

It will cost you "a good round sum of 40 or 50 millions" (George continues) and "40 or 50 thousands of your Constituents will get knocked on the head." Win or lose, the contest will exhaust the Treasury. When the Serpent whispered in my ear, "Let them feel that your little finger is thicker than the loins of all your ancestors," I sought out Lord Rockingham, who advised me "not to burn my fingers in the business." "It is your own business," my Lords and Gentlemen,

and if you are not content as you are, look to the rest for your-selves. But if I were to give you a word of advice it should be to re-mind you of the Italian epitaph upon a poor fool that kill'd himself with quacking

Stava ben, por star meglio, sto qui.

that is to say. I was well, I would be better, I took Physick and died.[10]

The earliest of the King's Friends was the Earl of Bute, for-merly his master's tutor and from 1761 to 1763 chief minister of state. Even after his influence ended, the several factions of Whigs continued in the belief that Bute, a disturbing and in-effective person whose fortune it was to be born a Stuart, was a secret adviser to George.[11] Americans infected with this whig-gish prejudice imputed to him the Stamp Act, the Quebec Act, and even the war itself when it came. A dream vision, which appeared shortly before the war, relates how at the upper end

[10] "The Intended Speech for the Opening of the First Session of the Present Parliament viz. Nov. 29, 1774," Library of Congress MS, 1774; printed in Smyth, VI, 299–301. Crane says the piece was "apparently not printed at the time" (p. 268); and Carl Van Doren: "The manuscript was left in England with David Hartley, who returned it after the Revolution had justified much of the prophecy which Franklin had put so ironically into the king's mouth," *Benjamin Franklin* (New York, 1938), p. 492.

[11] Namier, *England in American Revolution*, p. 70; Ritcheson, *British Politics*, p. 103. M. D. George, *Wm. & Mary Quar.*, ser. 3, X (1953), 515, writes, "For the cartoonist, Bute was the power behind the throne and the Ministry till the end of the war (though the King's relations with him ended in 1766)"—an observation that holds equally for satirists of this period in England and America.

of a fertile garden (America) there stands a "stately fabrick" out of whose foundations a serpent crawls; him the people dissever with a stone but do not quite kill. The serpent appears shortly at the window and "in a humane voice" pronounces himself a dead man. The author of this vision, here identifying American interests with British, piously explains, "The great serpent can be no other than his northern lordship [Bute], and his wicked coadjutors, who have been undermining this noble fabric; and having placed themselves on Magna Charta, that grand bulwark to the liberties of Englishmen, strive to deprive them of the benefit thereof." [12]

On January 31, 1770, Lord North succeeded the Duke of Grafton as chief minister. Some time after he had taken charge in Commons the event was derided in the press:

> O Thou, whom Placemen all adore,
> Of the Exchequer Chancellor,
>   And first Lord of the Treasury,
> How can a Muse in humble Strain,
> Pretend thy Merits to explain,
>   Or how in Numbers measure you!

"Let G— –ft–n, shunning public Strife, / Shrink in the Bosom of his Wife," "Whilst thou, like Falstaff, tak'st the Floor, / With Men in Buckram thirteen Score."

> With Crest erect, like Priam's Son,
> Lead but your trusty Trojans on,
>   Regardless of Desertion,
> Like Swiss they faithfully obey,—
> Like Swiss too they must have their Pay,
>   Post, Pension, and Reversion.
>
>   . . . . .
>
> Great polar Star, who now secure
> Beams in the Sky the Cynosure
>   Of courtly Navigation,
> Oh deign to shed thy *Influence* forth

[12] *Royal American Magazine*, I (Dec., 1774), 471–472, II (Jan., 1775), 3.

> On him whose Needle points at *North*
> Without a *Variation.*[13]

Lord North was well aware of his own limitations in statecraft but acceded when George called on him to serve. Frequently his name was linked with that of Bute, though there was no foundation for this supposed connection.[14] An English writer pictures North, who was in fact held responsible for the Boston Port Bill, as the exasperated victim of circumstances clinging desperately to office:

I was afraid of that d--n'd act at first—It was none of mine—I was not the father of it—I did not beget it—I only supported it according to the directions of the closet—It is confounded hard, that I must be responsible for obeying the commands of the Thane [Bute] —I should have been turned out if I had not.—But hold—let me consider—I shall be dismissed now if I complain—I must not recant—I must proceed, let the consequences be what they will.

In view of Boston's defiance, "we must force the Americans to submit by fire and sword." In addition to sending over officers obedient to "the private orders of the cabinet," we must "raise some regiments of Papists in Canada—they may also recruit our army there—they will be glad to cut the throats of those heretics, the Bostonians." "This must be my way—it will answer my end—it will be relished by the cabinet—and I shall keep my place." [15] Bute and Grenville, inveighs an American writer, laid grievous taxes on America, but "oh! ignoble NORTH, for thee / It was reserv'd, the curst decree, / To murder industry." Trade at Boston lies idle; young and old, sailors and landsmen, the teamster and even his beasts of burden curse "the tyrant North."

> Britain, ere long, shall execrate
> Your hated name, and death your fate,

[13] *New-Hampshire Gazette*, Feb. 22, 1771, p. 2 (undoubtedly from an English paper).

[14] Ritcheson, *British Politics*, p. 197; *DNB*, XIV, 606.

[15] "Lord NORTH's SOLILOQUY," *Essex Gazette*, Jan. 10, 1775, p. 4 (from a London paper).

By public justice done.
Satan, on his infernal throne,
Beholds, and marks you for his own,
   Yet trembles as he writes,
Lest you, when from the present world,
Abhorr'd by millions, shall be hurl'd
   To darkness and despair,
Should there, with BUTE, thy favorite friend,
For his authority contend,
   And drive him out of hell.[16]

The attack on North would continue during the war years, for in him satirists had found a convenient symbol of British tyranny.

Next to the King and his chief minister the member of the Ministry best known to the colonists was the American Secretary. Hillsborough (1768–1772) and Germain (1775–1782), members of the King's party both, were the two Secretaries most often satirized, during their terms in office and after. Hillsborough did not always act with sufficient wisdom, moderation, and tact. A rigid imperialist, he once declared, "The colonies are our subjects; as such they are bound by our laws, and I trust we shall never use the language of supplication to beg that our subjects will condescendingly yield obedience to our inherent pre-eminence." [17] His opinion of American affairs while in office was heavily colored by Francis Bernard's reports, and, after resigning, he continued to act and vote with the King's party. At the war's end there appeared a letter to the English press, in which the ghost of Botetourt, a former governor of Virginia, denounces Hillsborough to his face: "Recollect a little of your conduct, my Lord, since you first appeared as the GREAT MINISTER for American affairs, and see how well your plans, in opposition to wisdom, as well as justice have succeeded." When the entire province of Massachusetts petitioned for Governor Ber-

[16] *Pennsylvania Evening Post*, Mar. 30, 1775, p. 114.
[17] Hansard, *Parliamentary History*, XVI, 1019, quoted in Clark, *British Opinion*, p. 201.

nard's removal and—which proved his guilt—secured it, how did your Lordship act? "You caused him first to undergo a sham trial, and after acquitting him you caused him to be pensioned with the title of Baronet! He however, soon after died of a guilty conscience." Recollect, my Lord, how you condoned Wedderburn's harangue against Franklin and the conduct of "GAGE the MEACHING mercenary successor to Hutchinson." I predict that

if appearances may be depended upon, your measure is very near full! . . . you will soon see cause to curse the day you aspired to be a Minister, in this once great and glorious, but now falling kingdom! Your Lordship's dying, as I foresee you will, like Bernard and Hutchinson, of a guilty conscience will be no compensation, and but very little consolation to a ruined people.[18]

On January 29, 1774, Solicitor-General Alexander Wedderburn denounced Benjamin Franklin before the Privy Council for having purloined certain confidential letters, six of them written by Thomas Hutchinson. The harangue was one that many Americans took personally, and it strengthened perceptibly their grudge against the British government.[19] In the midst of the blasts and counterblasts which sounded in the Anglo-American press appeared an epitaph to the memory of Wedderburn:

> His Abilities and Eloquence soon procured him
>   A Seat in the HOUSE of COMMONS,
>   Where he embraced the Principles,
> And followed the Practices, of a Company
>   Of STATE PROSTITUTES.
>
>   . . . . .
>
> He was led on from one Degree of Venality to another;
>   Until he was at last prevailed upon

[18] *Connecticut Journal* (New Haven), Mar. 7, 1782, p. 1 (from the *London Courant*).

[19] Lecky, *American Revolution*, p. 152. A succinct account of the whole affair is given in Verner W. Crane, *Benjamin Franklin and a Rising People* (Boston, 1954), pp. 141–147.

To commit MURDER upon the Character
Of an illustrious AMERICAN PATRIOT AND PHILOSOPHER,
    And HIGH TREASON against
    BRITAIN AND HER COLONIES.

                . . . . .

He had no Friends to lament his Fate,
    For "Treachery would not trust him:"
He had no Enemies to forgive,
    For he was below Contempt.[20]

Nor was the episode soon forgotten. When Benjamin Vaughan reprinted Franklin's "Rules for Reducing a Great Empire to a Small One" in 1793, he dedicated the work to Wedderburn (now Baron Loughborough), explaining, "When I reflect on your Lordship's magnanimous conduct towards the author of the following Rules, there is a peculiar propriety in dedicating this new edition of them to a nobleman whose talents were so eminently useful in procuring the emancipation of our American brethren." [21]

II

While aiming shafts at the King and his ministers, the satirists reserved others for members of the official class who dwelt for a time on American soil. Some of these, it is true, "displayed their mental and moral inferiority," but many more were loyal and courageous defenders of ministerial interests.[22] One cause for grievance against Crown officials in America was the fear that if that part of the revenue from the Townshend Revenue Act so designated were actually used to pay the salaries of royal governors and judges, the colonial assemblies would lose much of the control they presently exercised over them. Such a fear was frequently voiced from the time of the Massachusetts Circular Letter on. Quick to sense the prevailing sentiment in the

[20] *Virginia Gazette* (Purdie & Dixon), June 2, 1774, p. 1.
[21] Quoted in Trevelyan, *American Revolution*, I, 163.
[22] Namier, *England in American Revolution*, p. 309.

colonies, Franklin, this time playing the role of "impartial historian," declared that one of "the wild ravings of the at present half distracted Americans" is their fear that

if by means of these forced duties Government is to be supported in America, without the intervention of the Assemblies, their Assemblies will soon be looked upon as useless. . . . At present they have no other means of getting rid of an ignorant or an unjust Judge (and some of scandalous characters have, they say, been sometimes sent them) but by starving him out.[23]

Another grievance, in Massachusetts at any rate, arose over the situation created by the passage on May 20, 1774, of the Massachusetts Government Act and the Administration of Justice Act, two of the Coercive Acts so-called. The first provided that members of the Council would henceforth be appointed by the King, that the governor might appoint and remove judges and certain other officials without the consent of the Council, and that town meetings, except for one annual meeting, might be called only with the governor's consent. The second, that at the governor's discretion the trial of British officials "for murther, or other capital offence" might be held "in some other of his Majesty's colonies, or in *Great Britain*." [24] In nearby Rhode Island "Beelzebub," in "humble commemoration of the unparalleled example of our most — sovereign *Fabulae factor primus*" and mindful of "the *venal wiseacres*" who had passed the Acts by and with the advice of the government party in Massachusetts, published a memento:

All judges, justices, sheriffs, and other officers . . . are hereby commanded to use their utmost endeavours to promote "vice and sedition," and "prevent religion and virtue" by their example. . . . The people of the province of *Massachusetts* are desired to stand ready at a moment's warning, and *jump* at the first opportunity they have, to promote what they can, "towards a general reformation of man-

[23] *London Chronicle*, Jan. 7, 1768, pp. 17–18; reprinted in the *Pennsylvania Chronicle*, Apr. 25, 1768, and again in Smyth, V, 89, 83–85.

[24] Commager, *Documents*, pp. 72–74.

ners, restitution of peace and good order," especially as his Majesty in his great goodness and clemency, has been at the pains and expence of sending such *flaming examples* for their imitation.

It is hoped that the people will be so foolish as "to shew a proper subjection" to the Coercive Acts "and all arbitrary laws of a *northern* institution." Accordingly, it is further declared

"that in the disposal of all offices of trust, and honor, within that province," the mockers of religion, the encouragers of false oaths, the factious promoters "of *vice* and *sedition*," the *worshippers* of that *idol* of *falsehood* — Hutchinson, all smugglers, &c. "shall be considered as fittest objects for such appointment." [25]

The position of royal governor in America was often more trying than that of minister at London since, in the words of John C. Miller, he had "to placate two jealous mistresses at once: the people and the King." [26] Under these conditions even a professional politician, which many of these governors were not, would frequently have failed. The three men who successively held the governorship of Massachusetts in the pre-Revolutionary decade—Francis Bernard, Thomas Hutchinson,[27] and Thomas Gage—were conservative and essentially fair-minded men who, though sometimes critical of ministerial policy, tried conscientiously to discharge their duties out of deference to King and Parliament. For their pains all three saw their initial popularity with the people slip away. It will be remembered that Bernard was not altogether diplomatic in his handling of the stamped paper. At that time and frequently thereafter he quarreled with the Assembly. His speeches before that body were liable to travesty, such as a mildly worded reprimand in 1767:

> My old Friend *Grenville* out of Place
> And dear Oppression in Disgrace;

[25] *Newport Mercury*, Aug. 22, 1774, Supplement, p. 1. Oblique reference is here made to Gage's proclamation of July 21, for the encouragement of virtue and suppression of vice.

[26] *Origins*, p. 33.

[27] Because he was Massachusetts born, Hutchinson will be considered in Chapter XI, on the loyalists, rather than in the present one.

> Staunch to the Cause; I'll bring alone,
> A world of Malice all my own.
>
> .   .   .   .   .
>
> Tho' you my wishes should fulfil,
> I mean to be *Bernardus* still.
> Therefore beware to *give Offence*,
> I shall not brook your Insolence;
> Pay due Submission to my Station,
> You'll find me then, *all Moderation*.[28]

So steadily did Bernard's situation in the province deteriorate that soon he was entreating his friend Lord Barrington: "It still becomes very adviseable to the Government, & desirable to me, that I should have leave to come to England. . . . The Times are growing so bad, that I am not like to have any Choice in it."[29] Shortly thereafter the press at Boston and New York published letters he had written advising the home government to put down faction in Massachusetts. Outraged and mortified, Bernard notified Barrington,

It is impossible for a Governor who has been engaged in such Contests as I have been, & has as well by special Orders as by his own Sense of His Duty, given free & full Information of the Proceedings of the factious Party, to think of staying in the Province, after his most confidential Letters are put in the Hands of the Faction and printed & dispersed among the People.[30]

An order for his recall went out in April, 1769, but word also that he was being created a baronet. Whereupon one who signed himself "the most servile of all your tools, A Tory" offered his congratulations: "Your promotion, Sir, reflects an honour on

[28] "Bernardus Francisco's SPEECH versify'd," *Weyman's New York Gazette*, June 8, 1767, p. 2. The text of this speech of May 28, 1767, is given in *Speeches of the Governors of Massachusetts, from 1765 to 1775* (Boston, 1818), p. 109.

[29] Bernard to Barrington, Apr. 20, 1768, *Barrington-Bernard Correspondence*, p. 153.

[30] Bernard to Barrington, Apr. 12, 1769, *ibid.*, pp. 200–201.

the province itself: An honour which has never been conferred upon it, since the thrice happy administration of Sir Edmond Andros, of precious memory who was also a baronet; . . ." The Tory continues:

Your own letters will serve to convince the world, and the latest posterity, that while you have constantly preserved a sacred and inviolable regard to punctilious truth, in every representation, which you have made of the people of you G—[sic], you have carefully endeavoured to give the most favourable colouring to their conduct and reputation. And the tenderness which you have ever remarkably felt for their civil rights, as well as their religion, will not admit of the least room to question, but that were the influence you have evidently employ'd with success to introduce a military power, and the unwearied pains you took to get them quartered in the body of the town, sprang from your piety, and benevolence of heart,— Pity it is that you have not a pension to support your title.[31]

On June 28 Bernard notified the Assembly that he was repairing to England at the King's request, "to lay before him the state of this province." [32] A Boston writer pictures him as boasting that he had been commanded to return to the English court—

> Where I Sir Mungo Nettle'em, Bart,
> By lying, pimping, fraud and art,
> Am now advanc'd to such great credit,
> "It must be true if Mungo said it."
> There I shall stubbornly relate
> Chimeras, for your real state;
> Legends of lies, my own creation,
> But don't be saucy—know my station,

[31] *New-York Journal*, June 22, 1769, Supplement, p. 1; reprinted in *Boston under Military Rule, 1768–1769*, comp. Oliver M. Dickerson (Boston, 1936), pp. 96–97. At intervals from Oct. 13, 1768, to Nov. 20, 1769, the *New-York Journal* carried this daily chronicle, known familiarly as the "Journal of Occurrences"; in Schlesinger's opinion the "Journal" is of plural composition (*Prelude*, p. 312). It is difficult to ascertain whether Bernard or the Boston customs commissioners had the larger hand in securing additional regiments for Massachusetts.
[32] *Speeches of the Governors of Massachusetts*, pp. 175–176.

>   Yet do not wickedly devise
>   When Mungo's gone, that Mungo dies.[33]

When Bernard sailed on July 25, celebration at Boston was wide-spread. "The Flag hoisted on the Liberty Tree—the Bells Ring-ing—Great Joy to the People," noted John Rowe in his diary. "A Great Bonfire in King St & on Fort Hill." [34] About this time another Boston writer inveighed:

>   Must it not fill all men of sense with scorn,
>   To see a muckworm of the earth, low born,
>   The chance production of some am'rous spark,
>   In ignorance supreme, profoundly dark?
>   To see him seat his mighty self in state,
>   With arms a-kimbo, deal to each its fate.
>
>   .   .   .   .   .
>
>   Go join in concert with the croaking frogs,
>   Or howl in chorus with a pack of dogs;
>   With monkeys go, and chatter on a stage,
>   Or turn a mastiff, and each curr engage.
>
>   .   .   .   .   .
>
>   Were I a K***! I'd think it noble sport.
>   To kick such mongril tyrants from my C****.
>   No knavish soul, that's aggrandiz'd by wealth,
>   Obtain'd by force, or got by meanest stealth;
>   Should tread the threshold of the R– – –l dome,
>   But like a robber, be exil'd from home;
>   Or share, what best become a thievish wretch,
>   A Tyburn salutation from a Ketch.[35]

[33] "A Message Sir!," *Boston Gazette*, July 3, 1769, p. 3. On his return to England, Bernard, now Sir Francis, sat in Lords "as of Nettleham in the county of Lincoln," *DNB*, II, 381.

[34] *Letters and Diary of John Rowe*, ed. A. R. Cunningham (Boston, 1903), p. 190.

[35] "On the Departure of an infamous B–R– – –T," Boston broadside, 1769; reprinted in *American Broadside Verse* (New Haven, 1930), p. 133, wherein Ola Winslow conjectures that it was "issued soon after Governor Bernard's departure."

III

Five years passed, during which time the native-born Thomas Hutchinson was governor. Then on May 17, 1774, Thomas Gage, temporary governor in Hutchinson's place as well as commander in chief in North America, arrived at Boston. Although Gage brought integrity and personal charm to the difficult task of seeing the Coercive Acts enforced, one writer remarked that "like unto a Pharisee, he prayeth with his windows open, and a two edged sword at our throats." [36] The fact that Gage's good sense and caution had much to do with delaying the outbreak of hostilities was lost upon the satirists, who were bent on character assassination.[37] In one poem an old farmer dreamed he went to see Tom Gage, who "of Wine and Genave so freely had drunk, / That he was scarce able to visit his punk"; after a time Tom found he could stagger again,

> And laying his course for crossing the hall,
> Unluckily met with an impudent fall;
> That brought him at last two yards on the floor,
> Which tickl'd me so I dreamed no more.[38]

In another, a traveler, stopping at a public house, explains that he is a sailor bankrupt in body and estate. When the master asks how the people stand disposed to "G**E and all his new attendants," the sailor doesn't mince words:

> In truth it's judg'd by men of thinking,
> That G**e will kill himself a drinking.
> Nay, I'm inform'd by the inn keepers,
> He'll bung with shoe-boys, chimney-sweepers.[39]

[36] *The first Book of the American Chronicles of the Times*, p. 5.
[37] John Richard Alden, *General Gage in America* (Baton Rouge, 1948), p. 222; Ritcheson, *British Politics*, p. 170.
[38] *Essex Journal* (Newburyport), Jan. 19, 1775, p. 4.
[39] *Essex Journal*, Feb. 22, 1775, p. 4.

As a maker of proclamations Gage gained a reputation second only to that of Burgoyne. Trumbull's Honorius, for one, recounts the annals of Gage's "first great year":

"While, wearying out the Tories' patience,
  He spent his breath in proclamations;
  While all his mighty noise and vapour
  Was used in wrangling upon paper,
  And boasted military fits
  Closed in the straining of his wits;
  While troops, in Boston commons placed,
  Laid nought, but quires of paper, waste;
  While strokes alternate stunn'd the nation,
  Protests, Address and Proclamation,
  And speech met speech, fib clash'd with fib,
  And Gage still answer'd, squib for squib." [I, 53–54]

It will be recalled that when the Port Bill went into force the Boston town meeting drew up a Solemn League and Covenant of commercial nonintercourse with England. On June 29, 1774, Gage issued an unenforceable proclamation "which denounced 'certain persons calling themselves a Committee of Correspondence for the town of Boston,' for attempting to excite the people of the province 'to enter into an unwarrantable, hostile and traitorous combination,' and which commanded all magistrates to arrest all persons who circulated the so-called Covenant." [40] In one travesty Gage declares that whereas certain persons who daringly call themselves a Committee have made an "*Agreement* subversive of commerce and trade,"

I think it my duty such steps to disprove;—
In obedience therefore to the King, whom I fear,
In *tenderness*, too, to the inhabitants here,
And to the end that the folks may be peaceably bent.
Nor commit what, perhaps, they may too late repent,
(For, so sure as a GUN, should they kindle my ire
I'll destroy them by famine, by sword and by fire.)

[40] Alden, *Gage*, p. 208; Schlesinger, *Merchants*, p. 323.

I've thought fit, *without asking my Council's advice*,
To publish my threats at this crisis so nice;
And to caution all persons 'gainst signing their names
To *leagues* counteracting the Ministry's schemes,
On pain of subjecting themselves, without measure,
To the wrath of *Lord North*, and my *hottest* displeasure;
And whatever his Lordship, at home, may propose
Tow'rds destroying their freedom and height'ning their woes;
Soon as pass'd into acts, be they e'er so unjust,
Execute them with *rigour* I will, and I must;

· · · · ·

And each Sheriff's requir'd, on pain of being roasted,
"To cause this Proclamation forthwith to be posted." [41]

Another writer addresses the petitions of three hundred thousand Americans to "his most exalted Highness, the most Potent, the most Omnipotent Bashaw THOMAS GAGE, lately appointed by the illustrious Sultan SALEM III, to the Subduction of the mighty Province of Boston."

Seeing, by your Proclamation of the 29th of June, that you must be vested with Powers to make Laws, and convert what you please into *Treason* and *Rebellion*, it is our Prayer that you may consider the Necessity of our exercising the common Functions of Animal Nature, those ancient and undisputed Privileges of the Beast of the Field, and not make it *Treason* and *Rebellion* for an American to make Water.

And whereas it is become necessary, by your most glorious Edict, that we should henceforth not speak our Sentiments, nor choose for ourselves whether we will *buy* or not *buy* your Master's Good, we do earnestly entreat that you would stretch forth your Arm, and by one Touch suspend also the Power of Thinking and Reasoning, and, in such Circumstances, give us the Privilege of being Beasts.[42]

[41] "A Rigorous Proclamation," *Pennsylvania Packet*, Sept. 12, 1774, p. 3. Signed "Explicator," one of William Livingston's pseudonyms says Frank Moore (*Ballad History*, p. 341n.).
[42] *Virginia Gazette* (Purdie & Dixon), Oct. 27, 1774, pp. 1–2.

Unaware apparently how deeply it would offend the piety ingrained in the American character, Gage issued a proclamation on July 21 for "the Encouragement of Piety, and Virtue, and for preventing and punishing of Vice, Profanity and Immorality." Once again he had laid himself open to travesty: "Humbly to imitate our Lord the King / (As Monkies do Mankind) in ev'ry Thing," I Thomas Gage

> Do *issue*, after mature Deliberation,
> In *our first Year*, a like *Proclamation*,
> Exhorting our Subjects to avoid and fly
> Licentiousness, Sedition, and Hypocrisy,
> Thankfully to God and Man expressing
> Of our *wise, mild* Government, the Blessing.[43]

In another travesty Gage, addressing his proclamation to "all the pretty Girls and Boys" that live in Boston, orders schoolmasters to teach them to avoid "Deceit, Hypocrisy, Sedi-ti-on and Strife": If you are obedient to this my will, dear Children, you shall have fine things to eat and wear,

> But if you should rebellious prove,
>   For all that do amiss,
> I keep at *Home* a monstrous *Rod*,
> A *Rod*, well soak'd in P– – –.[44]

But Gage's major responsibility was to see the Coercive Acts implemented and enforced. In August the Council, Gage presiding, convened at Salem, now the provincial seat of government, and decided that the Assembly should be called into session on October 5, for which purpose writs of election were signed. On September 28, alarmed by signs of disaffection in the province, Gage cancelled this order—an act which prompted one writer to represent him as blustering, "Each Noise and Word that's out of Season, / E'en to a F– –t, I deem it Treason"; I

[43] "A PARODY *on a* late PROCLAMATION," *Virginia Gazette* (P. & D.), Aug. 25, 1774, p. 2.
[44] "A Proclamation," *New York Journal*, Sept. 15, 1774, p. 4.

swear "The Court to Salem ne'er shall trot, / While People are so cursed hot." Elections were held in spite of this countermand and delegates sent to Salem. When Gage did not appear on the day appointed and formally dissolve them, the Assembly resolved itself into a Provincial Congress and adjourned to Cambridge, where it assumed the powers of government and placed the province in a state of defense.[45] The fact that Gage was simply complying with the terms of the Government Act failed to impress the author of this travesty:

> SINCE an Assembly most unlawful,
> At Cambridge met in Congress awful,
> October last, did then presume,
> The Powers of Government to assume;
> And slighting British Administration,
> Dar'd rashly seek their own Salvation.
>
> . . . . .
>
> I therefore issue Proclamation
> That Sheriffs, Constables, Collectors,
> Dispite the Men who I call Hectors,
> Even although their Country deem
> Them worthy of her best Esteem,
> Forbidding all to pay attention
> To said Provincial Convention,
> Exhorting Perjury to hate all,
> Except in Kings a Sin most fatal,
> That they to me may be more stable
> I promise them as soon as able
> The Congress, Gardiner, and so forth,
> I'll make Submit to good Lord North.[46]

All in all, the satirists handled Gage the governor as roughly before the war as they would Gage the general after it had begun.

[45] Alden, *Gage*, pp. 211, 216; *Essex Gazette*, Oct. 11, 1774, p. 4; Carl Becker, *The Eve of the Revolution* (New Haven, 1918), p. 228; *Commonwealth History of Massachusetts*, ed. A. B. Hart (New York, 1928), II, 551–552.
[46] *Connecticut Gazette* (New London), Nov. 18, 1774, p. 3.

Some eight months before Gage landed at Boston, Franklin published his "Rules for Reducing a Great Empire to a Small One." Addressed to the "late minister," Hillsborough, this letter to the English press constitutes a comprehensive review of colonial grievances which had accumulated during the decade just past, but falls short of the rhetorical unity which sustains "An Edict by the King of Prussia." To be sure, here as in the "Edict" Franklin exploits the historical situation—every one of these "rules" had its basis in fact—but the analogy he employs at the outset is a less efficient vehicle than the *reductio ad absurdum* which informs the "Edict," and soon he is forced to abandon it. "In the first place," the letter begins, "you are to consider, that a great empire, like a great cake, is most easily diminished at the edges. Turn your attention, therefore, first to your *remotest* provinces; that, as you get rid of them, the next may follow in order." Such a beginning promises well. "By carefully making and preserving such distinctions, you will (to keep to my simile of the cake) act like a wise gingerbread-baker, who, to facilitate a division, cuts his dough half through in those places where, when baked, he would have it *broken to pieces*." Still excellent. But then, apparently at a loss how to develop it farther, Franklin drops the trope altogether. The rules which follow read like a succession of colonial petitions—only inverted. The letter advises the minister to show only resentment for such military and commercial support as the colonies have afforded the mother country and to quarter troops in their midst; "by this means, like the husband who uses his wife ill *from suspicion*, you may in time convert your *suspicions* into *realities*." As for civil administration:

If you can find prodigals, who have ruined their fortunes, broken gamesters or stockjobbers, these may do well as *governors;* for they will probably be rapacious, and provoke the people by their extortions. Wrangling proctors and pettifogging lawyers, too, are not amiss; for they will be for ever disputing and quarrelling with their little parliaments. If withal they should be ignorant, wrong-headed, and insolent, so much the better. Attornies' clerks and Newgate solicitors will do for *Chief Justices*, especially if they hold their places *during your pleasure;* and all will contribute to impress those ideas of your government, that are proper for a people *you would wish to renounce it.* . . .

When such Governors have crammed their coffers, and made themselves so odious to the people that they can no longer remain among them, with safety to their persons, *recall and reward* them with pensions. You may make them *baronets* too, if that respectable order should not think fit to resent it.

Other rules are offered: Pursue without compromise a policy of mercantilism. Deny them their constitutional liberties, passing another "solemn declaratory act." Send over revenue officers, "the most *indiscreet, ill-bred,* and *insolent* you can find," and apply the produce therefrom "where it is *not necessary,* in augmented salaries or pensions to every governor, who has distinguished himself by his enmity to the people, and by calumniating them to their sovereign." Harass "the parliaments of your provinces . . . with *repeated dissolutions.*" "Convert the brave, honest officers of your *navy* into pimping tide-waiters and colony officers of the *customs.*" Redress no grievances, grant no requests.

Lastly, invest the General of your army in the provinces, with great and unconstitutional powers, and free him from the controul of even your own Civil Governors. Let him have troops enow under his command, with all the fortresses in his possession; and who knows but (like some provincial Generals in the Roman empire, and encouraged by the universal discontent you have produced) he may take it into his head to set up for himself? If he should, and you have carefully practised these few *excellent rules* of mine, take my word for it, all the provinces will immediately join him; and you will that day (if you have not done it sooner) get rid of the trouble of governing them, and all the *plagues* attending their *commerce* and connection from henceforth and for ever.[47]

[47] *Public Advertiser,* Sept. 11, 1773, pp. 1–2; reprinted in the *Pennsylvania Gazette,* Dec. 15, 1773, and again in Smyth, VI, 127–137.

Franklin's "Rules" served notice on a King and Ministry that were drifting—heedlessly, it seemed to many—toward civil war. Hopes for a peaceful settlement of Anglo-American differences were cut short when the King on August 23, 1775, issued a Proclamation of Rebellion. What impelled the British government to take this fateful step? For too long the officials in power had clung to the ideal of a mercantilistic empire of supreme center and subordinate parts; it was not until the war was three years old and the Americans had formed an alliance with France that they began to view the empire as a commonwealth of nations.[48] In 1774, a year of crisis after which there would be no turning back, the North Ministry did not fall at the general election as the Americans had hoped; in fact, after that time the Opposition was even less influential in Parliament and with the nation than before. On February 2, 1775, Lord North, enjoying the confidence of Parliament and the nation, urged the King "to adopt effectual measures for suppressing rebellion in the colonies." Six months later, news of Lexington and Concord and of Bunker Hill having reached England, George III notified a startled America:

Whereas many of our subjects in divers parts of our Colonies . . . misled by dangerous and ill designing men . . . have at length proceeded to open and avowed rebellion, . . . we have thought fit . . . to issue our Royal Proclamation, hereby declaring, that . . . all our subjects of this Realm . . . are bound by law to be aiding and assisting in the suppression of such rebellion.[49]

[48] Ritcheson, *British Politics*, traces the stages by which this revolution in the theory of empire came about.

[49] *Ibid.*, p. 170; Trevelyan, *American Revolution*, I, 124, 235–236; Commager, *Documents*, p. 96.

CHAPTER V

The British Government during the War

BETWEEN 1774 and 1776 British civil authority in America crumbled. The Declaration of Independence merely confirmed the fact that for almost two years Americans had been assuming political privileges and responsibilities previously reserved to the mother country. By this date practically all civil servants had withdrawn from American soil. Now the satirical attack was concentrated on the British government at home—on George III and his ministers and their several efforts to negotiate a peace which would reassert parental control over America.

I

When war came in the spring of 1775, the North Ministry hesitated momentarily and then decided on coercion. During the first years of the war the ministerial party received the support of the people, a majority of whom strongly favored seeing the colonies coerced.[1] Early in 1777, at a time when the war was still popular in Britain, Francis Hopkinson published what purports to be the translation of a letter written by a foreigner on his travels in England, in which the inhabitants there are shown to be politically naïve. So infatuated are they with their

[1] John C. Miller, *Triumph of Freedom* (Boston, 1948), p. 32.

patriotism, writes the traveler, that two popular songs, "Britons Strike Home" and "God Save the King," "are vociferated at taverns, over porter, punch and wine, till the imagination is heated, and the blood in a ferment, and then these pot-valiant patriots sally forth and commit all manner of riot and excess in honour of their king and country." When they "grow uneasy under the too barefaced encroachments of prerogative," half a dozen court scribblers "sing the sweet Lullaby of Liberty. . . . Just so a nurse rattles three pieces of tin in a little rush basket to amuse her crying child. The poor infant thinks it has the world in possession, and is satisfied." The people of England are so provincial as to be totally ignorant of matters political.

A manufacturer has been brought up a maker of pin-heads. . . . It is enough for him, that he believes in the *Athanasian Creed*, reverences the splendor of the court, and makes pin-heads. This he conceives to be the sum-total of religion, politics, and trade. . . . [That] the colonies, formerly belonging to Great-Britain, now *independent states*, are vastly more extensive than England, Wales, Scotland and Ireland, taken all together—He cannot conceive. . . . Talk to him of the British constitution, he will tell you it is a glorious constitution—Ask him what it is, and he is ignorant of its first principles; but he is sure that he can make and sell pin-heads under it.[2]

The popularity of the war seems the more surprising in view of the economic distress it caused at home, especially after the time of Saratoga and the French alliance. The landed classes in particular suffered, and costly loans added heavily to the na-

[2] "Translation of a Letter, Written by a Foreigner on his Travels," *Pennsylvania Packet*, Feb. 4, 1777, p. 2; reprinted in *The Miscellaneous Essays and Occasional Writings of Francis Hopkinson* (Philadelphia, 1792), I, 98–110. In two of the "Pilgrim" papers, which are an admixture of social and political satire, Freneau attacks the British nation: No. II, *Freeman's Journal*, Nov. 28, 1781, pictures the contentiousness, oppression, pride and greed of the people of "the island of SNATCHAWAY," and No. VII, *Freeman's Journal*, Jan. 2, 1782, the credulity and cruelty of Britons. See *The Prose of Philip Freneau*, ed. Philip M. Marsh (New Brunswick, 1955), pp. 212–216, 45–49, for the text.

tional debt.[3] Hopkinson allegorizes on the plight of the nation at this time: Wandering in "A lane of mire and clay,"

> 'Twas there a dirty drab I saw,
>   All seated on the ground,
> With oaken staff and hat of straw,
>   And tatters hanging round.

When I inquired, she told me how she came to this beggarly condition:

> "An orphan child fell to my care,
>   "Fair as the morn was she,
> "To large possessions she was heir,
>   "And friendly still to me.

> "But George, my son, beheld the maid,
>   "With fierce lascivious eye;
> "To ravish her a plan he laid,
>   "And she was forc'd to fly.

> "She's young and will no more depend
>   "On cruel George or me;
> "No longer now my boasted friend,
>   "Nor of my family.
>
>   . . . . .
>
> "*Britannia* now in rags you see;
>   "I beg from door to door—
> "Oh! give, kind sire for charity,
>   "A penny to the poor." [4]

For the government the winter of 1777–1778 marked the turning point in the war. The spectre of bankruptcy on the horizon and military mischance diminished the prestige of Britain at home and abroad. "Do not think me a cynic," writes Samuel Curwen, a loyalist then living in England, "when I say, I fear this nation has sunk into too selfish, degenerate, luxurious a sloth, to rise

[3] Clark, *British Opinion*, p. 141; Robertson, *England under the Hanoverians*, p. 273.

[4] "Date Obolum Belisario," *Pennsylvania Packet*, Apr. 22, 1778; reprinted in *Poems on Several Subjects* (Philadelphia, 1792), pp. 164–168.

into such manly, noble exertions as her critical situation seems to demand." [5] These *"political* annihilators," sneers William Livingston at the government, "these real *Don Quixots,* instead of relinquishing their folly, now address *Europe* with their high design of dashing *America,* land and sea, man and beast, fish and fowl, out of existence by one flourish of their *coruscarious* arm." Next we shall hear that they intend to annihilate Asia and Africa as well.

The number of inhabitants in *Asia* and *Africa* are about 200,000,-000, suppose one third of them should migrate to Europe, and each of these estimated at £. 10 yearly, the annual income to *Europe* will be above £. 666,666,660.—I expect before the revolution of another year, these almighty NOTHING-MAKERS, finding themselves galled by *France* and *Spain,* will be for deducing [reducing?] the continent of *Europe* to non-entity too, and they will then have in imagination what they desire, the whole wealth of the universe piled up on that little all-important spot called *Great-Britain.* But all these imaginary riches will not discharge the *real* national debt. . . . And when they have toiled out their days in *making nothing,* they will then spend one ghastly, tormenting, never-ending wish, "That they were nothing themselves." [6]

Public confidence in the North Ministry was not finally shaken until after Yorktown, an event which convinced all but the most stubborn that the American war was lost. The following spring Philip Freneau predicted the outcome of the war in "The Political Balance," a Hudibrastic poem in anapestic measure. Jove, determined to weigh the political fortunes of England and American, instructs Vulcan to fashion "a globe of shorter diameter"; "But its various divisions must so be designed, / That I can unhinge it whene'er I've a mind—." Vulcan complies. Then, adjacent to Europe he strikes up the island of Britain, whose inhabitants are pressing their imperialistic claims:

[5] Letter to William Browne, Jan. 30, 1778, *Journal and Letters of the Late Samuel Curwen* (New York, 1842), p. 169.
[6] *New-Jersey Gazette* (Burlington), Feb. 11, 1778, p. 2.

Like emmits or ants in a fine summer's day,
They ever were marching in battle array,
Or skipping about on the face of the brine,
Like witches in egg-shells (their ships of the line).

These poor little creatures were all in a flame,
To the lands of America urging their claim,
Still biting, or stinging, or spreading their sails;
(For Vulcan had formed them with stings in their tails).

Hermes fetches a balance, and together the gods finally mount America, comprising "one-eighth of the ball," on one scale. "Like a man that is searching his thigh for a flea," Jove fingers about the globe to find Britain and places her on the opposite scale. "Britannia so small, and Columbia so large— / A ship of first rate, and a ferryman's barge!" At Momus' suggestion the rest of the British Empire is added to the scale, but this only diminishes Britannia's weight. No longer does the issue hang in the balance.[7] This poem scatters its force somewhat by ridiculing George III and even the Irish and the Welsh. Always a good hater, Freneau here does not discipline himself to look steadily at what is clearly his target, the fact that the British cause in America is now lost. On the other hand, he has carefully constructed a Lilliputian world through which to view Britain at this juncture, and the fact that he refuses to take the epic elements of this world seriously helps drive the satire home.

II

After the time of the Proclamation of Rebellion the Anglo-American press stepped up its attack on the person and policies of George III.[8] He was the symbol and, as events were to prove,

[7] *Freeman's Journal* (Philadelphia), Apr. 3, 1782, p. 1; reprinted in Pattee, II, 130-139. Weighing the destinies of men and nations in golden scales is a familiar part of epic machinery; see *The Iliad*, VIII, 69-72, XXII, 209; *The Aeneid*, XII, 725-727; *Paradise Lost*, IV, 990-1015. Freneau was familiar with such epics.

[8] Hinkhouse, *Preliminaries*, p. 196; Trevelyan, *American Revolution*, III, 172.

the guiding power behind a Ministry whose American policy was constantly being called into question. One American, at a time when the sentiment for independence was mounting, relates how a cat waited to devour some mice who were entrenched in a rich Cheshire cheese. Finding all his tricks are useless—

Grimalkin, deep versed in political schools,
    Affected the siege to give o'er,
Supposing the mice were such ignorant fools,
    They would venture abroad as before.

But, as he retreated, a spirited mouse,
    Whom time had bedappled with grey,
Cried, "All your finesse we don't value a sous,
    No more to your cunning a prey.

"This cheese by possession we claim as our own,
    Fair freedom the claim doth approve;
Our wants are but few, and her blessings alone,
    Sufficient those wants to remove.

"No cat will we own; with ambition run mad,
    For our king—so move off in a trice;
If we find from experience a king must be had,
    That king shall be made by the mice." [9]

We have already seen how from the first George wished to exercise all the rights to which he was constitutionally entitled. Steadily he developed self-assurance, and when the war came he made it peculiarly his own. Knowing full well that the most important of these rights was the appointment of ministers, he sought men who would depend on him for guidance.[10] Thus it

[9] *Pennsylvania Evening Post*, Feb. 17, 1776, p. 86; reprinted in *Diary of the American Revolution*, ed. Frank Moore (New York, 1860), I, 203.
[10] Richard Pares, *George III and the Politicians* (Oxford, 1953), p. 67; Herbert Butterfield, *George III, Lord North, and the People, 1779–80* (London, 1949), p. 16; Vivian H. H. Green, *The Hanoverians* (London, 1948), p. 304.

was that Lord North, who had formed his first Ministry in 1770, was prevailed upon to continue in office until after Yorktown. In a political ballad of 1780 George declares:

> My Grand-Father reign'd like a silly old fool;
> On a different system my kingdom I'll rule,
> By maxims I've learn'd in a very good school.
> No parties of men shall have influence here;
> That they all are alike I would make it appear,
> So I'll have a new ministry every year.
>
>   .   .   .   .   .
>
> A Treasurer I'll have who will blindly agree
> Whatever his real opinion may be,
> To carry all measures adopted by me.
> If I knew of a Statesman, wise, honest and good,
> From his friends I'd detach him as soon as I cou'd,
> And if he sticks to them, why, G–d d– –n his blood.
> If I knew of a man ignominious and base,
> Who had bro't on himself and his country disgrace,
> I'd exalt him at once into power and place.
>
>   .   .   .   .
>
> And when I have got all these men to my mind,
> To my absolute pleasure compleatly resign'd;
> How well I can govern—my people shall find.

Should my enemies join those "mutinous rascals" the Americans, "I'll down on my knees / And offer them terms, which, as every one sees, / I may afterwards give them or not, as I please."

> For what tho' Great Britain decline every day,
> In spite of the world I shall have it to say,
> That the King of Great Britain has his own way.[11]

But for George's obstinacy the war might have ended sooner. Four months after Yorktown he could still assert, "I certainly till

[11] "R–y–l Resolutions," *Boston Gazette*, Aug. 14, 1780, p. 2. In this imitation of "Royal Resolutions," a ballad sometimes ascribed to Andrew Marvell, George III is substituted for Charles II; although it preserves the form and general idea of the original, there are no line-for-line borrowings.

drove to the Wall do what I can to save the Empire, and if I do not succeed I will at least have the self-approbation of having done my Duty and not letting myself be a tool in the Destruction of the Honour of the Country." [12] Unmoved by the courage and pride behind such a statement, the satirists travestied speeches like the one he delivered in Parliament on learning of Cornwallis' surrender. "I have no doubt," he told the members on that occasion, "but that by the concurrence and support of my Parliament, by the valour of my fleets and armies, and by a vigorous, animated and united exertion of the faculties and resources of my people, I shall be able to restore the blessings of a safe and honorable peace to all my dominions." [13] An American writer, in a travesty on this address, depicts George determined to subdue America but sorely troubled by the effect of the French alliance:

> To leave one great beyond th' Atlantic,
> Our wants consider'd, would be frantic.
> And till they're thoroughly subjected,
> All terms of peace must be rejected.
> But then those cursed imps of France
> Who first this squabble did commence,
> Tho' long the rebels stood alone
> (As oft' I've boasted from the throne)
> Still take my ships and beat my troops,
> And join th' insurgents thick as hops;
> Prolonging thus this plaguy war
> And all my peaceful systems mar.

The first minister, my Lords and Gentlemen, may have to answer for his talk of coercing the Americans—

> For North, you know, talk'd strong as mustard
> How we could eat the rogues like custard;

[12] George III to Lord North, Feb. 26, 1782, *The Correspondence of King George the Third from 1760 to December 1783*, ed. Sir John Fortescue (London, 1928), V, 374.

[13] As reported in the *Royal Gazette*, Feb. 12, 1782, quoted in Thomas J. Wertenbaker, *Father Knickerbocker Rebels* (New York, 1948), p. 249.

And setting thus the mob agig.
It wants some skill to stop their jig,
Lest they become all over treason'd
And seize on North to cut his weasand.

On hearing of our naval triumphs, "You will rejoice and skip like frog / That leap the first upon king Log,"

Yet as the frog who strove to be
An ox, by dint of essoufle,
Did blow and swell until he burst on't
Nor till too late, did know the worst on't,
So I allur'd by loyal stories
To amplify my territories,
(What adverss fate attends the righteous,
When France and Spain and rebels fight us!)
Did send Cornwallis to Virginia,
By length of sword, and charm of guinea,
To try rebellion to subdue
Among the old dominion crew,
For that alone's my peaceful view.

There "Washington and Rochambeau / Did give my fav'rite such a blow," "That maugre all his forts and ditches / He spoil'd the lining of his breeches." Nevertheless, with the support of the entire nation we can yet win.

I hope that every mother's son
Will to the royal standard run,
('Tis not the standard that's here meant
Which Washington to Congress sent)
And cuff and bruise, and claw and clatter,
And fight like punk by land and water
To finish this confounded matter.[14]

---

[14] *Pennsylvania Packet*, Mar. 9, 1782, p. 2. Freneau also travestied this speech, *Freeman's Journal*, Feb. 20, 1782, pp. 2–3 (reprinted in Pattee, II, 117–119). Another of George's speeches, that of Nov. 20, 1777, at the opening of Parliament, was travestied in the *Pennsylvania Packet*, Feb. 11, 1778, p. 2; and Livingston prepared ironical annotations on it, *New-Jersey Gazette*, Feb. 11, 1778 (reprinted in Moore's *Diary*, II, 18–21).

Soon after a screed on the person of George appeared in the Boston press. The Devil says of George in the year 1776:

There is not a character in Tophet stinks (above ground) worse than yours. . . . Instead of showing the spirit of a lion, you have the head of a goat and the heart of a sheep. . . . If you fail, what a deform'd mongrel puppy you will appear to all the world.

When George makes light of Cornwallis' predicament at York-town, the Devil cries:

George ye whoremonger, where are you? your kingdom totters while you are wenching. . . . You are a Scotch damn'd goat—who begat ye, or bore ye—you've no more political eye sight than a blind curst puppy, three days old—A Dutch bull frog would learn naviga-tion, sooner than you'll learn the first lesson in politicks.

George boasts how he will govern America when the rebellion is crushed:

I'll plant the provinces with loyal Scotchmen, and a due mixture of my royal breed among them for rulers. I shall have enough of my own for every office of consequence; my German rib (known by the name of Pug) has brought me upwards of a dozen.—I've five by a Quaker girl—three by a Drury Lane Bunter—four by Billings-gate Dab—several by Blue Moll, etc. etc. etc.—I've enough I'll swear, and more coming.

When report comes that Cornwallis has surrendered, the Devil declares:

O ye mongrel bastard, George, you'll turn out another bull headed cur like Charles Ist. I have been trying one hundred and fifty years to raise a tyrant out of the breed; but ye are a sap-headed generation, fit only for backlogs in tophet, and for mudboats in the Stygian lake.

George in turn blames his ministers and commanders for this dis-aster:

If I had rak'd hell, and skin'd the devil, I could not have found a worse set.

In order to silence him the Devil orders Tom Firetongs to "take George by the nose and give the scoundrel a twist" and Triphammer to "make a *tongue cuff*" instantly and "rivet it on red hot." And the ministers decide to "give the mule a dose of arsenic, and let him go off with the dry belly ache," so that they can "retire from the helm, and live in domestic peace." [15]

III

The satirists dealt with the ministerial party no less harshly than with the King himself. In the fall of 1775, while a British army lay besieged at Boston, an English writer, in what proved to be a skillfully conceived allegory, published an account of "the present POLITICAL RACE, that is now running in AMERICA, between TYRANT, a stallion belonging to a club of jockeys in Parliament-street, and LIBERTY, a horse belonging to America."

The judges of the race, on this side, are the Lords Bute, Mansfield, North, &c. &c. &c. the greatest jockeys in the kingdom, . . . as they have formerly been detected of unfair practices, in several scrub and petty stamp races, they have been concerned in, it is thought no harm to double the watch, as they probably may attempt the like again.

The judges of the race on the other side are (we hear) prime jockeys, perfect connoisseurs in horse flesh, and, we are told, hath met for some time past in the city stable in Philadelphia. . . .

TYRANT is a black, haughty, wanton, vicious, inflexable stallion,

---

[15] *A Dialogue, between the Devil, and George III* (Boston, 1782), pp. 4–21 *passim;* advertised as for sale in the *Boston Gazette,* Feb. 18, 1782. Satires on the person of George III are numerous; thus, the *Pennsylvania Packet,* Aug. 8, 1778, p. 3, punned on his shortsightedness, and a Philadelphia broadside of 1782 carved an epitaph for the "residuum and political remnant of GEORGE THE III." Other members of the royal family fared no better. The appropriateness of Queen Charlotte's thirteenth pregnancy was duly noted, *Boston Gazette,* Oct. 5, 1778 (reprinted from the *London Evening Post*). When Prince William Henry, George's third son, visited New York City late in 1781, General James Robertson's greeting on his arrival was travestied, *Pennsylvania Journal,* Nov. 21, 1781, p. 3, and Freneau twice satirized his stay there, *Freeman's Journal,* Jan. 30, July 23, 1782 (reprinted in Pattee, II, 112–114, 167–169).

a contumacious quadruped, remarkable only for getting colts out of a good breeding German mare, at least nineteen hands high, a little past the prime. . . . He was put while a colt into the Buteenian stable, and pampered like Pharoah's coach horses, too luxuriantly, out of the manger of bad policy, by the hands of Jacobite and Tory ostlers with food of deceit, flattery, falsehood, ignorance, infatuation, bluster, pride, and now and then a fricasee of BERNARD's abominable insinuations, a mess of HUTCHINSON's scorbutick "Taxation no Tyranny." . . .

LIBERTY is a most beautiful white, and modest looking horse, . . . despises a whip, and goes incomparably well, with a judicious rider, full of American blood, . . . has from a colt been as regularly and carefully fed as a Christian horse ought to be in moderation, out of the manger of wisdom, by the hands of loyal and whig ostlers, with food of sincerity, honesty, truth, knowledge, clearsightedness, modesty, meekness, and once in a while with a relish of Chatham's patriotic eloquence, a dish of Burke's constitutional boldness, and a sensible draught of "Taxation Tyranny." . . .

General Gage is TYRANT's rider, and dressed in deep blood red, and Oliver Cromwell is LIBERTY's rider, and dressed in a beautiful sky blue. . . .

Captain Darby says, that TYRANT was hard put to it this first heat and with the greatest difficulty reached Boston, considerably disabled, being obliged to run backwards upwards of twenty miles, and it was thought he had burst some blood vessel, as great quantities of blood exsudated from his breech; but as three quack horse doctors had arrived there very seasonably, it was thought they would patch him up for the second heat, which he was bound in honor to run or give up the stakes. . . .

Bets are now ten to one against TYRANT; the ministerial jockies are in a quandary, and beginning to hedge, and some of them attribute their miscarriage to the account of their rider, others of them to the d– – – –d phlebotomistical Yankee sons of w– – – –s, as they ludicrously term them.[16]

[16] *Pennsylvania Evening Post*, Nov. 18, 21, 1775, pp. 529–530, 533–534, with an explanatory note that this account first appeared in a letter "from a gentleman of eminence in London, dated September 14, 1775."

The topic of horse racing, aside from its obvious appeal to an Anglo-American audience of the eighteenth century, remains plausible at all times as a vehicle for the allegory. At no point do correspondences between the narrative and allegorical levels seem forced; consistency is maintained throughout; and the allegorical details are vivid and cumulative.

Although in actuality the British government was uncertain how to gauge the seriousness of the American revolt in its first stages and how best to subdue it, the impression left by *The Fall of British Tyranny* (1776) is that the ministerial forces to a man favored a policy of coercion while the Opposition stood just as firmly opposed.[17] So persistent was the Bute legend that, although his influence had ended a decade before, he is the central figure of the play. At the Court of St. James, Lord Paramount (Bute), in conference with Mocklaw (Mansfield), who swears to "screw, twist and strain the law as tight as a drumhead, to serve you," confides his plan to stir up a war in America and, while England is thus embroiled, to march on London with 30,000 Scottish troops, where with the support of the united fleets of France and Spain he will overthrow the government. More immediately to the purpose, however, is the expression of ministerial designs on America itself. Paramount soliloquizes:

The Americans from one end to the other shall submit, in spite of all opposition; I'll listen to no overtures of reconciliation from any petty self-constituted congress, they shall submit implicitly to such terms as I of my royal indulgence please to grant. I'll shew them the impudence and weakness of their resolves, and the strength of mine; I will never soften; my inflexibility shall stand firm, and convince them the second Pharoah is at least equal to the first.

And Lord Catspaw (North), in conference with other ministers, rants:

Barbarous nations must be held by fear, rein'd and spurr'd hard, chain'd to the oar, and bow'd to due control, till they look grim

[17] Troyer Steele Anderson, *The Command of the Howe Brothers during the American Revolution* (London, 1936), p. 41.

with blood; let's first humble America, and bring them under our feet; the olive-branch has been held out, and they have rejected it; it now becomes us to use the iron rod to break their disobedience; and should we lack it, foreign assistance is at hand.

Members of the Opposition counter. Bold Irishman (Burke), for one, who warns the Ministry:

Let the mighty Philistine, the Goliath Paramount, and his oracle Mocklaw, with their thunder bellowed from the brazen mortar-piece of a turn-coat lawyer, have a care of the little American David! . . . I can compare the whole herd of them to nothing else but to the swine we read of running headlong down the hill, Paramount their devil, Mocklaw the evil spirit, and Brazen [Wedderburn] their driver.[18]

Lord North, an even-tempered and indolent first minister who had little desire to prosecute the war in America with vigor, finally agreed to do so after news of Bunker Hill arrived. To further this determination, on November 10, Lord George Germain, a man who strongly favored coercion, was appointed American Secretary. Germain was a good administrator and, the memory of his behavior at Minden notwithstanding, no coward; but like Hillsborough before him, he did not possess the cool, far-sighted statesmanship so essential to his office.[19]

[18] *The Fall of British Tyranny* (Philadelphia, [1776]); reprinted in *Representative Plays by American Dramatists, 1765–1819*, ed. Montrose Moses (New York, 1918), pp. 283–350. Though advertised in the *Boston Gazette*, Sept. 16, 1776, as just for sale, Tyler infers from internal evidence that it was finished sometime between Jan. 10 and Mar. 17, 1776 (*Literary History*, II, 198–199n.). The play is generally attributed to John Leacock of Philadelphia and seems actually to have been staged in America during the war. At least Claude C. Robin, recollecting his visit to Harvard College, writes in 1781, "Their pupils often act tragedies, the subject of which is generally taken from their national events, such as the battle of Bunker's Hill, the burning of Charlestown, the Death of General Montgomery, the capture of Burgoyne, the treason of Arnold, and the Fall of British Tyranny," *New Travels through North America* (Boston, 1784), p. 17, quoted in C. M. Newlin, *West. Penn. Hist. Mag.*, X (1927), 231.

[19] Ritcheson, *British Politics*, p. 194; G. H. Guttridge, *Am. Hist. Rev.*,

Not long after his appointment an antiministerial writer, echoing the popular prejudice, gibed:

> Ye poor silly people, who foolishly think,
> That the glory of Britain is likely to sink;
> Your affairs will soon prosper, recover your frights,
> For the hero of Minden will set them to rights.
>
>   . . . . .
>
> His judgment, sometimes, when the enemy's near,
> Is weaken'd, 'tis true, by the passion of Fear;
> But now having th' Atlantic 'twixt him and his foe,
> All his talents for war he'll intrepidly show.
>
>   . . . . .
>
> How surpris'd will our Gen'rals his orders receive!
> With what joy they'll obey what he bids them achieve!
> Since they all must conclude from his being in place,
> To be broke and cashier'd is not thought a disgrace.
>
>   . . . . .
>
> Then droop not, Britannia, but lift up your voice,
> And join in applauding this excellent choice;
> For though *Sackville* once left on your glories a stain,
> Your disgraces will all be repair'd by *Germain*.[20]

Shortly before Yorktown, when Germain had weathered six years in office, Freneau pictured him instructing Lord Dunmore, the last colonial governor of Virginia:

> Virginia is conquered, the rebels are banged,
> You are now to go over and see them safe hanged:
> I hope it is not to your nature abhorrent
> To sign for these wretches a handsome death warrant—

XXXIII (1927), 42, 26; Gerald S. Brown, *Wm. & Mary Quar.*, ser. 3, IX (1952), 336, 334. From a careful examination of the circumstances surrounding the trial of Sackville (Germain) after the battle of Minden (Aug. 1, 1759), Brown concludes that "an interpretation in terms of personal cowardice is quite inadequate" (p. 334).

[20] *New York Journal*, Apr. 4, 1776, p. 4 (from a London paper). Lord Germain was born George Sackville.

Were I but in your place, I'm sure it would suit
To sign their death warrants, and hang them to boot.

. . . . .

And send us some rebels—a dozen or so—
They'll serve here in London by way of a show;
And as to the Tories, believe me, dear cousin,
We can spare you some hundreds to pay for the dozen.[21]

IV

On two occasions in particular the British government tried to effect a reconciliation with America. Both attempts failed, largely because Britain refused to acknowledge American independence. In the spring of 1776, when Americans were considering the wisdom of declaring themselves independent, Joseph Reed wrote Washington: "To tell you the truth, my dear Sir, I am infinitely more afraid of these Commissioners than of their Generals and Armies. If their propositions are plausible, and behaviour artful, I am apprehensive they will divide us." He had reference to Richard and William Howe, who on May 6 were appointed "Commissioners for restoring peace to his Majesty's Colonies and Plantations in North America, and for granting pardons to such of his Majesty's subjects there, now in rebellion, as shall deserve the Royal mercy." On September 11, Benjamin Franklin, John Adams, and Edward Rutledge, representing Congress, conferred with Richard Howe on Staten Island; Franklin interpreted the British terms to mean unconditional submission, and negotiations were broken off.[22] A week later the Howes issued a proclamation, whereupon a Bostonian mimicked, "Rebels of all ranks and ages" "Shall taste the blessings in profusion / Of

[21] "A LONDON DIALOGUE Between My Lords, Dunmore and Germaine," *Freeman's Journal*, Sept. 19, 1781, p. 2; reprinted in Pattee, II, 88.

[22] Joseph Reed to George Washington, Mar. 15, 1776, quoted in Edmund Cody Burnett, *The Continental Congress* (New York, 1941), p. 147; Lynn Montross, *The Reluctant Rebels* (New York, 1950), pp. 143-144, 177.

Britain's crazy constitution." "To all committees and conventions, / To Congresses of all dimensions" (the travesty continues),

> We now command that from this hour
> They quit their long usurped power,
> Of raising troops and fleets equipping,
> To levy money, men or shipping,
> Or to imprison or molest
> The subjects by the court caress'd;
> The tories, parricides and pimps,
> The placemen, pensioners and imps,
> The fell posterity of Cain,
> Who stab their country for gain;
> Through envy, malice, pride and strife,
> Who rob their brethren of life.

"Desist from your audacious views, / And round your necks affix the noose." If every man will swear allegiance to Britain,

> We promise pardon to all treason;
> Attainders, forfeitures shall cease,
> You may hereafter live in peace;
> The dupes, the sycophants and slaves,
> Of tories curs'd, or garter'd knaves.
> But if your Washington's and Lee's,
> Or other heroes like to these,
> With courage, dignity and might,
> Preferring death before a flight,
> Should animate you ne'er to yield,
> But bravely win and keep the field;
>
> .   .   .   .   .
>
> The prowess of my brother Will
> Shall plunder, burn, destroy and kill.
> We'll bounce and bark and cry bow wow,
> And stigmatise the name of Howe,
> 'Till every gen'rous noble brow,
> Detests the name of Howe and Howe.[23]

[23] *Continental Journal* (Boston), Jan. 2, 1777, p. 2.

On February 17, 1778, Lord North introduced a bill in Commons that led to the appointment of the Earl of Carlisle, William Eden, and George Johnstone as new peace commissioners; they were invested with broader powers than the Howes.[24] An American writer, the more vividly to expose what he interpreted as North's apostasy in introducing this bill, employs a metaphor thoroughly familiar to an Anglo-American audience of the day:

In the very midst of this furious career, this mighty huntsman of the humankind, all at once is at *fault;* turns short on his heel, and starts off with equal speed on his own back scent, swallowing as he goes, those very threats, still vibrating in the air, with the whole pack in full cry close behind him, as hasty and as loud as if their leader had never changed his course.

"Should any blind son of bondage," exhorts this author, "hanker after the stinking leeks and onions of Egypt, let him remember the double task of bricks without straw; and the slaughter of his male children; and rouse himself up to the dignity of an AMERICAN." [25] An Englishman observes that North, having long pursued a policy of coercion, must now recant:

> With his brother Burgoyne,
> He is *forc'd* now to join,
> And a *treaty of peace* for to want;
> Says he ne'er more will fight,
> But will give up his right
> To taxation, and freely *recant.*
> With the great Gen'ral Howe,
> He'd be very glad now,
> He ne'er had engag'd in the jaunt;
> And ev'ry proud Scot,
> In the *dev'lish plot,*
> With his Lordship are *forc'd* to *recant.*[26]

[24] Montross, *Reluctant Rebels*, p. 233.
[25] *New-Jersey Gazette* (Trenton), May 20, 1778, p. 3.
[26] "On Lord NORTH's Recantation," *Providence Gazette*, Aug. 29, 1778, p. 4 (from the *London Evening Post*).

On April 22, Congress declared "that these United States cannot, with propriety, hold any conference or treaty with any commissioners on the part of Great Britain, unless they shall, as a preliminary thereto, either withdraw their fleets and armies, or else, in positive and express terms, acknowledge the independence of the said states." [27] The Convention of Saratoga, rumor of a Franco-American treaty (confirmed before the commissioners reached America), and a British decision to evacuate Philadelphia strengthened Congress' hand. The Carlisle Commission, which arrived at Philadelphia on June 4, was not empowered to accede to either of the preliminary conditions Congress had imposed and so found itself doomed at the outset to almost certain failure. An American writer expresses the dilemma facing the commissioners:

> "How hard is your Congress' exacted Conditions!"
> Cry the gentlemen come with pacific commissions,
> Withdrawing our troops, they premise, and our fleet,
> And on no other terms will they deign for to treat!
> The word *Independence*, what can they intend in't?
> In spite of our efforts you are Independent.
> Were we left to ourselves, faith, ere now we had scamper'd;
> But consider, good folks, we are terribly hampered.
> True, an *army* we have—but completely invaded;
> And our fleet to the full is as nicely blockaded;
> Sure the world then can judge, and as readily say,
> If it's left at our option to go or to stay?
> Get consent from Estaing, and your chief Washington,
> And we need not a prompter to set off and run.[28]

On October 3, Carlisle, Clinton, and Eden, attempting to go over the head of Congress, issued a manifesto to the people at large expressing their willingness to exempt the colonies from taxation by Parliament. Congress countered, defending the rebellion and condemning British military and diplomatic pro-

---

[27] *Journals*, X, 379.
[28] "An Epigram," *New York Journal* (Poughkeepsie), Aug. 3, 1778, p. 2; reprinted in Moore's *Diary*, II, 78.

cedure.[29] Weary and discouraged, the commissioners embarked for England the end of November. Livingston opined that the manifesto of October 3 was "rather calculated for the meridian of London than that of America."

. . . I once thought of consecrating [it] to the Goddess *Cloacina*, but it being ornamented with his Majesty's own arms, and I having heard so much in times of yore about the *Lord's anointed*, . . . was struck with horror at the sacriligious (rebellious) impulse. I shall therefore paste it up over my chimney-piece, but in all probability *topsyturvy*, . . . [so] that if I am hang'd at last, my descendants may know it was thro' sheer love of hanging, by refusing so gracious and unmerited a pardon upon sincere repentance, with so grim-frowning a lion on the top, terrificly denouncing the royal vengeance against final contumacy and impenitence after the forty days *quarantine* mercifully allowed to air away all the infection of republicanism and rebellion.[30]

The refusal of the British government to recognize American independence foredoomed the Howe and Carlisle commissions to failure. Conversely, Americans never tired of reminding loyalists and Britons alike that the Declaration of Independence was a *fait accompli*. In the fall of 1779, William Livingston, exercising "the greatest decorum and impartiality," enumerates six "eminent advantages" of British government, of which we Americans "are most lamentably deprived by our independency and republicanism." First, unlike Britain whom the world knows to be insolvent and whose credit is always good, America, having contracted an enormous debt by the present war, can and will pay it.

[29] Nathan R. Einhorn, *Penn. Hist.*, XVI (1949), 209; Weldon A. Brown, *Empire or Independence* (Baton Rouge, 1941), p. 288. Johnstone, failing in his efforts to bribe several members of Congress, had returned to England in September.

[30] *New-Jersey Gazette*, Oct. 21, 1778, p. 1. The manifesto had proclaimed full pardon to all American soldiers and officials (with certain exceptions) who should ask it during the next forty days (Oct. 3–Nov. 11).

Would it not, therefore, have been infinitely better for us to have remained in subjection to a nation that can equip the most formidable fleets and armies on credit, and prosecute endless wars in every quarter of the globe, not only without any cash of her own, but without the least intention of repaying what she borrows from others for that purpose?

Second, the American Congress may eventually "betray their trust, and sacrifice our liberties"; the House of Commons can never serve their constituents so, "because the people selling their voices to the members on their election, the latter undoubtedly may, without the imputation of corruption, dispose of theirs to the ministry, to re-imburse themselves the expenditures. . . ." Third,

I am astonished that men of fashion and spirit should prefer our hotchpotch, oliverian, oligarchical anarchies, to the beautiful, the *constitutional*, the *jure divino*, and the heaven-descended monarchy of Britain. For pray how are the *better sort* amidst our universal *levelism*, to get into offices?

Fourth, notwithstanding "all our pompous declarations" of religious freedom, "our gentlemen of distinction" have to prove themselves "neither atheists nor deists," whereas in England no gentleman of fashion thinks "himself under the least obligation to give any proof, even of his faith in the existence of a Deity, except only that of profanely swearing by his name." Fifth, as long as

we received our governors and other principal officers immediately from the fountain-head of high life and polish'd manners, it was impossible for us to degenerate into our primitive clownishness and rusticity. . . . I *pertest*, were I a woman, I should instantly turn *tory* in revenge of the dismal prospect of our not having, by next Christmas, a single *red-coat* on the continent.

Finally, our printers not behind enemy lines "are cruelly restricted to plain truth and decency; while their brother-craftsmen in the enemy's lines, with the whole typographical fraternity on the *constitutional* island, are generously permitted to range uncontrolled thro' the boundless fields of imagination. . . ." Many gentlemen (concludes Livingston) are of the opinion that by our independence we have gained one material advantage over Britain:

> that no persons employed by the States are mistrusted for imitating her example in peculation, and defrauding their country in any the departments committed to their management, and that all continental property is husbanded with the greatest oeconomy; but this, without any predilection for Old England, I shrewdly suspect wants confirmation.[31]

In this ironic letter to the press Livingston assumes the mask of a well-meaning friend of government who opposes the "present republican and levelling systems." As lawyer, congressman, and wartime governor, he was familiar with the domestic and foreign scene, especially where legal distinctions were concerned, and brings this large understanding of his times into full play at that moment in history when America seemed on the threshold of securing the independence she had declared two years before. Until the final paragraph, which is labored and obvious by comparison, say, with the postscript to "An Edict by the King of Prussia," he manages the underlying irony with a sure and steady hand.

At a time when it remained only to sign the final treaty of peace Hopkinson, writing in a manner less subtle than Livingston's, professed to detect inconveniences attendant on American independence. In the first place, he declares, how happy we were in our dependent state! for then Britain told us "that the *French* are a trifling and contemptible nation; that the *Spaniards* are proud, sullen, and revengeful; the *Germans*, ostentatious; the *Hollanders*, boors; the *Russians*, savages; and, in short, that the English were themselves the only people fit to live and govern the world, as if all other nations held their dominions by usurpation." But now we are compelled

[31] *New-Jersey Gazette*, Sept. 9, 1778, p. 4.

by actual experience to acknowledge, that the *French* are a brave, generous, and polished people: and that none of the other nations are, in truth, such as they have been represented to us. . . . That good and bad men are to be found in every climate; and that the people of England have not actually monopolized all the virtue and wisdom of the world.

In the second place, whereas once it was not "thought disreputable for the merchants to evade the payment" to Britain of imposts and duties, now that we are independent "it would be dishonourable, and even wicked, to evade the duties laid by our own laws, and for the support of our own government."

If, notwithstanding all I have said, and all I might have said, you will be so blind as to prefer a state of freedom, with all its cares and troubles, to a state of dependence and slavery, which required nothing but implicit faith, and obedience: if you will persist in maintaining a right to make your own laws, and levy your own taxes, although a foreign power so kindly offers to take this trouble off your hands, you must e'en abide by the consequence, and enjoy the events as well as you can.[32]

The two years following Yorktown saw the resignation of Lord North, twelve years in power, and a peace settlement, in which among many other terms Britain officially recognized American independence. Britons experienced a sense of relief, "relief from the burdens of the war, from the ordinary expenses of maintaining the colonies even in times of peace, and from the continuous controversy that for many years past had destroyed all possibility of imperial harmony."[33] The picture the satirists drew of the corruption and near bankruptcy of the

---

[32] "On PEACE, LIBERTY, and INDEPENDENCE," MS [Philadelphia, 1783]; probably written, says Hastings, for the commencement exercises at the College of Philadelphia on July 4, 1783 (*Hopkinson*, p. 412). It was printed in *Miscellaneous Essays*, II, 13-23, wherein Hopkinson explains, "The arguments used in this speech are manifestly *ironical*, but the professors considered it as burlesquing the subject, and would not permit it to be delivered."

[33] Clark, *British Opinion*, p. 280.

British government did not alter the fact that losing the American war, British arms scored so signally against France, Spain, and Holland as to all but win the European peace. George III not only survived the satirical assault, with the emergence of the younger Pitt he found a chief minister who suited both himself and the English nation at large.[34] For their part, the free and united states of America, exulting in their hard-won independence, yet fearing it too, walked the ever trackless way into the future.

[34] Green, *Hanoverians,* pp. 304–305.

CHAPTER VI

The Continental Congress

THE period 1774–1776, during which British civil authority in America disintegrated, witnessed the first sustained effort
at colonial federation. The continuing presence of a revolutionary congress at Philadelphia impelled loyalists to close ranks
at last. While they did not, during the almost two years of grace
before the adoption of the Declaration of Independence forced
them on the defensive, take full advantage of the opportunity
to attack the Congress, increasingly they added their voice to
that of ministerial writers. In the Anglo-American press from
1774 on, but especially in Rivington's *Royal Gazette* (established at the end of 1777), ridicule was heaped on the delegates
and their efforts to secure independence, foreign alliances, and
a stable currency.

I

On September 4, 1774, the First Continental Congress convened at Philadelphia, in response to proposals by town meetings and committees of correspondence that immediate action
be taken in the cause of Massachusetts. Whereas the radical delegates bound themselves to protest British oppression and secure
liberty, the conservatives sought to re-establish harmonious relations with the mother country, by compromise if necessary.[1]

[1] Cornelia Meigs, *The Violent Men* (New York, 1949), p. 39.

This division within the Congress was only resolved two years later with the unanimous adoption of a declaration of independence, committing the delegates thenceforth to a hazardous course of action. At this first session in 1774, Congress, agreeing to make the cause of Massachusetts its own, endorsed the Suffolk Resolves, wherein a county convention at Milton had adjudged the Coercive Acts unconstitutional and declared its unwillingness to obey them. While Congress in due course respectfully addressed the inhabitants of Great Britain and pledged allegiance to the King, unquestionably its most far-reaching pronouncement was the Association for Nonintercourse (October 20), informing the colonies that "to obtain redress of these grievances, which threaten destruction to the lives, liberty and property of his majesty's subjects, in North America, we are of the opinion that a non-importation, non-consumption, and non-exportation agreement, faithfully adhered to, will prove the most speedy, effectual, and peaceable measure." [2]

The Association was at once travestied by the Anglican minister Jacob Bailey. Congress, after drinking *"Bumpers, thirty-two,"* agrees upon *"Import—Export—Consump-non."* That body recites the fourteen articles in anapestic measure and closes with this rousing chorus addressed to all Americans:

> And now we do, in solemn dumps,
> Bind us and you from heads to rumps
> In cords like hempen, tight and strong
> To stand by stiffly, right or wrong,
> Th' aforesaid mulish Association,
> Till we have brought the British Nation,
> To us, their betters far, to buckle,
> And on their marrow-bones to truckle.
> We'll starve ourselves and them, by Jove!
> So mighty is our country's love,
> Until we make the Parliament,
> Those haughty Lordlings, to repent,

[2] *Journals,* I, 76.

Repeal, and re-repeal those acts,
Which they have pass'd like saucy jacks.

. . . . .

For nature's law is clear and plain,
That parents should their brats maintain.

. . . . .

The Parliament shall straight repeal
All tax acts on our common weal;
All acts imposing dues or custom,
For which we've bully'd cheated, curs'd em.[3]

And in *The Americans Roused* (1775) Parson Sharp, a loyalist bent on converting lukewarm patriots, cries that the Association

recommends robbery to the whole continent; it is calculated to reduce thousands of families to poverty and ruin; it tends directly to quarreling, fightings and murders; it is a scheme, in the fixed nature of things, impossible to be executed; it must render us contemptible in the eyes of Britons, a reproach, a laughing-stock and a bye-word, among all civilized nations.[4]

As the first session drew to a close, John Adams complained:

In Congress, nibbling and quibbling as usual. There is no greater mortification than to sit with half a dozen wits, deliberating upon a petition, address or memorial. These great wits, these subtile critics, these refined geniuses, these learned lawyers, these wise statesmen, are so fond of showing their parts and powers, as to make their consultations very tedious.[5]

Although some of the delegates would have agreed with Adams, the accomplishments of the Congress in the space of six short

[3] "The Association, etc. of the Delegates of the Colonies," [Philadelphia] broadside, 1774; reprinted in Moore's *Ballad History*, pp. 349–360.

[4] Boston, 1775; reprinted in the *Magazine of History*, XX (1922), 148–149. In the *New York Gazette*, Mar. 25, 1775, a New York reprint is advertised as for sale. A. H. Quinn, *A History of the American Drama from the Beginning to the Civil War* (New York, 1943), p. 57, attributes the play to Jonathan Sewall, a Massachusetts lawyer.

[5] Diary entry for Oct. 24, 1774, *Works of John Adams*, II, 401.

weeks were substantial enough to alarm the loyalist community.[6]
The wife in *A Dialogue between a Southern Delegate and his
Spouse*, for example, jeers at her husband's too eager offer "to
be led by the Nose" rather than have the world think they've
"come to Blows." Loath to begin, he tries nevertheless to clear
himself:

> You mistook me, my Dear, I did not pretend
> Every Measure of Congress, right or wrong to defend;
> Many Things they've left undone they shou'd surely have done,
> Many Things they have done, they shou'd have sure let alone:
>
>   .   .   .   .   .
>
> But grant their Resolves were more absurd than they are,
> Could you really expect your meek Husband would dare
> Oppose such a Torrent, when its very well known,
> He dare not say to your Face, his Soul is his own?

Ignoring his command to "Mind thy Household-Affairs, teach
thy children to read," she declares it would be much better if
"instead of Delegates, they'd sent Delegates' Wives," and concludes with this unassailable argument:

> Instead of imploring their Justice, or Pity,
> You treat Parliament like a Pack of Banditti:
> Instead of Addresses, fram'd on Truth and on Reason,
> They breathe nothing but Insult, Rebellion, and Treason;
> Instead of attempting our Interests to further,
> You bring down on our Heads Perdition, and Murder.
>
>   .   .   .   .   .
>
> In all the Records of the most slavish Nation,
> You'll not find an Instance of such Usurpation.
> If Spirits infernal, for dire Vengeance design'd,
> Had been nam'd Delegates, to afflict Human kind,
> And in Grand Continental Congress, had resolv'd
> "Let the Bonds of social Bliss be from henceforth dissolved,"
> They could not have plann'd, with more exquisite Skill,

[6] Miller describes the nature and extent of this loyalist reaction (*Origins*,
pp. 388–392).

Nor have found a tame Race, more submiss to their Will.
Let Fools, Pedants, and Husbands, continue to hate
The Advice of us Women, and call it all Prate:
Whilst you are in Danger, by your good Leave, my Dear,
Both by Night and by Day, I will ring in your Ear—
Make your Peace:—Fear the King:—The Parliament fear.[7]

This Hudibrastic writer has fairly mastered the more difficult anapestic measure, heightening thereby the burlesque tone of the poem.

The King's response to the actions of the First Congress was immediate and forthright. Regarding the Association as seditious, he informed North, "The New England Governments are in a State of Rebellion, blows must decide whether they are to be subject to this Country or independant." [8] On May 10, 1775, three weeks after the skirmishing at Lexington and Concord, the Second Continental Congress met. This time the delegates understood their objectives much more clearly; furthermore, they had been instructed by their colonies to support any measures which would promote the general welfare. James Duane put into words what were the hopes and fears of most Americans at this juncture:

The eyes of Europe and America are fixed on this Assembly, and the fate of one of the greatest empires on earth, in no small degree, depends on the issue of their deliberations.

We are contending with the State from whence we spring, with those who were once our fathers, our guardians, our brethren, with those fleets and armies which were lately our protection. . . .

Cemented by the ties of blood, religion and interest, victory itself however decided must be fatal: and whichever side prevails must weep over its conquests. . . .

Let this ever be considered as a *family quarrel, disgraceful* and

---

[7] [New York], 1774; reprinted in the *Magazine of History*, XVIII (1920), 287–297.

[8] George III to Lord North, Nov. 18, 1774, *Correspondence of King George the Third*, III, 153.

ruinous into which we are innocently plunged by intolerable oppression, and which we are sincerely disposed to appease and reconcile, whenever the good providence of God shall put it in our power, consistent with the preservation of our just rights.[9]

Congress, looked upon formerly as little more than an advisory council, now became the central government of an embattled America.

The personnel of the Second Congress remained substantially unchanged, though in the years immediately ahead some of its ablest talent would be drawn into the army, back into provincial politics, or abroad on diplomatic missions. One loyalist describes the delegates, who have left "Life's low, unambitious State" and hied themselves to Philadelphia, as

> Men deprav'd, who quit their Sphere
> Without Remorse, or Shame or Fear,
> And boldly rush, they know not where;
> Seduc'd, alas! by fond Applause
> Of gaping Mobs, and loud Huzzas.
>
> . . . . .
>
> In Politics mere Punchinellos,
> Yet pass for rare, for clever Fellows;
> Like Punch, who struts, and swears and roars,
> And calls his Betters, Rogues and Whores.
>
> . . . . .
>
> Shall we applaud this vagrant Crew,
> Whose wretched Jargon, crude and new,
> Whose Impudence and Lies delude
> The harmless, ign'rant Multitude:
> To Varlets, weak, impure, unjust,
> The Reins of Government entrust[?]
> Will Raggamuffins bold like these,
> Protect our Freedom, Peace, or Ease?

[9] James Duane, Notes on the State of the Colonies, May 25, 1775, *Letters of Members of the Continental Congress*, ed. E. C. Burnett (Washington, D.C., 1921–1936), I, 98–99. Hereafter referred to as *Letters*.

Men such as these, ignorant of the nature, conditions, and ends of government, are

> Like Pettifoggers, pert and raw,
> Who grope in Indexes for Law,
> Prating of Books they never read,
> Toiling o'er Parchment for their Bread;
> Form'd at the most to scrawl a Lease,
> Yet dare to judge of War, and Peace.

When these "Men to Atlantic Empire born" fall to quarreling like "giddy Eton Boys" and are suddenly brought to task by the schoolmaster, they cry, "T'was H–n– – –k, A– – –s, led the way." The author concludes,

> Let Coblers, Tinkers, Butchers, prate
> At Will, of deep Affairs of State;
> Relate their Suff'rings o'er and o'er,
> Of Tea, of Tax, and Compacts roar,
> Till Pow'r supreme to Babes devolves,
> And every Suckling lisps Resolves.[10]

Whereas the conservatives under Joseph Galloway had tried to dominate the First Congress and failed, under John Dickinson they were sufficiently powerful in the Second to resist for a year the cry for independence. A second petition addressed to the King was in effect rejected by the news, which came the end of October, that he had called on all British subjects to help suppress the rebellion to which the American colonies, "misled by dangerous and ill designing men," had proceeded. Congress promptly answered this Proclamation of Rebellion, in order "to wipe off, in the name of the people of these United Colonies, the aspersions which it is calculated to throw upon our cause; and to prevent, as far as possible, the undeserved punishments, which it is designed to prepare for our friends." Parliament's

---

[10] *The Patriots of North-America* (New York, 1775); reprinted in the *Magazine of History*, VII (1914), 813–847. Attributed to Myles Cooper, an Anglican clergyman at New York.

answer to the Association for Nonintercourse was the passage
on December 22, 1775, of an act "removing the colonies from
the protection of the crown, forbidding all trade with them, and
authorizing the seizure and confiscation of American ships at
sea." Congress countered, authorizing the issuance of letters of
marque and reprisal against British shipping (March, 1776) and
opening American ports to the ships of all nations except Great
Britain (April). The prospect of reconciliation growing ever
dimmer, John Adams saw more clearly than most that Congress
should always, as Cornelia Meigs has paraphrased him, keep
three objectives in view: "There must be independence, there
must be foreign alliances, there must be a confederation of the
colonies into united and permanent government. Of these, independence was the first and paramount issue; the others would
be possible only when independence was achieved. But one must
not greatly outstrip the other." These objectives constituted the
main order of business in Congress during the war years.[11]

II

During 1774 and 1775, Congress took no action whatsoever
upon the question of independence. On January 8, 1776, news
came of the King's speech of the previous October charging
that the colonies aimed at independence. Two days later *Common Sense* was published, wherein Paine attempted to shift the
ground of the Anglo-American dispute from reconciliation—
the end which the declarations of Congress and the provincial
assemblies had in view—to independence. Though radical delegates like Samuel Adams and Richard Henry Lee heralded
Paine's pamphlet as an important step toward realizing John
Adams' first objective, the majority of the Congress received
it with fainter heart than the nation at large. "The People are
now ahead of you," Joseph Hawley informed Samuel Adams,

[11] Dec. 6, 1775, *Journals*, III, 409–410; Montross, *Reluctant Rebels*,
p. 120; Miller, *Origins*, p. 482; Meigs, *Violent Men*, p. 176.

and the only way to prevent discord and dissension is to strike while
the iron is hot. The Peoples blood is too Hot to admit of delays—
All will be in confusion if independence is not declared immediately.
The Tories take courage and Many Whiggs begin to be chagrined
—the Speech in Many parts is what is our Congress about? they are
dozing or amusing themselves or waiting to have a Treaty with
Commissioners which will end in our destruction.

As spring advanced, the desire for independence was voiced ever
louder in assembly and at town meeting.[12]

Josiah Tucker in *An Humble Address and Earnest Appeal*
(1775) told fellow Britons that it was to their best interests to
promote the cause of independence, that in fact the mother country should strive to prevent reunion in the event that the colonies
later sought it.[13] In the spring of 1776 a sarcastic countryman
produced this trope by way of answer:

> Crown'd be the man with lasting praise,
>   Who first contriv'd the pin,
> To loose mad horses from the chaise
>   And save the necks within.
>
>   . . . . .
>
> With ready foot the spring we press;
>   Out jumps the magic plug;
> Then, disengag'd from all distress
>   We sit quite safe and snug.
>
> The pamper'd steeds, their freedom gain'd,
>   Run off full speed together;
> But having no plan ascertain'd,
>   They run they know not whither.
>
>   . . . . .
>
> Each claiming now his nat'ral right
>   Scorns to obey his brother:

12 John H. Hazelton, *The Declaration of Independence* (New York,
1906), pp. 7, 38; Burnett, *Continental Congress*, p. 129; Miller, *Origins*,
p. 471; Joseph Hawley to Samuel Adams, Apr. 1, 1776, Adams MSS, New
York Public Library, quoted in Miller, *Origins*, p. 485.
13 Clark, *British Opinion*, pp. 276-277.

So they proceed to kick and bite
  And worry one another.

Hungry at last, and blind and lame,
  Bleeding at nose and eyes,
By suff'rings grown extremely tame,
  And by experience wise:

With bellies full of *liberty*,
  But void of oats and hay
They both sneak back; their folly see;
  And run no more away.[14]

On June 7, Richard Henry Lee, acting on instructions from home and speaking for the Virginia delegation, offered a resolution, "That these United Colonies are, and of right ought to be, free and Independent States." Consideration of this resolution was postponed until July 1 and a committee appointed to draft a written declaration so that, if independence were actually voted, no time would be lost. In debate on July 1, Dickinson argued that the establishment of a confederated government and the securing of foreign alliance should precede a declaration of independence. John Adams replied, in effect, that "if independence, confederation, and foreign alliance could not all come at once, then independence must assuredly come first." The next day twelve colonies voted for independence; New York gave its assent a week later. Carl Becker has observed that "the primary purpose of the Declaration was to convince a candid world that the colonies had a moral and legal right to separate from Great Britain" and that "rebellion was not the proper word for what they were doing." The strategy in the Declaration, like that in *Common Sense*, was to attack the institution of monarchy and the person of George III and affirm

[14] "America. Addressed to the Rev. Dean TUCKER," *Gentleman's Magazine*, XLVI (Mar., 1776), 133; reprinted in the *Pennsylvania Ledger*, Feb. 21, 1778, and again in *The Loyalist Poetry of the American Revolution*, ed. Winthrop Sargent (Philadelphia, 1857), pp. 77–79. Attributed to the English poet, Soame Jenyns.

the idea of political autonomy. Given an ideal worth fighting for, many Americans who had held back were won over to the patriot cause. Those who chose to remain loyal to the King were placed outside the pale of the law, subject to whatever punitive measures governmental agencies saw fit to take.[15]

Late in the war there appeared in the New York press a travesty on the Declaration, in which the members of Congress are substituted for King George. After the familiar preamble a long train of their abuses is enumerated.

They have by mobs and riots awed Representative Houses, repeatedly into a compliance with their resolutions, though destructive of the peace, liberty, and safety of the people.

They have by their misconduct reduced us to all the dangers and distress of actual invasion from without, and to all the horrors of a civil war within. . . .

They have driven many of our people beyond sea, into exile, and have confiscated their estates and the estates of others, who were beyond sea before the war, or the existence of Congress, on pretence of offences, and under the sanction of a mock trial, to which the person condemned was neither cited nor present.

They have abolished the true system of the English constitution and laws, in thirteen of the American provinces, and established therein a weak and factious democracy, and have attempted to use them as introducing the same misrule and disorder into all the colonies on the continent. . . .

They have involved us in an immense debt, foreign as well as internal, and did put the best port and island on our continent into the hands of the foreigners, who are their creditors.

They have wantonly violated our public faith and honor, and destroyed all grounds for private confidence, or the security of private property; have not blushed to act in direct contradiction to their most solemn declaration, and to render the people under their government "a reproach and a bye-word among the nations."

[15] *Journals,* V, 425; Meigs, *Violent Men,* pp. 223–224, 225; Carl Becker, *The Declaration of Independence* (New York, 1940), pp. 203, 7; Burnett, *Continental Congress,* p. 188; Miller, *Origins,* p. 493.

"We think it not too severe to say," the travesty continues, "that we find them as intoxicated with ambition of independent sovereignty, as that execrable Roman daughter, who drove the wheels of her chariot over the mangled body of her murdered father, in her way to the capitol"; and concludes,

We therefore . . . do renounce and disclaim all allegiance, duty, or submission to the Congress, or to any government under them; and declare that the united Colonies, or States so called, neither are, nor of right ought to be, independent of the Crown of Great-Britain, or unconnected with that empire, . . . and in the support of this Declaration, with a firm reliance on the blessings and protection of Divine Providence, We mutually pledge to each other, and to the Crown and Empire of Great-Britain, our lives, our fortunes, and our sacred honour.[16]

A Continuation of Hudibras (1778), published anonymously in London, relates how Sir Hudibras rises to tell a Presbyterian meeting, at which the Adamses, Hancock, Otis, Cushing, Deane, and Franklin have assembled, that he foresees the growing prosperity of colonial America. He is convinced that like Satan the Americans will revolt and gain their independence, for already they

> Insist that all men are born free,
> And have a right to liberty:
> Some meaning liberty of taking,
> Part of what fortune made mistake in,
> Bestowing blindly upon others,
> Less worthy than themselves our brothers,
> Some meaning liberty of living,
> By law protected—without giving,
> Or being made to give or grant,

[16] *A Counterdeclaration* (New York, 1782), pp. 1-11. Variously attributed to Silas Deane and Arthur Lee. Tullia, daughter of king Servius Tullius and wife of Tarquinius Superbus, "stirred her husband to oust her father from the throne, and when the latter had been murdered, drove her chariot over his dead body," *The Oxford Companion to Classical Literature* (Oxford, 1937), p. 440.

One penny to the nation's want,
To pay th' expences of that state,
Under whose influence they grow great.
Most meaning liberty of using
The name—all order to confuse in,
Thus anarchy and mischief brewing,
And rising on the realm's undoing.
By fools they may be understood,
To act on grounds and reasons good;
Make them believe they have a reason,
That war against the king's no treason.

Sophistically Sir Hudibras justifies rebellion. When it breaks out in America,

Tradesmen of ev'ry occupation,
Shall be the lords of a new nation,
Members of Congress,—by the fates,
Doom'd to be rulers of the states.
Lawyers and their attendant bums
Shall turn their parchment into drums,
Instead of bags, long briefs and deeds,
Shall think of banners—neighing steeds,
Swords gun-powder and cannon shot,
To send poor Englishmen to pot.—
Some gen'rals too of matchless skill,
Shall rise from brothers of the quill,
And ruin'd men, releas'd from duns,
Shall live by rifle barrell'd guns.

Those at the meeting concur in these views and prepare forthwith to settle in the American colonies, a few remaining behind to "watch the guiders of the helm." In 1755 (the poem continues) Great Britain helps the Americans defeat the French but incurs a heavy war debt in the process. The filial ingratitude of the colonies after the war calls forth successive low-burlesque similes: like the viper whom the farmer sheltered, America tries to sting her British savior; furthermore, Americans are worse than baby hawks ready to kill the mother sparrow that nursed them, for they are *rational* creatures who would wound their *natural* mother.

In the second canto Sir Hudibras, never more than a shadowy figure, drops out of sight altogether. The goddess Discord visits her son, an archpatriot, in his London room late at night, where he is "penning false items" for tomorrow's paper, "mischief and faction to infuse." Suggesting that the Whigs in Parliament may encourage the Americans to revolt, she urges him to foment rebellion by writing still bigger lies. Abroad, his specious arguments prompt American patriots to exile loyalists. They then issue a declaration of independence which asserts their natural rights:

> First, let this downright maxim strike,
> That all men are born free alike,
> And are undoubtedly allow'd,
> By providence to be endow'd,
> (As many a learned author writes)
> With some unalienable rights;
> 'Mong these we lay the greatest stress,
> On life, pursuit of happiness,
> And (what is best of all the three)
> Of uncontrouled liberty.
> For surely no one can believe,
> But he's a certain right to live,
> Without receiving check or stop here,
> As long as ever he thinks proper;
> Neither is life like chair or table,
> To one another alienable,
> Neither can any mortal have,
> The right to make himself a slave,
> (Altho' by thieving we must say
> Some people do it ev'ry day)
> Neither can anyone entrap ye,
> From the just right of being happy:
> (Tho' your chief happiness in life,
> Should be to kiss your neighbour's wife.)

Especially do we Americans cherish the right to revolution:

> The people have a right t'abolish,
> Alter, relinquish, and demolish,
> By methods novel and surprizing,
> New states and powers organising,
> In such a form and figure drest,
> As the wise authors shall think best.

After a list of grievances charged to George III comes the declaration proper:

> We therefore jointly acquiesce,
> (As it is plain we cant do less)
> To separate ourselves by force,
> Pronouncing sentence of divorce,
> Looking upon Them as you'll find,
> We mean to look at all mankind,
> On plans of ancient Rome and Greece,
> Foes when at war—and friends in peace.
> We then the lawful Delegates
> Of the American joint States,
>
>   .   .   .   .   .
>
> Do, by the pow'r that in Us lies,
> Acting for All these Colonies,
> Solemnly publish and declare,
> That these same Colonies now are,
> And from henceforth of right shall be,
> States Independent Great and Free.

With which declaration the poem comes to an end.[17]

While falling short of *M'Fingal* and "The Political Balance," this Hudibrastic poem has much to recommend it. It too explores low-burlesque situations to good advantage. Thus, when the author, travestying the Declaration of Independence, names happiness an inalienable right and adds parenthetically, "Tho' your

---

[17] *A Continuation of Hudibras in Two Cantos* (London, 1778), pp. 1–76; I consulted a longhand copy at the New York Public Library. Attributed to Joseph Peart, who was probably an English solicitor.

chief happiness in life, / Should be to kiss your neighbour's wife," the effect is bathetic. Never so fully developed a character as M'Fingal, Sir Hudibras' bluster and sophistry make him a convincing hero nonetheless. The author establishes his point of view more clearly and consistently than either Trumbull or Freneau by concentrating his attack on the natural rights doctrine, more especially the rights to revolution and national independence that Americans had been asserting for many years past.

III

By the summer of 1776, less than two years after first convening at Philadelphia, the Continental Congress had gained such power and influence that now the prosecution of the war depended on its continuing in existence. Twice during the year ahead, as the British pressed toward the city, the delegates were forced to flee and convene elsewhere, once at Baltimore, once at York. "Meer personal safety I suppose would not have induced many of them to fly," wrote Robert Morris after the first flight, "but their security as a body was the object. had any number of them fallen into the Enemies hands so as to break up the Congress, America might have been ruined before another choice of Delegates could be had and in such an event that would have been deemed criminal and rash to the last degree." Starting about this time, two persistent ills—absenteeism and maladjusted finances—began to reduce the efficiency of Congress and morale itself. "The Congress do worse than ever," declared a member in 1778; "We murder time, and chat it away in idle impertinent talk: However, I hope the urgency of affairs will teach even that Body a little discretion." [18] One writer at this time inveighs against the "obscure pettifogging attorneys, bankrupt shop-

[18] Robert Morris to John Jay, Jan. 12, 1777, *Letters*, II, 214; Montross, *Reluctant Rebels*, p. 187; Charles Carroll to Thomas Johnson, Jr., Apr. 21, 1778, *Letters*, III, 181.

keepers, outlawed smugglers" who compose the Congress.[19] Another calls it "an hydra-headed form, with harpies' claws."

> Lo! num'rous mouths hiss, chatter, bark, or croak:
> Here, one like Cacus belches fire and smoke;
> The second like a monkey grins and chats;
> A third squalls horrible, like angry cats:
> Here, you've the growls and snarlings of a dog;
> And there the beastly gruntings of a hog.
> Others affect the puritanic tone;
> The whine, the cant, the snuffle, and the groan.[20]

More pointedly than before the Declaration of Independence, individuals were now singled out. "Low and lousy beggars, rebel tailors, lawyers, pimps, parsons, and cobblers" (inveighs one writer)

Since by your machinations you have led us into difficulty with our just and gracious King George the Third, and now have left us at the mercy of a worse than lord protector, we humbly *veouw* we will see you all to the devil before we'll continue our allegiance to you. . . . And we further advise and declare, that if you don't "disband, and at once return to the peaceful employments" discerning nature hath pointed out for you, (you, W[ilson?] to your ink and horn book; you, A[dams?] to your cheating; you, H[untington?] to your goose, and you, D[eane?] to your wax,) you must expect to receive unseasonable things at unseasonable hours.[21]

In another satire the narrator dreams that he is in a spacious apartment before the infernal judges. Savage, cruel McKean appears first and is "condemned to assume the shape of a blood-

[19] "A MODERN CATECHISM," *Royal Gazette*, May 23, 1778, p. 1.

[20] "The Word of Congress," *Royal Gazette*, Sept. 18, 1779; reprinted in *Loyalist Poetry*, pp. 48–49.

[21] Moore's *Diary*, I, 443, for May 29, 1777; quoted from the "Journal of Captain Smythe" of the British Army, p. 61. These are possible identifications: James *W*ilson of Pennsylvania, who had been an accountant for a time; Samuel *A*dams of Massachusetts, who was almost always bankrupt; Samuel *H*untington of Connecticut, who had spent much of his boyhood working in his father's clothier shop; and Silas *D*eane of Connecticut, who had once been a blacksmith.

hound." "Next appeared the polite and travelled Mr. Deane, who from a tricking, hypocritical, New England attorney, was metamorphosed into a French marquis, with all the external frippery that so eminently distinguishes the most trifling characters of that trifling nation . . . and the most excellent ambassador to his most Christian majesty, skipped off, with very little change in the character of 'The monkey who had seen the world.'" "The black soul of Livingston . . . was condemned to howl in the body of a wolf; . . . he retained the same gaunt, hollow, and ferocious appearance, and . . . his tongue still continued to be red with gore." Finally, the court orders President Jay to "transmigrate into the most insidious and most hateful of animals, a snake; but to prevent his being able any longer to deceive, and thereby destroy, a large set of rattles was affixed to his tail, that it might warn mankind to shun so poisonous a being." [22]

The author of "The American Times" attacks still other of these "senators" who "infest the land." "Ye priests of Baal, from hot Tartarean stoves," "Haste to attend on *Witherspoon* the great."

> Scotland confess'd him sensible and shrewd,
> Austere and rigid; many thought him good.
> But turbulence of temper spoil'd the whole,
> And show'd the movements of his inmost soul.
> Disclos'd machinery loses of its force:
> He felt the fact, and westward bent his course.
>
> . . . . .
>
> Meanwhile unhappy Jersey mourns her thrall,
> Ordain'd by vilest of the vile to fall;
> To fall by Witherspoon—O name, the curse

[22] *Royal Gazette*, Jan. 23, 1779, p. 2; reprinted in Moore's *Diary*, II, 120–124, where it is ascribed to John André. Thomas McKean sat in Congress for Delaware (1775–1776, 1778–1782); Silas Deane, for Connecticut (1774–1776), after which he became an agent to France; William Livingston, for New Jersey (1774–1776); and John Jay, for New York (1774–1779; President, 1778–1779).

Of sound religion, and disgrace of verse.
Member of Congress we must hail him next:
Come out of Babylon, was now his text.
Fierce as the fiercest, foremost of the first,
He'd rail at Kings, with venom well-nigh burst:

. . . . .

I've known him seek the dungeon dark as night,
Imprison'd Tories to convert or fright;
Whilst to myself I've humm'd, in dismal tune,
I'd rather be a dog than Witherspoon.

Jay, Laurens, Roberdeau, and Wilson are also painted in spirited
invective. The following portrait completes this gallery of senators:

Ev'n while I write, a monster fierce and huge
Has fix'd his station in the land of Googe;
Virginian caitiff! *Jefferson* by name;
Perhaps from Jefferies sprung of rotten fame.
His savage letter all belief exceeds,
And Congress glories in his brutal deeds.[23]

IV

As early as December, 1775, France began to sympathize with
the American cause, unofficially to be sure. The following March
Congress authorized Silas Deane to dangle the prospect of American independence before Comte de Vergennes, foreign minister
of Louis XVI. In the summer of 1776 a bogus Spanish firm,
Roderique Hortalez and Company, was formed to ship French

[23] *Royal American Gazette* (New York), July 6, 13, Aug. 10, 1779;
reprinted in *The Cow-Chace, &c.* (New York, 1780), and again in
Loyalist Poetry, pp. 1–37. Italics mine. Variously attributed to John
André, Jonathan Odell, and Daniel Batwell; see *Am. Lit.*, II (1930),
79–82. John Witherspoon sat for New Jersey (1776–1782) and Thomas
Jefferson for Virginia (1775–1776). Julian P. Boyd conjectures that the
"savage letter" here alluded to may be either Jefferson's *Summary View*
(1774) or his letter of Aug. 25, 1775, to John Randolph; see *The Papers
of Thomas Jefferson* (Princeton, 1950), I, 121–137, 669–676, 240–243.

munitions and clothing to America in exchange for American produce—a move which, by contributing to the success of American arms at Saratoga and the stout defense offered against Howe by Washington, opened the way for a Franco-American alliance. That September Congress appointed Franklin, Deane, and Arthur Lee commissioners to negotiate such an alliance.[24]

Ministerial and loyalist writers warned Americans that foreign alliances were not to be depended on, that should America win the war her allies would turn and conquer her. In the first of two fables published in 1776 the beasts, finding themselves at war with the birds, who are the aggressors, make a treaty with the fish, who later explain that their Constitution will not allow them to aid the beasts on land.

> The fable teaches to beware
> Of false dependencies in war,
> Of faithless treaties, treach'rous friends,
> Who seek alone their private ends,
> Who would betray the common cause,
> To gain a tyrant's vile applause;
> Or, brib'd by fair and sordid gold,
> Have liberty and conscience sold.[25]

The second relates how, after a war in which they were saved from the foxes (France) and the wolves (Spain) by the dogs, the sheep, urged on by "some old stinking rams" (patriot leaders), proclaimed themselves "a commonwealth of free people."

The dogs, upon this, resolved to bring them back to obedience, but the sheep implored the foxes, the wolves, and the boars [Holland] to attack the dogs, which they gladly performed; and while the best mastiffs were in the country of the sheep, these different tribes so violently attacked their old formidable enemies the dogs, that they utterly broke their strength, and ruined them as a people. But the sheep did not long boast of their profound politics; the foxes, the

[24] Montross, *Reluctant Rebels*, pp. 116, 118, 170, 253–254; Burnett, *Continental Congress*, p. 208.
[25] *Pennsylvania Ledger*, June 22, 1776, p. 4.

wolves, and the boars poured in upon them, and soon rendered them the most abject and miserable of all animals.[26]

On May 4, 1778, Congress hastened to ratify two treaties that the commissioners had struck with France in February, one of alliance, the other of amity and commerce. "They are founded upon the broad Basis of Mutual Interest and Security," declared Oliver Wolcott, "and Nothing in them which indicates any Design of obtaining any Advantage over us, But seem adapted to secure a lasting Friendship which it is certainly the highest Interest of France to Cultivate." The French ambassador Gérard reached Philadelphia in July. The following February he informed Congress that probably Spain would soon declare war on Great Britain and asked point-blank what America expected to get from the war. By way of reply Congress resolved that "the liberty, sovereignty, and independence absolute and unlimited of these United States, as well in matters of government as of commerce, shall be assured on the part of Great Britain." [27]

Satirists reiterated their early warning and suggested further that the alliance would catholicize Americans.[28] One tells how, having overthrown the logs (colonial governors), the frogs make a treaty with King Stork. Then, having urged them bid the world defiance,

> The Stork grew hungry, long'd for fish;
> The monarch could not have his wish;
> In rage he to the marshes flies,
> And makes a meal of his allies.

[26] *Middlesex Journal*, Dec. 26, 1776; reprinted in the *Newport Gazette*, Oct. 16, 1777, and again in Moore's *Diary*, I, 355–357.

[27] Montross, *Reluctant Rebels*, pp. 234–235, 267; Oliver Wolcott to Mrs. Wolcott, May 9, 1778, *Letters*, III, 225; Aug. 4, 1779, *Journals*, XIV, 920.

[28] The alliance provoked satire in the European as well as in the Anglo-American press. Two of the liveliest of these are Delauney's *Histoire d'un pou français* (Paris, 1779) and [Richard Tickell's] *La cassette verte de Monsieur de Sartine* (The Hague, 1779), which ridicule Franklin and the other American commissioners, the boorishness of the Congress, and the designs of America and her allies on the British Empire.

Then grew so fond of well-fed frogs,
He made a larder of the bogs!
Say, Yankees, don't you feel compunction,
At your unnatural, rash conjunction?

Can love for you in him take root,
Who's Catholic, and absolute?
I'll tell these croakers how he'll treat 'em;
Frenchmen, like storks, love frogs—to eat 'em.[29]

Another composes a dream vision in which the narrator sees Louis XVI in the Hall of Justice upbraiding his fleet commander, D'Estaing. Louis is metamorphosed into a cat, D'Estaing into a village cur. Robert Morris, being accused by Thomas Paine of "negligence and dishonesty in his dealings with the *Public,*" delivers a harangue:

Having finished this effusion he look'd *up* for applause to *Mons. Gerard,* who had thrown off the mask, and openly assumed the dignity of *President,* vacated by the transformation of Mr. Jay. But this representative of his most Christian Majesty began to *hoot* like an owl, and *whoo, whoo, whoo,* resounded through the dome. . . . At this instant I heard the sound of rattles, and being informed it was some of the *Congress,* changing into *Rattle-Snakes,* like their President, . . . I awoke.[30]

V

The source of inflation, which Congress and the state governments found it increasingly difficult to check as the Revolution ran its course, was rooted in the past. The fact that in the colonial period export value usually fell short of import had led to a scarcity of specie and a consequent demand for paper emissions. As early as 1690, Massachusetts issued bills of credit to pay the

[29] *Scots Magazine,* XL (Aug., 1778), 439; reprinted in the *Royal Gazette,* Dec. 8, 1778, and again in Moore's *Songs,* pp. 237–240, where it is attributed to David Matthews, mayor of New York City during the war.
[30] *Royal Gazette,* Jan. 30, 1779, p. 2.

soldiers in King William's War; eventually all the colonies adopted the practice of issuing paper money to finance government in time of peace as well as war. In 1773, Parliament finally legalized this practice. Congress was acting on precedent as well as need, therefore, when it resolved on June 22, 1775, that "a sum not exceeding two millions of Spanish milled dollars be emitted by the Congress in bills of Credit, for the defence of America" and that "the twelve confederated colonies be pledged for the redemption of the bills of credit, now directed to be emitted." During the next four and a half years and at steadily shorter intervals Congress authorized forty emissions totaling nearly $250,000,000. The states, meanwhile, aggravated the situation by issuing almost an equal amount of paper in their own right. State legal-tender laws and congressional resolutions to insure the use of paper currency and fix its price failed to head off inflation.[31] Late in the war "State Money" set forth the "advantages" of continuing the Pennsylvania tender law in force.

1. It will deprive the State of all the benefit to be expected from taxes. 2. It will starve all the officers and members of the government, except the *Assemblymen*. 3. It will prevent loans, so injurious to agriculture, commerce and manufacturers. 4. It will destroy widows, orphans, and the aged members of the community, who can neither work nor fight. . . . 6. It will enable the good Whigs to punish the Tories, by cancelling their bonds with depreciated money. 7. It will encourage speculation and monopoly, and thereby enable staff officers to rise into rank and importance by trading with public money. . . . 9. It will promote resignations among our officers, and mutiny among our soldiers, for neither of them can live upon *nominal* dollars. . . . 12. It will satisfy the British, that their emissaries are doing their duty, in the most effectual manner, and that Gov. Johnstone did not carry his guineas back with him.[32]

[31] Davis Rich Dewey, *Financial History of the United States* (New York and London, 1907), pp. 8, 21–24, 36, 37–39; E. James Ferguson, *Wm. & Mary Quar.*, ser. 3, X (1953), 172, 178–179; *Journals*, II, 103.
[32] *New-York Gazette: and the Weekly Mercury*, Apr. 30, 1781, Supplement, p. 1.

Inflation began late in 1776 and accelerated until the collapse of Continental paper in the spring of 1781. Counterfeiting, the failure of the states to fulfill their pledges or meet the requisitions Congress made of them, spending foreign loans before they were secured, the British blockade which cut America off from a cash market eager for her products—all contributed to the collapse. In 1779, a year in which the value of Continental paper currency in specie sank to 40 for 1, one delegate wrote from Philadelphia: "Speculation here has arrived to such a height, and prices in three weeks encreased 100 per Ct. This has made those Vermins the Speculators become the object of resentment, and a Mob has assembled to regulate prices. what will be the issue God knows." [33] A political arithmetician calculated:

SUPPOSE the congress emitted two years ago thirteen millions, but now the emissons amount to one hundred and eighty millions of congress paper dollars. At two years ago one million was worth twenty millions of this day's congress paper dollars; then it geometrically follows, that the said one hundred and eighty millions is worth no more than nine millions was two years ago, and by such depreciation the congressal [sic] government can never get in debt; consequently there is no need of a tax; for one hundred and eighty millions divided by twenty quotes nine millions only; ergo said congressal government have gained by said depreciation four millions of congressal paper dollars.[34]

In a move that was tantamount to an admission of bankruptcy, Congress on May 18, 1780, made provision for accepting paper in place of silver at 40 for 1 and urged the states to repeal their legal-tender laws.[35]

In view of America's shaky finances during the war, it is small wonder that the hard-money advocates spoke out against fiat money. "Paper money," wrote Pelatiah Webster, "polluted the equity of our laws, turned them into engines of oppression,

[33] Dewey, *Financial History*, p. 39; Daniel of St. Thomas Jenifer to Thomas Johnson, Jr., May 24, 1779, *Letters*, IV, 232.
[34] "TAXATION ROYAL TYRANNY," Philadelphia broadside, Sept. 22, 1779.
[35] Dewey, *Financial History*, pp. 39–40.

corrupted the justice of our public administration, destroyed the fortunes of thousands who had confidence in it, enervated the trade, husbandry, and manufactures of our country, and went far to destroy the morality of our people." [36] Early in the war one of these advocates sneers:

Suppose the Congress finds it advisable to attain [obtain?] foreign assistance; will their PAPER DOLLARS go down with the mercenaries or auxiliaries? I fancy CONGRESS MONEY will appear to the Spaniard a poor representative of the hard Peruvian and Mexican dollar, a Helvetian would curl his nose at it, the phlegmatic Netherlander would light his pipe with it, and a French man will scarcely think it fit for papering his hair.[37]

Prematurely the loyalist merchant Joseph Stansbury describes Paper Money's final illness:

> Seiz'd by a Fit of Opposition
> Which baffled ev'ry State Physician;
> Each Lenitive was tried in vain
> To bring her back to Health again:
> Her Nerves now firm, now weak, by spells—
> It pox'd the Doctors Smith and Wells,
> And when they order'd stronger Med'cines,
> She languish'd—puked—in fine, is dead since!

Upon her urn shall be inscribed:

> Here rest, in Hope some future Day to rise
> With former lustre in these Western Skies,
> A Heap of Paper; once by Britain made
> The Life of Agriculture, Arts, and Trade;
> The Sign of Wealth, and all that wealth could grant;
> The Friend of Man, the Antidote to Want!
>   Tho' by Rebellion now intomb'd a while,
> This seeming lifeless Heap again shall smile—
> Again revive—exert her native Fire,
> And shall, with Britain flourish or expire.[38]

[36] Quoted in *ibid.*, p. 41.
[37] *Virginia Gazette* (Norfolk), Feb. 3, 1776, p. 35.
[38] "A Fragment," Dec. 10, 1777, in "Loyalist Rhapsodies," pp. 63–65.

In 1781, the year that saw the final collapse of Continental paper, "Old Continental Currency" petitions Congress that his

son NEW EMISSION lately employed in the service, may have the patronage to deliver him from the many enemies now planning his ruin; and young as he now is, may he receive strength from thee, and by thy goodness and conduct may he retain a credible character in the discharge of his important trust. . . . Hear this request, and comply but with this my petition in his favour, and his aged though injured parent will retire from this stage of political confusion, resigned to his cruel fate.[39]

The son replies:

> We begin to grow faint, and our cause of complaint
> is the want of a free circulation.
> Our dad old emission was in this condition,
> who true to your cause did abide,
> Tho' by the foe taken, his faith was not shaken,
> And never would turn to their side.

He pleads with Congress,

> Most worthy *Fathers* we on you rely,
> and you great *sponsors* all our wants supply,
> *Pay one year's board*, and then *each quarter pay*,
> we'll chear your friends, and drive your foes away.[40]

The most elaborate hard-money attack is "The Representation and Remonstrance of HARD MONEY," which Brackenridge seems to have "planted" in the January, 1779, issue of the *United States Magazine*, hoping to elicit a reply. Angry at being replaced by "that paper-wasted, ragborn, kite-faced fellow, *Continental Currency*," Hard Money declares:

Winthrop Sargent entitles it "On the Downfall of Legal Paper Money" in his collated text, *The Loyal Verses of Joseph Stansbury and Doctor Jonathan Odell* (Albany, 1860), pp. 29–31. The first of the two doctors alluded to is the Rev. William Smith of Philadelphia.

[39] *Massachusetts Spy* (Worcester), July 19, 1781, p. 1.

[40] *Continental Journal*, Sept. 6, 1781, p. 4. Actually no issue of Continental paper was authorized after Nov. 29, 1779 (Dewey, *Financial History*, p. 36).

I saw the airs which he gave himself at his first appearance, vapour-
ing and affecting an importance, as if he had been equal to the
solid coin. I did not wonder that he imposed himself upon the common people; for with these, as with young women, a stranger is
always a *divine creature.* . . . I had the satisfaction very early to
observe, that many shop-keepers began to ask two to one for any
article on his credit. In this case it was ridiculous enough to see him,
like the frog in the fable, endeavouring to stretch and distend himself. . . . I am well convinced that it was the frequency of his attempt to enlarge himself, that encreased the circle of his belly, and
left him to walk about the country with a paunch like a drum, or
the cask of a wine-cellar merchant.

Hard Money wonders what Congress can see in him: "It cannot be his great family that so highly recommends him to their
notice; for we know that he is a fellow of obscure birth, the
son of one Lamp-black, a worker at the press in a printing-
office of this city [Philadelphia]." Nor can it be his "vast erudition" or his "fine-breeding and polite accomplishment of manners."

He is certainly a fellow of a bad moral character. It is well known
that he spends his time, almost constantly in ordinaries, and beer-
houses, calling for bowl after bowl, and pledging his hat and wig
for the reckoning. I am well informed that he is also a frequenter
of the bawdy-houses: several thirty dollar bills have been seen going
to a certain *Charlotte.*

The Congress must also have heard of his dishonest business
dealings:

He values himself upon his whiggism; but is it not a fact, that he
has been several times within the British lines? and whether to gain
intelligence or to communicate it, may be matter of enquiry. I do not
like his sitting for his picture, and leaving many of these among the
enemy; so that spread about the country by the tories, many honest
men have taken them for the real currency, and paid the same attention to an image, which they had intended for a servant of the
public.

Hard Money finds it mortifying to be ranked with this fellow:

My birth, in all respects, is honourable. I am descended of the sunbeams; I am related to the family of the pearls and diamonds; I am refined by proper course of education; I am taught to speak every language; I have been companion to philosophers; I have lived in kings palaces; I have travelled over every country. . . . No man can say a word against my character. The scripture bears a very honourable testimony in my favour. . . . I have been in no small repute among good men in all ages. They have parted with country, with family, with pleasure, but very seldom quitted their attachment to HARD MONEY.

While Continental Currency passes freely in public, I have been "shut up in desks, and old chests, and mens pockets." "Is it to be born[e], that a freeman of *sterling value*, should see himself degraded from the office which properly belongs to him, by a fellow, who, if things were on a right footing, would scarcely be accounted good enough to use for my wrapping paper?"[41]

The advocates of paper money, less vocal than their hardmoney opponents, had been driven to their conviction by facts that seemed to them incontrovertible. After all, other than Continental emissions Congress had only two practicable methods of financing the war: loans and taxation. Voluntary loans from abroad could not be hoped for until after independence had been declared and were not certain even then. During the war years Congress had no power under the plan of confederated government to lay taxes, and the states guarded carefully against possible encroachments on their right of taxation. The remaining alternative was paper money, one for which a great number of Americans never lost their ancient affection even after inflation set in.[42]

[41] *United States Magazine*, I (Jan., 1779), 28–31. "One or more of our ingenious correspondents," remarks Brackenridge in an editorial note, "will please furnish us with answers to the Representations and Remonstrances of *Hard-Money*, for our next Magazine."

[42] Dewey, *Financial History*, p. 42; Ferguson, *Wm. & Mary Quar.*, X, 167.

For one thing, paper money often favored the debtor class, a situation attested to in the following dialogue. Sharpshins calls on Sandby to pay off an eight-year-old debt in what Mrs. Sandby calls "depreciated money—trash—paper rags—good for nothing, or next to nothing!" Sandby, descending from the garret where he has been hiding from his debtor, tries desperately to avoid the subject: "O Mr. Sharpshins, how are you, sir? How are all at home? How does your good family? How is Madam Sharpshins? How is Billy, and Sam, and Dolly, and Bridget? Has Jemima got well of her cold?" But Sharpshins, who will not be put off, asks whether Sandby is prepared "to receive that four hundred pounds I owe you and give me up the Bond." "I am ready at any time to receive the money," Sandby replies, "but then it must be in *chinkum*. I suppose you have heard how things are going. I hope you mean to settle with me in money of the same value, stamp and description with that I lent you *in your day of distress*. . . . I hope you intend to pay me in gold or silver, or at least in the real value thereof in paper, which is nearly about sixty five thousand dollars, if I calculate right." "Sixty five thousand devils!" cries Sharpshins. "Is the man mad? I intend to do no such thing. It is my determination to pay you one thousand dollars, the principal, and seventy paper dollars, being one year's interest: and you can have no further claims or demands on me." When Sandby refuses to receive payment, Sharpshins, who has brought witnesses for this purpose, declares, "Then, here is your money, old fox, and I leave it with you on your table, in presence of these two very respectable witnesses, whose oaths will be recorded, and when at any time, or before any court of Justice, will nullify the Bond—Good bye to ye—Madam Sandby, good bye." [43]

Brackenridge's representation and remonstrance of Hard

[43] *The True American* (Trenton), XX (July 6, 1822), 1. This dialogue is supposed to have taken place in July or August, 1780; Lewis Leary interprets the signature "R" as that of Philip Freneau (*That Rascal Freneau* [New Brunswick, 1941], p. 477).

Money at the beginning of 1779 called forth not one but three early replies. "Continental Currency," in the first of these, retorts that "though to the words *rag-born, paper-wasted, kite-faced*, which [Hard Money] very courteously throws out, it might be in my power to re-join those of *copper-nosed, yellow-visaged, jaundice-faced*, yet I wave every epithet of this nature, and leave them to my adversary, who in this kind of eloquence is so greatly and so confessedly my superior." At the beginning of the present war, when Congress "stood in need of some *monied* man," Hard Money found it "more safe to be silent, and to retire into *old chests* and *mens pockets*, where he now complains that he is obliged to conceal himself." Whereupon I, though but a young trader at this time, stepped forth and offered my services. "Where in the mean time was Hard Money? was he not chiefly in the cities of Boston, Philadelphia, and Baltimore, sending out his sloops to the West-Indies, or *speculating with the Tories?* Did he ever take a gun in his hand, or go out with the militia, or was he ever so much as seen in the continental army?" He has charged me with *"want of family."* "The circumstance of family is so adventitious and disconnected, that no one will value himself upon it, who has any thing else to boast of; and no one will value another for it, but the fool or the parasite."

My adversary is careful to inform us that he is *descended of the sun-beams*, but at the same time does not tell us that *fogs* and *pestilential vapours* are of the same original. He acts in this case like most others of your lineage-boasting people, who pitch upon the great name of some uncle, brother, cousin, or other person in the line of consanguinity, but never think of all the illegitimate descendents that are equally co-relative, and place their family on a level with the lowest.

I am by the mother's side of the family of *Paper;* a family that has been of more service to the commonwealth of letters than all of the name of Hard-Money that ever have existed. How many fine editions of the classics and of other books have they given to the world? It is true they have associated more with philosophers and poets than with crowned heads; and have been oftener in the bowers and grottoes of sages and wise men, than in the palaces of kings; but whether it is to their credit or discredit, I will leave you to judge.

He has further charged that because I have not travelled, I am unacquainted with the world. "What does it profit many persons that they have seen the lions in the tower of London, have been in a bawdy house at Paris, and can tell (after some hesitation) which way the river Rhine runs in Germany?" As for his accusation that I have sat for my picture within the British lines—

It is a testimony even from an enemy, that I am of some value. Whoever heard of any one counterfeiting the appearance of a mean person, in order to advance himself? Any one may be a mean person in reality, and therefore there is no necessity of any counterfeit. It is a king or a great man of whom the pretender or impostor takes the name and appearance. Perkin Warbeck was not set up to be the son of an oyster-monger, but of the duke of York Richard Plantagenet. It is, therefore, a direct, though not intended reflection of honour on me, that as the devil sometimes assumes the shape of good men, so the wicked of the world have taken pains to counterfeit my likeness.

This same Hard Money who charges me with immorality "has been at all times the great and standing cause of thefts, and robberies, and murders, and almost every attrocious and wicked action."

When I call to mind the great rascallity of his behaviour, I check myself, lest I enflame your virtuous breasts to such resentment, that in the manner of Lycurgus the rigid legislator of the Spartans, you exclude him from your commonwealths intirely, and make use of iron-money, as less colleaguing with the devil to seduce the hearts of mankind. . . . It is well known, that Spain was great and powerful in the time of Charles V. but has been greatly injured since that period, by her over-fond caresses of this fellow, whom with the *venereal complaint,* a very hopeful companion, she introduced from the countries of Peru and Mexico.

When American liberty has been secured, I mean to "return to the calm shades of private life" and "spend the remainder of my days in the company of literary men, bearing in my mind a happy recollection of this country, which I have assisted to preserve, and whose best interests still lie so near my heart." [44]

William Livingston carried the debate forward, strengthening the argument of paper-money advocates. "Continental Currency" explains:

In the beginning of the contest with Great-Britain, this *Hard-money* was apparently a warm and decided Whig. When I first entered into public life I found him flourishing away in the patriotic style, cherishing and guiding the spirit of resistance, and uttering high terms of defiance against the British Ministry. He had peremptorily declared his disinclination from being sent any longer to Great-Britain for goods, an occupation he used to follow; he had made a journey to Boston, shortly after the port-act took place, where he spirited up the people against the British government and the East-India company; and when the army was embodied at Cambridge, entered forwardly into the service.

His "blazing patriotism" consumed itself "as soon as the aspect of affairs became doubtful." "Whether he skulked among the disaffected, or passed over to the enemy, is not worth enquiry." Realizing now that the patriots will prevail, "like a frozen snake scaringly peeping forth in the spring to get a little sunshine, he comes sneaking out with a half knavish and half foolish look" and tells a "dolorous tale . . . of hard restraints." What impudence for him now to talk of "being the *nerves* of government"!

The apostate talks of my credit being slender and unequal: another mark of the society he is connected with.—Among the disaffected I am so happy as not to be in credit: I never wish to be. . . .

This aukward braggadocio has the effrontery to talk big of his

[44] "Reply of CONTINENTAL CURRENCY, *to the Representation and Remonstrance of* Hard Money," *United States Magazine*, I (Feb., 1779), 72–81.

birth, education, figure and breeding, partly in direct terms and partly under the colour of discussing mine. . . . Among my fellow-citizens have I openly led my life; I have never concealed myself from public view, I have never owl-like shunned the face of day-light, or left my country to seek safer and better times in the in-terest and service of its enemies. . . . This *Hard-money*, amidst all his straining at high figure to cover real fact, and pretending to derive his genealogy from the *sun-beams* is well known to be de-scended of as low, obscure, mongrel and motley a mixture as any to be met with. The old man of the family is a mulatto, the mother an Indian; one only of the race has any tolerable pretensions to whiteness of complexion, and this must be the effect of bastardism or of some wild anomalous lusus naturae, . . . which however has no influence upon his low manners and native stupidity. . . . I shall only say that having lately happened within ken of him on one of his by-road excursions I had an opportunity of observing, but such a rusty, old-fashioned, squalid, bizarre, lousy object never did I meet with in the traverse of a Bedlam. An old worn-out weather-beaten, long-bearded miser who had not seen the sun in a twelvemonth, but had been bending, peering and brooding over his rusty bags, could not have exhibited a more outlandish caricatura.

He has often "secretly traversed our country in order to sow the seeds of bribery, corruption and venality among us," as in the case of the British Commissioners. He still hesitates to declare himself Whig or Tory though there can be no doubt which he is from the company he keeps. On the other hand, "the Congress have seen me tried. The brave and patient soldiery and their worthy General have seen me tried. They have seen my con-duct in the day of peril, and in the day of triumph. Let them be my witnesses." [45]

[45] "The currency of the United States in answer to the representation and remonstrance of Hard-money," *United States Magazine*, I (Mar., 1779), 110–121; reprinted in the *New-Jersey Gazette*, Mar. 24, 1779, pp. 1–2. It should be added, however, that Livingston "opposed the cheap-ening of the currency by unrestricted issues of paper money," *DAB*, XI, 326.

In the third reply, which closed out the debate, "Continental Dollar" relates that he had the honor of being born "not in the stinking, smoaky, foggy city of London, but in the cleanly, sweet, and wholesome city of Philadelphia, . . . on the 10th day of May 1775":

At my first appearance in the world, the family of Discontents, and the family of Tories in our neighbourhood, said, scoffingly, that I hung my lip like a motherless colt, and turned their backs on me with scorn and contempt, declaring I was an upstart coxcomb, a mushroom that soon would wither. . . . Some shunned me as a porcupine, others caressed me.

The members of Congress stood as godfathers to me.

As soon as I began to chatter and prattle a little, I was handled and dandled, and carried about by almost every one, and was made a mere pet of. This was a sad mortification to some of my elder brethren, to find themselves supplanted, daily losing ground, and getting out of credit; particularly my eldest brother Twenty Shilling Will.

I was sent by Congress

to thirteen different schools, academies, colleges, and universities in America, and gained such a fund of knowledge and wisdom, civil and military, political, both speculative and practical, as caused astonishment in all ranks of people, on account of the early pregnancy of my understanding.

The Declaration of Independence and the French alliance enhanced my reputation and worth. But then,

a couple of worthless rascals [Howe and Galloway] procured and introduced another vile scoundrel, of obscure parentage and spurious birth, if it were possible more brazen than themselves, by the name of *Counterfeit Dollar* to personate me, to bastardise me, and come in as true heir of all my estate. They had the assurance to dress him in my cloaths (or others very like mine) and indeed as to his size and features, and in some few other respects, there was a pretty near resemblance (excepting his gallows look) which was as visible, on a close inspection as the mark of Cain.

Argus-like, Congress detected Counterfeit Dollar and put him to the torture, whereas they clothed me "anew from head to foot . . . not, like Adam, with an apron only, but with a full suit, which made a much gayer appearance than the former, the trimmings being in part red," and arranged a tour of America suitable to my birth.[46]

This series of four adventure essays, appearing over a nine months' period in Brackenridge's *United States Magazine*, must certainly have appealed to contemporary readers, who had long been familiar with this species of periodical essay in the English press. One is tempted to say that Brackenridge himself, in initiating this debate between Hard Money and Continental Currency at a time when inflation in America was getting out of hand, undertook the role of *advocatus diaboli* with considerable relish. (The fact that he published three replies to Hard Money suggests that actually he favored the cause of paper money.) By and large, the authors of these four essays demonstrate a comprehensive but somewhat superficial grasp of the currency question at this time. The persuasiveness of this debate lies in the skill with which they project the genealogy, birth, early life, education, and breeding of coin and paper money alike against an appropriately American setting, and present portraits that are individualized and full-bodied.

The satirical attack began the moment Congress started to sit at Philadelphia and continued heavy throughout the war. Loyalists mounted it and supervised it at every important turn —independence, foreign alliance, inflation. At every turn but one. Their failure to ridicule the struggle for confederation can be explained in part by the fact that this step was so long drawn out in debate and politicking and seemed to them inherently less dramatic than the other problems confronting Congress. It

[46] "*The* ADVENTURES of a CONTINENTAL DOLLAR," *United States Magazine*, I (June, Sept., 1779), 264–268, 385–387.

is altogether natural that much of this satire should have been personal. In the course of civil war social and political divisions are apt to express themselves in a personal as well as in a general way, the more so if such war witnesses the birth of a revolutionary assembly whose members commit themselves soon after to a radical course.

CHAPTER VII

The British Army

WHAT drew the heaviest satirical fire during the war years was the British military establishment, notably certain campaigns, battles, and raids, high-ranking officers in the army, and the employment of German mercenaries and Indian allies. One reason for this is not far to find. During the Seven Years' War and again in the decade following the Stamp Act crisis, British soldiers had been quartered at various points in North America, chiefly at New York and Boston, so that even before the outbreak of hostilities the British army in America, constituting an important segment of the official class as defined by Namier, offered a more immediate target than a stubborn King and a short-sighted Ministry.

In 1774, for example, Franklin took the opportunity to expose Britain's air of superiority toward America when a certain General Clarke was so rash as to boast that "with a Thousand British grenadiers, he would undertake to go from one end of America to the other, and geld all the Males, partly by force and partly by a little Coaxing." [1] In view of the fact, writes Franklin, that "our rebellious Vassals of North America" may eventually deny our authority altogether, "more especially when

[1] Franklin to William Strahan, Aug. 19, 1784, Smyth, IX, 261. Verner Crane says, "General Clarke was probably Col. Thomas Clarke, aide-de-camp to the King, commissioned Major-General in 1777 and Lieutenant-General in 1782," *Letters to the Press*, p. 263n.

it is considered that they are a robust, hardy People, encourage early Marriages, and their Women being amazingly prolific, they must of consequence in 100 years be very numerous, and of course be able to set us at Defiance," it is humbly proposed that "a Bill be brought in and passed, and Orders immediately transmitted to G——l G—e, our Commander in Chief in North America, in consequence of it, that all Males there be c—st—ed."

Let a Company of Sow-gelders, consisting of 100 Men, accompany the Army, On their Arrival at any Town or Village, let Orders be given that on the blowing of the Horn all the Males be assembled in the Market Place. If the Corps are Men of Skill and Ability in their Profession, they will make great Dispatch, and retard but very little the Progress of the Army. . . . The most notorious Offenders, such as Hancock, Adams, &c. who have been the Ringleaders in the Rebellion of our Servants, should be shaved quite close. . . . It is true, Blood will be shed, but probably not many Lives lost. Bleeding to a certain Degree is salutary. The English, whose Humanity is celebrated by all the World, but particularly by themselves, do not desire the Death of the Delinquent, but his Reformation.

Consider the advantages arising from the execution of this scheme:

In the Course of fifty years it is probable we shall not have one rebellious Subject in North America. This will be laying the Axe to the Root of the Tree. In the meantime a considerable Expence may be saved to the Managers of the Opera, and our Nobility and Gentry be entertained at a cheaper Rate by the fine Voices of our own C—st—i, and the Specie remain in the Kingdom, which now, to an enormous Amount, is carried every Year to Italy. It might likewise be of service to our Levant Trade, as we could supply the Grand Signor's Seraglio, and the Harams of the Grandees of the Turkish Dominions with Cargos of Eunuchs, as also with Handsome Women, for which America is as famous as Circassia.[2]

Franklin exploits the implications of Clarke's *faux pas* with ingenuity, taking care at every ironic turn to stay within the realm

[2] *Public Advertiser*, May 21, 1774, p. 2; reprinted in Crane, pp. 262–264.

of the possible. His sense of timing here, as in the "Rules" and
the "Edict," is faultless: a letter to the English press at the time
the Coercive Acts were being made law might give many Britons
pause.

I

Campaigns, battles, and raids, generally speaking, are too im-
personal and too complex to be the object of satire. It is sometimes possible, though, to hold eccentricities in military maneuver
up to ridicule. Between the day of Lexington and Concord and
the surrender at Yorktown writers on both sides of the Atlantic
made capital of a number of such occasions.

The opening encounter between British regulars and provincials demonstrated that, as Allen French puts it, "in spite of his
lack of training the American was, because of his traditions and
his cast of mind, potentially the more dangerous man with a
gun." [3] This fact was evident not so much in the American advance at Concord Bridge as during the British retreat to Boston.
The next day no less a witness than Lord Percy, whose provi-
dential arrival at Lexington had saved the regulars from disaster,
said of the Americans:

Whoever looks upon them as an irregular mob, will find himself
much mistaken. They have men amongst them who know very well
what they are about, having been employed as Rangers agst the
Indians & Canadians. . . .

You may depend upon it, that as the Rebels have now had time
to prepare, they are determined to go thro' with it, nor will the insurrection here turn out so despicable as it is perhaps imagined at
home. For my part, I never believed, I confess, that they wd have
attacked the King's troops, or have had the perseverance I found in
them yesterday.[4]

"Paddy" recalls the events of that day in a disparaging letter addressed to the British troops now besieged at Boston:

[3] *The Day of Concord and Lexington* (Boston, 1925), p. 36.
[4] Quoted in *ibid.*, pp. 269–270.

By my faith but I think ye're all makers of bulls,
With your brains in your breeches, your guts in your skulls.
Get home with your muskets, and put up your swords
And look in your books for the meaning of words.
Ye see now my honies, how much you're mistaken,
For CONCORD by *Discord* can never be beaten.

How brave you went out with muskets all bright,
And thought to befrighten the folks with the sight;
But when you got there how they powder'd your pums,
And all the way home how they pepper'd your bums,
And is it not, honies, a comical farce,
To be proud in the face, and be shot in the a–se.

How come ye to think now, they did not know how,
To be after their firelocks as smartly as you.
Why ye see now, my honies, 'tis nothing at all,
But to pull at the trigger, and pop goes the ball.

And what have you got now, with all your designing,
But a town without victuals to sit down and dine in;
And to look on the ground, like a parcel of Noodles,
And sing, How the Yankies have beaten the Doodles.
I'm sure if you're wise you'll make peace for a dinner,
For fighting and fasting will soon make ye thinner.[5]

The regulars, reviewing their record from the time of Preston-
pans, boast:

No troops perform better than we at reviews,
We march and we wheel, and whatever you choose,
George would see how we fight, and we never refuse,
There we all fight with courage—you may see 't in the news.

Contrary to Gage's expectations, it was the *Yankees* who surprised *us* at Lexington:

For fifteen miles, they follow'd and pelted us, we scarce had
time to pull a trigger;

[5] "*The* IRISHMAN'S EPISTLE *to the Officers and Troops at Boston,*"
Pennsylvania Magazine, I (May, 1775), 232; reprinted in Moore's *Songs,*
pp. 92–93.

But did you ever know a retreat perform'd with more vigor?
For we did it in two hours, which saved us from perdition;
'Twas not in *going out,* but in *returning,* consisted our EXPE-
DITION.

.   .   .   .   .

That they had not much to brag of, is a very plain case;
For if they beat us in the fight, we beat them in the race.[6]

The British troops at Boston suffered great physical distress.
As weeks lengthened into months they raided the countryside
and the islands in the harbor for food, principally cattle. Freneau
imagines himself an invisible spectator at General Gage's resi-
dence. The time is midnight, and here the British high command
has congregated. Losing patience with the endless wrangling
about military strategy, Gage at length interjects into the discussion what is after all their major concern:

"But now attend—a counsel I impart
That long has laid the heaviest at my heart—
Three weeks—ye gods!—nay, three long years it seems
Since roast-beef I have touched except in dreams.
In sleep, choice dishes to my view repair,
Waking, I gape and champ the empty air.—
Say, is it just that I, who rule these bands,
Should live on husks, like rakes in foreign lands?—
Come, let us plan some project ere we sleep,
And drink destruction to the rebel sheep.
"On neighbouring isles uncounted cattle stray,
Fat beeves and swine, an ill-defended prey—
These are fit visions for my noon day dish,
These, if my soldiers act as I would wish,
In one short week should glad your maws and mine;
On mutton we will sup—on roast beef dine."

6 "The King's Own Regulars," *Boston Gazette,* Nov. 27, 1775, p. 4;
reprinted in Moore's *Diary,* I, 214-216. In a letter of Apr. 15, 1775,
Charles Carroll told his wife that Franklin was the author, Carroll Papers,
VIII, 335, cited in Davidson, *Propaganda,* p. 163n.—an attribution I have
not been able to substantiate.

All applaud this plan, and Wallace is appointed to execute it. Directly Gage sinks into a slumber so profound that "even his guts" sleep.[7] In *The Fall of British Tyranny* Lord Boston (Gage) summons his officers to consider the same problem. When he declares that they must act on the defensive this winter, Admiral Tombstone (Graves) wryly observes: "Defensive? aye, aye— if we can defend our bellies from hunger, and prevent a mutiny and civil war among the small guts there this winter, we shall make a glorious campaign of it, indeed—it will read well in the American Chronicles." "I expect to be recalled this winter," Lord Boston continues, "when I shall lay the case before Lord Paramount, and let him know your deplorable situation." "Don't forget to tell him," replies Tombstone, "the poor worms are starving too, having nothing to eat, but half starv'd dead soldiers and the ships' bottoms. . . . I think we're all a parcel of damn'd boobies for coming three thousand miles upon a wild-goose chase—to perish with cold—starve with hunger—get our brains knock'd out, or be hang'd for sheep-stealing and robbing hen-roosts."[8] And in the opening scene of *The Blockheads: or, The Affrighted Officers*, a farce laid at the time of the British evacuation of Boston, a group of officers are discovered complaining of the extremities to which the siege has reduced them. Compared to the condition of us who are besieged, says Lord Dapper (Percy), Churchill's description of Scotland (in *The Prophecy of Famine*) is a shadow: "He represents their *flies* and *spiders*, &c. as *starving*, but here they are absolutely starv'd—poor innocent insects, I forgive ye your former tormenting of my legs; ye suck'd 'till you could find no nourishment, and then fell at my feet and died." Shallow (Grant) concurs: "*Hard crusts* and *rusty bones* have never till *now* become my diet; they do not suit my *digestion.*—My *teeth* are worn to stumps, and my *lips* are swell'd like a blubber-mouth negro's, by thumping *hard*

[7] *A Voyage to Boston* (New York, Sept., 1775); reprinted as "The Midnight Consultations," Pattee, I, 162–178.
[8] Philadelphia [1776]; reprinted in Moses' *Representative Plays*, p. 339.

bones against them; my *jaw bone* has been set a dozen times, dislocated by chewing *hard pork*, as tough as an old swine's ass." [9]

Elsewhere in New England military incidents were satirized. A cushion battle during a British raid on Dartmouth, Massachusetts, was matter for low burlesque. "With soldiers, tories, many score," "brave *Gray*" sets sail to burn and plunder. Advancing on the town,

> No opposition do they meet,
> Till they approach the second street,
> And now begins the mighty fray;
> A CUSHION there obstructs the way.
> They well draw up the battle-line,
> With caution, prudence, vast design:
>
> . . . . .
>
> The action's warm, the battle strong;
> The Cushion could not stand it long:
> No reinforcement coming in,
> And Cushion's number being thin;
> The battle's won by gallant *Gray*,
> Who now pursues without delay,
> His grand design to burn and steal,
> Fat sheep and oxen, lamb and veal.[10]

The bathos present in the final line reinforces the low-burlesque situation.

In another piece the captain of a British frigate tells a tory refugee of the "strange infernal tragical machine" he encountered during a cruise against the rebels in Connecticut, "A new invented sort of whirligig, / Which play'd and danc'd a hornpipe and a jig."

[9] Boston, 1776, pp. 4, 5. W. C. Ford, *Proc. Mass. Hist. Soc.*, LXII (1928), 20–21, suggests that this play was published on June 17 and rejects the assumption that Mercy Warren is the author; "the vulgarity of the text precludes her being entirely responsible for it."
[10] "The Cushion Battle," *Massachusetts Spy*, Nov. 26, 1778, p. 4.

My people found it floating on the water,
I thought 'twas something for the world hereafter;

. . . . .

One of the men officious at the work,
To put it into motion in a jirk,
Begun to wind it round and round and round,
At length it burst and with a horrid sound,
It hurried three or four of my Jack Tars,
Instantly up to heav'n to count the stars.[11]

One loyalist sneered at what he construed to be William Howe's lackadaisical manner of conducting the New York–New Jersey campaign of 1776–1777.

Didn't He give to the Rebels a total Defeat
At Brooklyn, and cut off all hopes of Retreat,
Had they not cross'd a *Stream* that run close by their Side!
—Some call it a *River*—about a *Mile* wide!

Didn't He land at New York, and that Capital get;
Where he had all the Rebels inclos'd in a Net;
But, like Peter, afraid of the wonderful Draught
He let them escape as—a proof of his Craft!

At Trenton again, in a Season severe,
The Rebels were here—and Howes Army was there—
Behind them the River—the Bridge—hereabout—
You know *how* he put this whole Army to rout! [12]

Howe's Philadelphia campaign of 1777–1778 was also the object of satire. In his progress up Chesapeake Bay Howe boasts:

The Warwick Guy, with me can't vie,
Tho' his fame's on record wond'rous high,
For killing the dun cow;
At Elk Head, I made thousands fly,

[11] "A DIALOGUE *between* the CAPTAIN *of a* BRITISH FRIGATE *and a* TORY REFUGEE on LONG ISLAND," *Norwich Packet*, July 13, 1778, p. 3.
[12] "Genl. Howe vindicated," Dec. 14, 1777, in "Loyalist Rhapsodies," pp. 86–89.

> Plunder'd each hen roost, cribb, and sty,
> And made whole herds to low!

I vowed I would go to Philadelphia, there to "make the broad brims bow."

> At Chesnut hill, 'spite of my skill,
> They made me halt against my will,
> It grieves me to tell how;
> They drove me down, thro' Germantown,
> Which sully'd much, the great renown,
> Just sprouting on my brow.
>
> My troops thus beat, and scant of meat,
> We to the city, did retreat,
> In woeful plight I trow;
> To get out again, gives me great pain,
> So many of my soldiers slain,
> Curse me if I know how.[13]

Francis Hopkinson's well-known "Battle of the Kegs," the most enduring of several satirical ballads set to the tune "Yankee Doodle," had its origin in the following incident, which occurred during the British occupation of Philadelphia:

. . . Mr. [David] Bushnell [writes James Thacher] contrived another ingenious expedient to effect his favourite object. He fixed a large number of kegs under water, charged with powder, to explode on coming in contact with anything while floating along with the tide. He set his squadron of kegs afloat in the Delaware, above the English shipping, in December, 1777. The kegs were in the night set adrift, to fall with the ebb, on the shipping; but the proper distance could not be well ascertained, and they were set adrift at too great a distance from the vessels, by which means they were obstructed, and dispersed by the ice. They approached, however, in the day time, and one of them blew up a boat, and others exploded, which occasioned among the British seamen the greatest alarm and consternation. They actually manned the warves and

---

[13] "On the Grand AMERICAN EXPEDITION, in the Year 1777," *Maryland Journal*, Nov. 18, 1777, pp. 2–3.

shipping at Philadelphia, and discharged their small arms and cannon at everything they could see floating in the river, during the ebb tide.[14]

In the ballad a soldier spies "a score of kegs or more" floating down the river early one day. A sailor, seeing them too, suspects mischief:

> These kegs, I'm told, the rebels bold,
>   Pack'd up like pickled herring,
> And they're come down t'attack the town,
>   In this new way of ferrying.

Scared almost to death, they race to spread the news. The noise soon wakens Howe.

> Sir William, he, snug as a flea,
>   Lay all this time a snoring,
> Nor dream'd of harm as he lay warm,
>   In bed with Mrs. L——g.

At the waterfront the British stand, "All ranged in dread array."

> The cannons roar from shore to shore,
>   The small arms make a rattle;
> Since wars began I'm sure no man
>   E'er saw so strange a battle.
>
>   .   .   .   .   .
>
> The kegs, 'tis said, tho' strongly made,
>   Of rebel staves and hoops, sir,
> Could not oppose their powerful foes,
>   The conqu'ring British troops, sir.
>
>   .   .   .   .
>
> Such feats did they perform that day,
>   Against those wick'd kegs, sir,

[14] *Military Journal during the American Revolutionary War* (Hartford, 1854), pp. 125–126; see E. F. MacPike, *Notes and Queries*, CLXXV (1938), 354–355. A prose account of this incident, probably written by Hopkinson himself, appeared in the *New-Jersey Gazette*, Jan. 21, 1778; the *Pennsylvania Ledger* republished this account, "along with a more sober and no doubt more accurate account of its own" (Hastings, *Hopkinson*, p. 292).

That years to come, if they get home,
They'll make their boasts and brags, sir.[15]

In the spring of 1776 a British attack on Charleston was repulsed, Clinton leading the land forces and Sir Peter Parker the
naval. Clinton was unable to enter effectively into the action
because the passage to Sullivan's Island, across which he had
planned to lead his men, was found to be seven feet deep at low
tide.[16] Parker, meanwhile, could not get his fleet past Fort
Moultrie and into the harbor. When he informed the Admiralty
of this reverse, the press carried a mock paraphrase of his letter.

With much labor and toil,
Unto Sullivan's Isle,
I came firm as Falstaff or Pistol,
But the Yankees, 'od rot 'em,
I could not get at 'em:
Most terribly maul'd my poor Bristol.

Bold Clinton by land,
Did quietly stand,
While I made a thundering clatter;
But the channel was deep,
So he only could peep,
And not venture over the water.

. . . . .

But my Lords, do not fear,
For before the next year,
Although a small island could fret us,
The Continent whole,
We shall take, by my soul,
If the cowardly Yankees will let us.[17]

[15] *Pennsylvania Packet*, Mar. 4, 1778, p. 4; reprinted in *Poems*, pp. 169–
173. "Mrs. L——g" is Elizabeth Loring, presumably Howe's mistress,
the wife of a loyalist officer whom Howe appointed commissary of prisoners.

[16] A. T. Mahan, *The Major Operations of the Navies in the War of
American Independence* (Boston, 1913), p. 32.

[17] "A New War Song. By Sir Peter Parker," *Scots Magazine*, XXXVIII

Although the British did not succeed in taking the "Continent whole," within four years they had captured Charleston and Savannah. When word went out that the British at Sunbury, a garrisoned town south of Savannah, had captured a children's fort, one writer, seeing an opportunity to indulge in low burlesque, invoked his own genius:

> Oh! Pungency extol my Lays!
> And to pathetic Rapture raise
> My nervous style, and string my hand
> To write the glory of FORT-SAND,
> Who brav'd the foe, despising death,
> Immortaliz'd to latest Breath.

A "*young ambitious growing Corps*" of children erect an imposing fort, whose roof is "Bomb proof" and whose cannon are "dead old bones."

> An huge, unmoved magazine,
> Stood threat'ning 'midst the awful scene;
> Whose pregnant, and capacious womb,
> Bore deathful stores, for years to come,
> Of oyster-shells, long pikes and grubs,
> Promiscuous heap'd with staves and clubs.

Frightened by this stupendous work and by so formidable a force, the British in council finally decide it "best a guileful war to wage," for which purpose a sergeant's guard is detached. "The Serjeant, then at dead of night,"

> At head of 'squad, with caution creeps
> And as predicted—fortress sleeps,
> The *bones* are spik'd—the file returns—
> And chief with expectation burns.

Next morning the children scorn the command to surrender, whereupon the sergeant is again dispatched

---

(Sept., 1776), 495; reprinted in the *Pennsylvania Journal*, Feb. 26, 1777, p. 3, and again in Moore's *Songs*, pp. 135–137. The "Bristol" was Parker's flagship.

At head of the immortal squad,
In open day, and open road,
With baynets fix't to urge again,
And strike decisive cope de main.
The squad, in all the pomp and pride
Mov'd to the fife with Martial stride;
Demolish'd all the works of fort—
To spite the little childrens sport.[18]

In the fall of 1781 a sarcastic invitation was issued to Cornwallis' army at Yorktown, then invested by Franco-American forces:

The Monsieurs, Mynheers, Yankees and Dons, present their compliments to the My Lords, and being desirous of entertaining them in a manner suitable to their taste, are happy in making them the following invitations:—Monsieur has the honor to invite them to a grand concert on the water, when the power of music will be shown in a manner never heard of since the days of Timotheus and Alexander. They hope it will be such as to make the My Lords acknowledge his superiority in musical composition and performance.

Yankee intends to present them with a grand firework, to be performed at London, or some other great seaport town in Great Britain or Ireland, but much superior to those which the My Lords pretended to exhibit at Norfolk, Kingston, New London, etc. For the sake of those who are in this country and cannot transport themselves over to England, they will shortly be shown a new Bear Trap, wherein five thousand of those obnoxious animals are to be caught at once. This entertainment was exhibited to them about four years ago, and they were pleased to appear highly satisfied with it. The present one is on a new plan, in which friend Monsieur has had some share.

Mynheer and Don do not chose, as yet, to let them know what will be the nature of their entertainment, being desirous of affording them the pleasure of *surprise.*[19]

[18] "ELUCIDATION OF FORT-SAND-REDUCED," *Charleston Gazette,* Jan. 18, 1780, p. 2.

[19] "A Card to the British at Yorktown," *Pennsylvania Packet,* Oct. 6, 1781, p. 1; reprinted in Moore's *Diary,* II, 503–504.

Another writer, choosing to ignore Cornwallis' victories in
the Southern campaign of 1780–1781 now come to an end at
Yorktown, described the dances he had performed so nimbly.

Cornwallis led a country dance,
    The like was never seen, sir,
Much retrograde and much advance,
    And all with General Greene, sir.

. . . . .

Greene, in the South, then danc'd a set,
    And got a mighty name, sir,
Cornwallis jigg'd with young Fayette,
    But suffer'd in his fame, sir.

Then down he figur'd to the shore,
    Most like a lordly dancer,
And on his courtly honor swore,
    He would no more advance, sir.

. . . . .

Now hous'd in York he challeng'd all,
    At minuet or all 'amande,
And lessons for a courtly ball,
    His guards by day and night conn'd.

De Grasse, Rochambeau, and Washington accept the challenge.

Now hand in hand they circle round,
    This ever-dancing peer, sir;
Their gentle movements, soon confound
    The earl, as they draw near, sir.

His music soon forgets to play—
    His feet can no more move, sir,
And all his bands now curse the day,
    They jiggèd to our shore, sir.[20]

[20] *Pennsylvania Packet*, Nov. 27, 1781, p. 1; reprinted in Moore's *Songs*,
pp. 363–366.

II

A number of British officers, notably Gage, Howe, Tryon, Burgoyne, Cornwallis, Clinton, and Carleton, were vilified and ridiculed in the American press. Although these men were simply executing orders from home, orders the wisdom of which they sometimes questioned, their very presence in America made them just as vulnerable as civil officials before the war had been. As commander in chief of the British forces in North America and acting governor of Massachusetts at the outbreak of the war, Thomas Gage was vulnerable on both counts. At beleaguered Boston he proclaimed martial law on June 12, 1775, and offered pardon to all Americans (except Samuel Adams and John Hancock) who would lay down their arms.[21] The turgid, pompous style of this proclamation—actually Burgoyne was its author— invited travesty. One writer announced it as "Tom Gage's Proclamation"

> Or blustering denunciation
> (Replete with defamation)
> Threatening devastation,
> And speedy jugulation,
> Of the new English nation,

and proceeded:

> I'm able now by augmentation,
> To give a proper castigation;
>
> .   .   .   .   .
>
> Yet, e'er I draw the vengeful sword,
> I have thought fit to send abroad,
> This present gracious proclamation,
> Of purpose mild the demonstration,
> That whosoe'er keeps gun or pistol
> I'll spoil the motion of his systole;
>
> .   .   .   .   .

[21] Alden, *Gage*, pp. 263–264.

But every one that will lay down
His hanger bright, and musket brown,
Shall not be beat, nor bruis'd, nor bang'd,
Much less for past offences hang'd;
But on surrendering his toledo,
Go to and fro unhurt as we do:—
But then I must, out of this plan, lock
Both SAMUEL ADAMS and JOHN HANCOCK.[22]

The most that can be claimed for Gage's generalship is that, whereas he excelled as a drillmaster and disciplinarian, in the field he was merely competent. Thus modestly endowed, he was unequal to the task of command in a town, invested from the land side, whose inhabitants were many of them hostile. "He is amiable for his virtues," wrote Burgoyne, "but he is not equal to his situation." [23] Freneau's judgment was hardly so generous. Pictured in soliloquy soon after the time of Bunker Hill, Gage is despondent, ready to give over the command at Boston:

What if we conquer this rebellious town,
Suppose we burn it, storm it, tear it down—
This land's like Hydra, cut off but one head,
And ten shall rise, and dare you in its stead.

. . . . .

A viceroy I, like modern monarchs, stay
Safe in the town—let others guide the fray:
A life like mine is of no common worth,
'Twere wrong, by heaven, that I should sally forth!

It may well be that the cause for which I fight is unrighteous.

I speak the language of my heart—shall I
Steal off by night, and o'er the ocean fly,
Like a lost man to unknown regions stray,

[22] *Pennsylvania Journal*, June 28, 1775, p. 1; reprinted in Moore's *Diary*, I, 93-94. The *Connecticut Courant*, Aug. 7, 14, 1775, p. 4, carried Trumbull's travesty of this proclamation, some fifty lines of which reappeared in the first edition of *M'Fingal* a few months later.

[23] Alden, *Gage*, p. 295; Burgoyne to Germain, Sept., 1775, quoted in Henry Belcher, *The First American Civil War* (London, 1911), I, 194.

And to oblivion leave this stormy day?—
Or shall I to Britannia's shores again,
And big with lies, conceal my thousands slain?—

. . . . .

Ye souls of fire, who burn for chief command,
Come! take my place in this disastrous land;
To wars like these I bid a long good-night—
Let North and George themselves such battles fight.[24]

On September 26, 1775, Gage was recalled. Little wonder! In letters to his superiors he had placed the responsibility for the situation in which his army now found itself exactly where it belonged, on the shoulders of the Ministry.[25] "Philoleutheros Americanus" taunted the departing commander:

many talk of Robbin-Hood we know,
Who never yet so much as bent his bow,
As by this hero is exemplify'd,
Who eighteen months or something better try'd
By all his forces to obtain his will.
At length he got as far as Bunker's Hill;
Tho' he himself would never take the field,
But like a valiant coward kept conceal'd.

. . . . .

Thus disappointed of his expectation,
His little heart was fill'd with perturbation.
He walk'd the streets, not knowing what to do,
Look'd like a spector from the pit below.
Some days he walk'd in this distress'd condition,
Then like a coward, quitted his commission,
Which when his royal master came to hear,
He order'd he should speedily appear
Before his betters, give a reason why,
He thus behav'd, or like a cowar'd die.[26]

---

[24] *General Gage's Soliloquy* (New York, Aug., 1775); reprinted in Pattee, I, 152-157.
[25] Alden, *Gage*, pp. 283, 280.
[26] "A Poem, Upon the present Times," Boston broadside, 1776.

And in a poetic dialogue by Freneau, Gage rejoices, "Boston, farewell, thy final doom is pass'd, / North hears my prayers, and I'm recall'd at last," and turns to his father confessor:

> Come, Father Francis, be my heart display'd,
> My burden'd conscience asks thy pious aid;
> Come, if confession can discharge my sin,
> I will confess till hell itself shall grin,
> And own the world has found in me again
> A second Nero; nay, another Cain.

The friar replies, "Your sins are venial—trust me when I say / Your deepest sins may all be purged away." Gage concedes, "This faultless country ne'er deserv'd my hate; / Just are its pleas; unmerited its fate," but explains that when North "ordained" him to Boston, he yielded even though his conscience troubled him at the time. The friar assures him:

> All should be well—from sins like this, I ween,
> A dozen masses shall discharge you clean;
> Small pains in purgatory you'll endure,
> And hell, you know, is only for the poor.

He agrees that Gage has not been guilty of murder: "Some few Americans have bled, 'tis true, / But 'twas the soldiers killed them, and not you." Gage admits that he proclaimed martial law, crowded his "dungeons dark and low / With wounded captives of our injur'd foe," and stuffed "the epistolary page / With vile invectives only worthy Gage." The friar offers to pardon him "before we sup," to which Gage replies, "Nay, clear me not"; "my monarch I've obey'd, / And now go home, perhaps to lose my head."

> Come, let's embark, your holy whining cease,
> Come, let's away, I'll hang myself for peace:
> So Pontius Pilate for his murder'd Lord
> In his own bosom sheath'd the deadly sword—
> Tho' he confess'd and wash'd his hands beside,
> His heart condemn'd him and the monster dy'd.[27]

[27] *General Gage's Confession* (New York, Oct. 25, 1775); reprinted in Pattee, I, 189–195.

Gage's successor, Sir William Howe, was satirized in both his private and his military character. Actually there was some basis for attacking his private life—he did keep a mistress and was addicted to gambling—though it should be added that his pursuit of pleasure at Philadelphia was probably intensified by the realization that his military position was deteriorating through, as he felt, no fault of his own.[28] Hopkinson, a native of that city, judged the man severely:

> Howe with his legions came,
> In hopes of wealth and fame.
>   What has he done?
> All day, at Faro play'd,
> All night, with whores he laid,
> And with his bottle made,
>   Excellent fun.[29]

In the summer of 1777, the memory of the British army's march through northern New Jersey still fresh in the minds of all thereabouts, a reward was posted in the Philadelphia press:

Whereas a certain William Howe, alias General Howe, alias Sir William, alias any thing or nothing, has lately gone off, greatly in debt to sundry persons in New Jersey and other parts of the continent, and has not left wherewithal to make payment for the same; this is therefore to caution all persons not to trust him on any account, as they will certainly lose their money. Said Howe is charged with having, in company with one Cornwallis, not yet taken, broken into several houses in New Jersey, and stolen and carried off many valuable effects; likewise with being concerned in counterfeiting the currency of this continent, and of having starved to death several good subjects of the States, while he was chief jailer at New York. He is a very ill-looking fellow, and is an indented servant to a certain George Whelp, alias Guelph, alias King George.

Whoever will secure said Howe in any of the jails of this con-

---

[28] Anderson, *Command of Howe Brothers*, p. 302.

[29] "A Tory Medley," Philadelphia broadside, [1780?]. Although this broadside is dated 1777, a manuscript copy at the Huntington Library bears the subscription: "Written in the Year 1780."

tinent, or will give notice where he is to the American army, shall
be handsomely rewarded.

N. B.—He was lately seen skulking about Amboy, Westfield,
and Spanktown, in the Jerseys, and has not since been heard of.
Should he attempt to practice any more of his villanies, 'tis hoped
all persons will be on their guard to apprehend him.[30]

In the fall of 1775 William Tryon, governor of New York
early in the war, took refuge aboard a British ship in the harbor,
awaiting the arrival of the Howes in those waters. His proclamation of March, 1776, promising the loyalists relief and protection, was promptly travestied at New York:

> I WILLIAM TRYON on board the Dutchess,
> Safe from the Whigs and Yankees clutches,
> Being moor'd beyond their utmost furies;
> Send this with greetings to the Tories.
>
> . . . . .
>
> Go on as steady friends to George,
> New lies to fabricate and forge,
> Proceeding on from fast to faster.
> Untill you match our common master.
>
> . . . . .
>
> In a few months I prophecy
> There'l be a turning of the die,
> When British troops and British vessels
> Will bring relief to British vassals,
> And drive the Rebels helter skelter
> To rocks, and nooks, and holes, for shelter.
> When ever[y?] Tory if it please him,
> May cut his whiggish neighbours weason
> And all his goods and chattles seize on.
> Encouragement I cannot proffer,
> More great and glorious than this offer,

[30] *Pennsylvania Evening Post*, July 10, 1777, p. 366; reprinted in Moore's
Diary, I, 453.

To keep your zeal still hot and burning
And banish ev'ry tho't of turning.[31]

The following April Tryon landed on the Connecticut coast
with 2,000 troops and marched upcountry to Danbury, where
he destroyed revolutionary provisions and stores and set fire to
the homes of nonloyalists; during his return march the Connecticut militia inflicted heavy losses on his force.[32] Here again was
matter for low burlesque, cast this time in galloping anapests. At
New York the gallant Howe, "who fights all by proxy," tells his
soldiers, "My boys, I'm a going to send you with Tryon, / To
a place where you'll all get as groggy as I am"; he's just been
informed by a tory from Danbury "That there's *nobody there,
so the place shall be storm'd.*" Tryon replies, "If there's nobody
there, sir, and nobody *near it*, / Two thousand will conquer the
whole, never fear it." But when his troops land in Connecticut,
he tells them,

> In cunning and canting, deceit and disguise,
> In cheating a friend, and inventing of lies,
> I think I'm a match for the best of my species,
> But in this undertaking I feel all in pieces;
> So I'll fall in the rear, for I'd rather go last;—
> *Come, march on, my boys,* let me see you all past;
> For his Majesty's service (so says my commission)
> Requires that I *bring up* the whole expedition.

At Danbury his troops get drunk and grow noisy, and houses
and stores are set on fire. An alarm is sounded, and a report goes
out that the provincials have cut them off from their boats. Away
the British troops gallop, Tryon in the van. At the boats he cries,
"My belly's full of balls—I hear them rattle," whereupon a
surgeon assures him, " 'Tis only, sir, the echo of the battle."
Tryon finds it difficult to believe he is not wounded, for, as he
stood uncertain what to do, "A cannon ball, of two and thirty

---

[31] "The last most excellent Address of William Tryon, Esq.," *Constitutional Gazette* (New York), Apr. 13, 1776, p. 1.
[32] Trevelyan, *American Revolution*, IV, 116–117.

pound, / Struck me just where Sir Peter got his wound; / Then passing on between my horse's ears—" [33]

Of all the British generals who fought in the American war the one who earned the greatest notoriety through satire was John Burgoyne. Playwright and dandy, he possessed charm and wit in the field and in the drawing room equally. On his arrival in America Freneau asked pointedly:

> Is he to conquer—he subdue our land?—
> This buckram hero, with his lady's hand?
> By Cesars to be vanquished is a curse,
> But by a scribbling fop—by heaven, is worse! [34]

And Trumbull added:

> Behold that martial Macaroni,
> Compound of Phoebus and Bellona,
> Equipp'd alike for feast or fray,
> With warlike sword and singsong lay,
> Where equal wit and valour join!
> This, this is he—the famed Burgoyne!
> Who pawn'd his honor and commission,
> To coax the patriots to submission,
> By songs and balls secure allegiance,
> And dance the ladies to obedience. [I, 138–139]

Having won a modest reputation at home as a man of letters, abroad Burgoyne was to win another—less enviable, to be sure —as a maker of proclamations. His language in such compositions was characteristically high-flown and stilted.[35] It will be recalled that the order proclaiming martial law and general amnesty at Boston, which he drafted at Gage's request, provoked travesty. No utterance of his illustrates this penchant for bom-

[33] "The Expedition to Danbury," *Pennsylvania Gazette*, May 14, 1777, p. 3; reprinted in Moore's *Diary*, I, 428–432. During the naval bombardment at Charleston in the spring of 1776 Sir Peter Parker had the seat of his trousers torn off by shot or splinters.

[34] *A Voyage to Boston*; reprinted in Pattee, I, 165.

[35] Hoffman Nickerson, *The Turning Point of the Revolution* (Boston, 1928), p. 34.

bast more forcefully than the proclamation Burgoyne addressed
to the Americans in late June, 1777, as he stood ready to push
south toward Albany. After listing all his titles pretentiously, he
promises those "faithful servants of the Crown" who, opposing
"the present unnatural rebellion," will co-operate in every way
with his present campaign, protection of "their lands, habitations, and family." [36] Can't you see, mimics a writer at New
York, "what a dust your leaders kick up, / In this rebellious
civil hickup"?

> But now inspired with patriot love
> I come th' oppression to remove;
> To free you from the heavy clog
> Of every tyrant demagogue.
>
> .   .   .   .   .
>
> A Tory cannot move his tongue,
> But whip, in prison he is flung,
> His goods and chattels made a prey
> By those vile mushrooms of a day.
>
> .   .   .   .   .
>
> These things are done by rogues, who dare
> Profess to breathe in freedom's air.
> To petticoats alike and breeches
> Their cruel domination stretches.
>
> .   .   .   .   .

I issue now my manifesto,

> I, the great knight of de la Mancha,
> Without Squire Carleton my sancho,
> Will tear you limb from limb asunder,
> With cannon, blunderbuss and thunder;
> And spoil your feathering and your tarring;
> And cagg you up for pickled herring

[36] Edward Barrington de Fonblanque, *Political and Military Episodes
. . . Derived from the Life and Correspondence of the Right Hon. John
Burgoyne* (London, 1876), pp. 490–492.

> In front of troops as spruce as beaux,
> And ready to lay on their blows.

. . . .

From him who

> With neutral stomach eats his supper,
> Nor deems the contest worth a copper,
> I will not defalcate a groat,
> Nor force his wife to cut his throat.

. . . . .

But "Who e'er secrets cow, bull, or ox, / Or shall presume to hide his flocks," "I'll hang him as the Jews did Haman; / And smoke his carcass for a gammon."

> If any should so harden'd be
> As to expect impunity,
> Because *procul a fulmine,*
> I will let loose the dogs of Hell,
> Ten thousand Indians, who shall yell,
> And foam, and tear, and grin, and roar,
> And drench their moccasins in gore;

. . . . .

> If after all these lovely warnings,
> My wishes' and my bowels' yearnings,
> You shall remain as deaf as adder,
> Or grow with hostile rage the madder,
> I swear by George and by St. Paul
> I will exterminate you all.[37]

More reprehensible than this proclamation to the Americans was Burgoyne's speech a few days earlier, exhorting the Indians

---

[37] "Proclamation," *New York Journal* (Kingston), Sept. 8, 1777, p. 4; reprinted in *Ballads and Poems Relating to the Burgoyne Campaign,* ed. W. L. Stone (Albany, 1893), pp. 7–15. Variously attributed to Livingston and Hopkinson. "Squire Carleton" is Sir Guy Carleton, governor of Canada at this time. Hopkinson furnished sarcastic annotations on this same proclamation, *Pennsylvania Packet,* Aug. 26, 1777, p. 3 (reprinted in *Miscellaneous Essays,* I, 146–150).

to "strike at the common enemies of Great Britain and America —disturbers of public order, peace, and happiness—destroyers of commerce, parricides of the States." Though he forbade them to shed blood when "not opposed in arms," this prohibition, as events proved, could not be enforced.[38] "We are credibly informed," inveighs a Philadelphia writer, "that Burgoyne, the chief and director of the King of Great Britain's band of thieves, robbers, cutthroats, scalpers, and murderers of every denomination, now infesting the northern and western frontiers of several of the American United States, has not only discontinued the reward he had offered" for scalps, "but has strictly prohibited, for the future, under a severe penalty, the practice of scalping."

He had found by experience, that his rewards lessened the number of his emissaries, who not only scalped some of his Tory friends, concealed among the inhabitants, but also scalped one another; and that a scalping party of a lieutenant, and about thirty men, he lately sent out, with a large number of Indians, were by the latter all killed and scalped, none of the party having been since seen or heard of. . . . It is not improbable he might be apprehensive, that some of the dexterous hands about him, might take an opportunity, one time or another, and slip off his own night-cap.[39]

During midsummer Burgoyne's army moved steadily southward; then in September it ground to a halt near Saratoga. Unable to advance or retreat, Burgoyne finally signed an agreement that his troops would not serve again in America. The more vividly to dramatize this defeat, one ballad writer chooses a metaphor highly appropriate to a commander with parlor manners:

Jack, thinking of cribbage, all fours, or of put,
With a dexterous hand, he did shuffle and cut,
And when likely to lose—like a sharper they say—
Did attempt to renege—I mean, run away.

[38] De Fonblanque, *Correspondence of Burgoyne*, p. 489.
[39] *Pennsylvania Journal*, Sept. 10, 1777, p. 2; reprinted in Moore's *Diary*, I, 491–492.

But watch'd so closely, he could not play booty,
Yet to cheat he fain would, for George—'twas his duty;
A great bet depending on that single game;
Dominion and honor—destruction and shame.

Examin'd with care his most critical hand,
At a loss, if better to beg or to stand,
His tricks reckon'd up; for all sharpers can jangle;
Then kick'd up a dust, for his favorite wrangle.

'Twas diamond cut diamond, spades were of no use,
But to dig up the way for surrender and truce;
For he dreaded the hand that dealt out such thumps;
As the hearts were run out, and clubs were then trumps.

Thus he met with the rubbers, as the game it turn'd out,
Poor Jack, although beat, made a damnable rout,
Complain'd he was cheated, and pompously talks;
Quit the game with a curse, while he rubb'd out the chalks.[40]

If the report be true, writes Livingston in all innocence after the surrender at Saratoga, that Burgoyne is being held prisoner for having violated the terms of the treaty, I think him "the most profitable prisoner we could have taken, having . . . more titles, than any gentleman on this side the Ganges." Against the time when an exchange shall be contemplated, I humbly propose to the Congress and to General Washington that a suitable equivalent for each of his titles be specified. This modest proposal concludes:

For John Burgoyne, &c., &c., &c., Some connoisseurs in hieroglyphics imagine that these three *et ceteras* are emblematical of three certain *occult* qualities in the general, which he never intends to exhibit in more legible characters, viz.: prudence, modesty, and humanity. . . . Certain it is that these three *et ceteras* must stand for three

[40] "A New Song," [1778?]. Frank Moore, who reprinted this song, writes, "The following ballad appeared before the royal commissioners returned to England, in a double-columned sheet, adapted to the tune, 'A late worthy old Lion,'" *Songs,* p. 191; I have not been able to locate this contemporary printing. "All Four" (or Seven Up) and "Put" (Put and Take?) are card games.

somethings, and as these three somethings must, at least, be equal
to three somethings without rank or title, I had some thoughts of
setting them down for three privates; but then as they are three
somethings in General Burgoyne, which must be of twice the value
of three anythings in any three privates, I shall only double them,
and demand in exchange for these three problematical, enigmatical,
hieroglyphical, mystic, necromantic, cabalistical and portentous *et
ceteras,* six privates.[41]

Not quite so notorious as Burgoyne was Charles, Lord Cornwallis, who campaigned in America through five years of war.
During the night of January 2, 1777, Washington slipped around
Cornwallis at Trenton and on the following day put to flight
a body of British troops at Princeton. If his own troops had
not been so fatigued, Washington might well have captured the
military stores at New Brunswick seventeen miles away; as it
was, he decided to turn north and go into winter quarters at
Morristown. Even so, the complexion of the war changed over-
night, and the British were forced to abandon their western
positions in New Jersey. "The Cornwalliad," an "Heroi-comic"
poem in four cantos, celebrates this British reverse:

A major of a Scottish brigade at New Brunswick, mindful
that the recent defeat at Trenton "impairs our strength," boasts
nevertheless that "The great Cornwallis amply shall repay, / The
sad misfortunes of that hapless day." Learning of the rout at
Princeton, Cornwallis hastens north to intercept Washington. In
the vicinity of New Brunswick mistaken identity leads to fear:
the Scotsmen in the town suppose Cornwallis' troops to be
Washington's forces in disguise, while Cornwallis on the wooded
heights nearby thinks that the Americans have captured the
town and its stores. At daybreak Cornwallis gives the signal for
attack, but his men cannot hear him, "For as that morning he
had caught a cough, / His voice was scarcely clear and loud
enough." When finally they are deployed, he addresses his men:

---

[41] *New Jersey Gazette* (Burlington), Dec. 17, 1777, p. 2; reprinted in
Moore's *Diary,* II, 12–15.

"Brave veterans keep your fire,
In full reserve till we have marched nigher,
But halt one moment till I shall apply
My grass green spectacles to either eye."
    The hero look'd, and thought he saw a row
Of cannon placed upon the bending brow.
His fears deceived him for they were the crowns
Of some poor Scotsmen on the distant downs,
Just half inclined upon their hams to pray,
And ask forgiveness of their sins that day.

He looks again and thinks he sees

        some wheeling to the right
In furious onset to begin the fight,
And with light infantry in many a rank,
To pierce with columns his unguarded flank.

            . . . . .

        what he saw was but five Scottish swains,
Who step'd aside upon the bending plains,
In social mood, and great good nature, there
To ease themselves of something else than care.

A wandering Scotsman is captured, and finally the confusion is
dispelled. Cornwallis' reunited forces assemble in the barracks
at New Brunswick. "On a fair bench exalted sat the chief, / And
with much grog washed down departing grief." Prevailed upon
to tell where he has recently been, he relates how, on learning of
the disaster at Trenton, he hurried there:

        Each veteran soldier bore a large knapsack
        With change of raiment on his weary back,
        But I, unhappy, this misfortune had,
        My shoes were clouted, and my breeches bad.
        For as to you it is already known,
        Sometime last autumn I had swap'd my own
        For that rent pair which Peter Parker wore,
        When a sad ball unbreech'd the commodore.

As we lay across stream from Washington at Trenton Bridge, we could scarcely sleep for imagining the enemy would stab us if we did.

> I once myself in dreary vision saw
> The raging Mifflin his fierce bayonet draw,
> And as he push'd at my posterior thigh,
> I felt my heart and fainting spirits die;
> But what the flush and pleasure of the soul
> When I awoke, and felt my backside whole.

At this point the poem breaks off, unfinished.[42]

This long poem in heroic measure lies squarely in the mock-epic tradition. The anonymous author explains in a preface that as Vergil sang in praise of Augustus, he, wishing to be reconciled with George III, has "earnestly invoked the muse who at length has favoured me with the following Cantoes in honour of the great Cornwallis. . . . It has always been my resolution, that if ever I should undertake to compose an epic poem, I would choose a suffering hero. . . . In this situation, that is struggling with adversity, I found the great Cornwallis in his retrograde manoeuvre from the Delaware to the banks of the Raritan at Brunswick." [43] While the poem opens in the manner of *The Aeneid*:

> I sing the prowess of that martial chief,
> Who bravely patient bore a weight of grief,
> On that sad eve that closed the march he made,
> From Trenton hills to Brunswic, retrograde,

its author, in keeping with the low-burlesque tradition, does not take seriously this or any of the several other epic and romantic conventions he employs. Thus, when Cornwallis learns that the troops in the town are his own, the poet sings:

42 *United States Magazine*, I (Mar.–July, Sept., Oct., 1779), 133–134, 181–182, 232–233, 278–279, 317–318, 394–400, 431–433.

43 "Apology for the *Cornwalliad*," *United States Magazine*, I (Jan., 1779), 16, 17.

Rehearse, O muse! for how shall I explain,
The joy that rushed upon the warrior train.
Had I a mouth as friar Bacon's was,
Scooped hollow out in a round bomb of brass;
Ten iron throats, and just ten thousand tongues,
Loud as street-watchmen with ben-leather lungs;
I could not number, or in words explain
The many mouths that gaped upon the plain.
No; I myself could not one hundredth stare
Of each long visage through the camp declare.
Yet might I call the muse, the queen of rhime,
To set them forth, but that I have not time,
And therefore this and other things shall leave
To each man's thought to guess at and conceive.

Owing perhaps to the complexity of the historical incident on which the poem is based, Cornwallis does not clearly emerge as the hero until the third canto, and only in the fragmentary fourth is attention focused on him. Still, the author's clearly defined point of view and sure grasp of prosodical and other verse features make "The Cornwalliad" one of the most successful long poems of the period covered by this study.

After campaigning vigorously and for the most part successfully in the South later in the war, Cornwallis withdrew to Virginia in 1781. Freneau, recalling his marauding there, inveighs:

None e'er before essay'd such desperate crimes,
Alone he stood, arch-butcher of the times,
Rov'd uncontroul'd this wasted country o'er,
Strew'd plains with dead, and bath'd his jaws with gore?

. . . . .

Convinc'd we are, no foreign spot on earth
But Britain only, gave this reptile birth.
That white-cliff'd isle, the vengeful dragon's den,
Has sent us monsters where we look'd for men.

. . . . .

Now curs'd with life, a foe to man and God,
Like Cain, I drive you to the land of Nod.

He with a brother's blood his hands did stain,
One brother he, you have a thousand slain.
And, O! may heaven affix some public mark
To know Cornwallis—may he howl and bark!—

. . . . .

Haste to the rocks, thou curse to human kind,
There thou may'st wolves and brother tygers find;
Eternal exile be your righteous doom
And gnash your dragon's teeth in some sequester'd gloom.[44]

Time and circumstance worked against Cornwallis, and by September he found himself totally invested at Yorktown. Not long after his surrender on October 19 a Boston writer ridiculed his overweening confidence throughout the Southern campaign.

No longer he sits, with his thumb in his mouth,
Like prudent Sir Harry—but *conquers* the south—
And soon having *victory* bound in his chain—
Inclos'd her in letters, he sent to Germain.

. . . . .

Thus deck'd with the plumage of eagle-wing'd fame
He swore there was conquest annex'd to his name;
For fortune the wanton voluptuous Gypsey—
Had pledg'd him her cup 'till his Lordship was tipsey.

So rising in wrath like Achilles at Hector,
He swore he wou'd turn every whig to a Spectre;
And bloodily threaten'd to peirce Mr. Greene,
And shiver more rebels than ever were seen.

Then came Yorktown. "The hands of bold freemen surrounded the shore, / And 'tis said the Earl never will conquer us more." [45]

In the spring of 1778, Sir Henry Clinton succeeded Howe as

[44] "On the Fall of General Earl Cornwallis," *Freeman's Journal*, Nov. 7, 1781, p. 1; reprinted in Pattee, II, 92–93, 94, 99.
[45] "NEW SONG. Occasioned by the surrender of Earl *Cornwallis* and his whole army, to General WASHINGTON," *Independent Chronicle* (Boston), Nov. 8, 1781, p. 1. "Sir Harry" is Sir Henry Clinton, then commander in chief of the British armies in America.

commander in chief in America. In this capacity he was color-
less and unimpressive, thin-skinned, at times almost a defeatist.
"I know I am hated, nay, detested in the Army," he once remarked, "but I am indifferent about it, because I know it is
without a cause." To state the case fairly, Clinton as a serious
student of warfare was alive to the realities of the situation but
was at the same time the victim of mistakes forced upon him by
the home government.[46] Assuming command at a time when the
tide of war had begun to run against Britain, it was inevitable
that Clinton, a political scapegoat at home, should have become
a butt for satire abroad. General Howe, jeers a Boston writer,
gained victory after victory,

> And what has Harry done, contemptuous knight?
> At day he fought and ran away by night:
> On Monmouth's plain, with blood of Britons dyed,
> Brave Monckton fell, a son of Britain's pride;
> But Harry fainted with fatigue, 'twas said,
> And wisely fled beneath the moonlight shade.
> Manhatten's island now affords him shelter,
> From whence; as yet, he's nothing done but pilfer,
> A few score sheep, and now and then a hog,
> Serve for to fatten this ignoble dog.
>
>   .   .   .   .   .
>
> A pettifogger in the art of war,
> William would go, where Henry never dare.
> Your army all despise the filthy dwarf,
> Whose heart's as rank as weeds on Lethe's wharff;
> Whose filthy carcass too, of equal stench,
> May coupled be to some old greazy wench.[47]

Another writer burlesques what he interprets to be Clinton's in-
ertia within the British lines at New York:

[46] Alden, *Gage*, pp. 260, 261; Miller, *Triumph*, pp. 44, 392, 393 (quoted);
John William Fortescue, *A History of the British Army* (London, 1911),
III, 403.

[47] "*A contrast between* Sir William Howe *and* Sir Henry Clinton,
dedicated to Lord North," *Boston Evening-Post*, Aug. 7, 1779, p. 4.

What's odd for Sir Harry, he nothing begun,
Kept close to his works—without firing a gun.
But, perhaps, th' poor man could not get on his legs,
After sitting so long—like a hen o'er spoil'd eggs.

. . . . .

The Knight he is either involv'd in deep gloom,
When no mortal but Andre dare enter his room;
Or careering, whip stich, with a dozen o' fools,
Like children astride upon switches or stools,
Hot after a dog who has tied to his tail
A herring, as boys tie a bladder or rail.[48]

An ill-fated British expedition on the lower Hudson in 1779 was promptly exposed in a letter to the Connecticut press: You, Clinton, like your predecessors, "have adventured your character, in the execution of delusory objects; but like them, you may not return to reap the reward of your labor." Having decided that the securing of West Point would end the war, you approached within nine miles and "halted before a small work at King's-Ferry."

Sir William Howe could not have invested this insignificant place with more unmeaning formality. . . . The capture of fifty men, after a foolish variety of movements, and under a vain pomp of capitulation, must appear to all the world a strange effort towards the reduction of America; and but a poor recompence for the millions voted by parliament, and which you have chearfully expended for this single purpose. . . .

It is a maxim *Rochefoucault*, "that fortune turns every thing to the advantage of her favourites." By this rule it would seem, that neither you nor your nation are within her patronage, for the business of both, since the beginning of this *happy contest*, has been constantly going backwards. Nay, as if she had placed you at the extremity of her malice, she has even made the blunders of your directors, serve as the steps to your ruin; and to complete the cata-

[48] *New-York Packet* (Fishkill), Nov. 9, 1780, p. 1. The following note is offered in explanation of the last four lines quoted: "A substitute for fox-hunting,—or a favorite and constant diversion of the Knight's."

logue of your evils, she hants your bewildered imagination with the
fate of Burgoyne.

The Americans captured Paulus Hook soon after and forced you
to withdraw from King's Ferry. "It is, however, a just punishment, that what was occupied from folly, should be evacuated
through fear."

Alas, Sir Harry! in aiming at a campaign, you have rendered yourself ridiculous to the world. . . . The momentary hopes you had
raised, like the fugitive gleams of a winter's sun, have been scarcely
felt, before they were succeeded by all the severity of disappointment. . . . You have suffered yourself to be successively defeated,
by a people, boastingly called cowards, and ridiculously rebels—
You have taken away from your Prince the chief support of his
speeches—He will be no longer able to tell his parliament of his
reliance on the bravery of his troops, and the courage and conduct
of his commanders.[49]

Shifting the seat of war to the South, at the end of 1779
Clinton sailed for South Carolina with 7,000 men. The following
spring, while Charleston lay under siege, he issued a proclamation

denouncing the severest punishments against those who should still
persist in their treasonable practices and promising the most effectual
countenance, protection, and support to the King's faithful and
peaceable subjects, together with a restoration of their former civil
government whenever the situation of the country would permit
it.[50]

Whereupon a writer gibed,

> HARK, Rebels hark! Sir Harry comes,
> With proclamation, sword and drums!
> A General who commands in chief
> The British troops, and like a thief

[49] "To Sir HENRY CLINTON," *Connecticut Courant*, Nov. 23, 1779, pp.
1–2.
[50] *The American Rebellion: Sir Henry Clinton's Narrative of his Campaigns, 1775–1782*, ed. W. B. Willcox (New Haven, 1954), p. 175.

> Steals Sheep and Negroes, Wood and Hay,
> Then jumps on board and sails away,

and proceeded to travesty:

> My name is Harry, each man knows
> This Nick-Name, by which Satan goes;
> Such as will serve this man of sin
> Are pick'd to serve the British King!!
>
> .   .   .   .   .
>
> "Under Great-Britain's royal seal,"
> Murder and bloodshed I conceal.
>
> .   .   .   .   .
>
> "A free and general pardon" here,
> To all that will Allegiance swear!
> Your King is very loth to lose you,
> Tho' he in anger did abuse you!
>
> .   .   .   .   .
>
> You shall no more for Rebels pass
> But honor'd, kiss his Royal – – –,
> If in your pocket close you keep
> The King's protection, 'wake or sleep
> No Ball that strikes can kill or wound,
> In it such mighty power is found.[51]

For once Clinton had the last laugh, though, for the American garrison surrendered after all.

On learning of Clinton's recall, Freneau jeered:

> The dog that is beat has a right to complain—
> Sir Harry returns a disconsolate man,
> To the face of his master, the Lord's oil-anointed,
> To the country provided for thieves disappointed.

Just what have you accomplished in America, Sir Harry?

> At the taking of Charleston you cut a great figure,
> The terms you propounded were terms full of rigour,

[51] "The Title," *Boston Gazette*, May 8, 1780, p. 1.

> Yet could not foresee poor Charley's disgrace,
> Nor how soon your own colours would go to the case.
>
> .   .   .   .   .
>
> Whoever the Tories marked out as a Whig,
> If gentle, or simple, or little, or big,
> No matter to you—to kill 'em and spite 'em,
> You soon had 'em up where the dogs couldn't bite 'em.

You thought to capture West Point and thus seize control of the Hudson:

> So off you sent André, (not guided by Pallas)
> Who soon purchased Arnold, and with him the gallows;
> Your loss I conceive than your gain was far greater,
> You lost a good fellow, and got a vile traitor.
>
> Now Carleton comes over to give you relief,
> A knight like yourself, and commander in chief,
> But the chief he will get, you may tell the dear honey,
> Will be a black eye, hard knocks, and no money.[52]

Sir Guy Carleton superseded Clinton on May 5, 1782, and remained in command until peace was concluded. An able administrator and officer who like Burgoyne held the Americans in contempt, Carleton had previously been governor of the province of Quebec. He it was who repulsed the desperate American assault on Quebec early in the war. On November 22, 1775, while preparing his defenses to meet this assault, he ordered all those who would not bear arms to leave Quebec within four days.[53] Two months later, in some successful broken rhymes, this order was travestied.

> Whereas I'm *chas'd* from place to place,
> By rebels, void of sense and grace;
> Crown-Point, Montreal and Chamblee,

[52] "On Sir Henry Clinton's Recall," *Freeman's Journal*, May 22, 1782, p. 2; reprinted in Pattee, II, 153–156.
[53] Willard M. Wallace, *Appeal to Arms* (New York, 1951), p. 69; Justin H. Smith, *Our Struggle for the Fourteenth Colony* (New York and London, 1907), II, 95.

By Arnold and Montgomery,
From GEORGE and PETER are set free,
In spite of *Indians*, *D– – –l* and me;

. . . . .

Each one who wont swear he's a tory,
I *sw– –r* shall go to *Purga*-tory,
There to reform *in limbo patrum*,
And those who blame me may go a'ter 'em.
Let those who go take wives and children,
And haste forthwith into the wildern-
Ess, 'most *savages*, God knows,
They'll find for *cheer* frost, ice and snows;

. . . . .

Given at St. Lewis Castle, in
Quebec, the year of GEORGE sixteen,
Of Britain, France and Ireland King,
(Of *Rome*) the faith's defender being,
And so forth—by me GUY CARLETON,
Kennell'd and toothless, yet I snarl on.[54]

In command at New York, Carleton by exercising clemency did
much to conciliate the Americans,[55] but Freneau imagines him
addressing them in quite another tone:

Our king, I must tell you, is plagued with a phantom
(Independence they call it) that hourly doth haunt him,
And relief, my dear rebels, you only can grant him.

Tom Gage and Sir Harry, Sir William, (our boast)
Lord Howe, and the rest that have travelled the coast,
All failed in their projects of laying this ghost:

So unless the damned spectre myself can expel
It will yet kill our monarch, I know very well,
And gallop him off on his lion to hell.

[54] *Providence Gazette*, Feb. 3, 1776, p. 2. "PETER" is a reference to
the Pope.
[55] *DNB*, III, 1003.

But I heartily wish, that, instead of Sir Guy,
They had sent out a seer from the island of Skie,
Who rebels, and devils, and ghosts could defy.

Nevertheless we will attempt to negotiate a settlement; remember "I am an honest, well-meaning old man."

Too proud to retreat, and too weak to advance,
We must stay where we are, at the mercy of chance,
'Till Fortune shall help us to lead you a dance.

Then lay down your arms, dear rebels—O hone!
Our king is the best man that ever was known,
And the greatest that ever was stuck on a throne.

. . . . .

Break the treaties you make with Louis Bourbon;
Abandon the Congress, no matter how soon,
And then, all together, we'll play a new tune.

. . . . .

So, quickly submit and our mercy implore,
Be as loyal to George as you once were before,
Or I'll slaughter you all—and probably more.

What puzzled Sir Harry, Sir Will, and his brother,
Perhaps may be done by the son of my mother,
With the Sword in one hand and a Branch in the other.[56]

III

So distasteful was the prospect of serving in America that not 20,000 British soldiers were available in 1776, whereupon the government applied to certain German states for mercenaries.[57] As early as January treaties were concluded with Hesse and Brunswick. From the time of the New York campaign German

[56] "Sir Guy Carleton's Address to the Americans," *Freeman's Journal*, June 5, 1782, p. 4; reprinted in Pattee, II, 156–158.

[57] Claude H. Van Tyne, *England and America: Rivals in the American Revolution* (New York, 1927), pp. 124–125.

192 POLITICAL SATIRE IN THE REVOLUTION

mercenaries, to the number of 30,000, served in America, with
the same vigor and courage as British regulars.

It was not cowardice but negligence on the part of the garrison commander that led to the capture, on the morning of December 26, 1776, of almost a thousand Hessians at Trenton with
only seventeen killed. In what purports to be a letter of February
18, 1777, from Rome, the Count de Schaumbergh commends
Baron Hohendorf commanding the Hessian troops in America
for his prudence in sending the minister in London an exact list
of the 1,605 men killed at Trenton:

"This precaution was the more necessary, as the report sent
to the English ministry does not give but 1,455 dead. This would
make 483,450 florins instead of the 643,500 which I am entitled
to demand under our convention." Don't economize the new
recruits I am sending you.

Do you remember that of the 300 Lacedaemonians who defended
the defile of Thermopylae, not one returned? How happy should
I be could I say the same of my brave Hessians!

It is true that their king, Leonidas, perished with them: but things
have changed, and it is no longer the custom for princes of the empire to go and fight in America for a cause with which they have
no concern. . . . You did right to send back to Europe that Dr.
Crumerus who was so successful in curing dysentery. Don't bother
with a man who is subject to looseness of the bowels. That disease
makes bad soldiers. . . . Better that they burst in their barracks
than fly in a battle, and tarnish the glory of our arms. Besides, you
know that they pay me as killed for all who die from disease, and
I don't get a farthing for runaways. My trip to Italy, which has
cost me enormously, makes it desirable that there should be a great
mortality among them. . . . Let it be your principal object to
prolong the war and avoid a decisive engagement on either side,
for I have made arrangements for a grand Italian opera, and I do
not wish to be obliged to give it up.

The letter closes on this ominous note: "Meantime I pray God,
my dear Baron de Hohendorf, to have you in his holy and gracious keeping." [58]

[58] "The Sale of the Hessians," written originally in French, probably

Picture the Count, wintering in Italy, eager to see his troops in America cover themselves with glory—and him with florins. He is the direct opposite of Leonidas, a fact in which he obviously takes pride. Like Swift in *A Tale of a Tub*, Franklin here devises a situational mask the better to objectify and give bite to the satire; outraged in his heart of hearts by the inhumane practice of hiring out mercenaries, he would seem not to trust himself to speak out effectively unless disguised.

Franklin's manner resembles that of Swift, moreover, in "letting the same words express incompatible values," in presenting simultaneously "the 'official version' and the 'real meaning' in the same term." [59] Having commended the Baron on his careful reckoning of the casualties, the Count informs him of new recruits that are being sent to America. "Don't economize them," he writes. "Remember glory before all things. Glory is true wealth. There is nothing degrades the soldier like the love of money." Officially, the epigram "Glory is true wealth" suggests that military glory is above all else even though it cost a man his life on the field of battle. Actually, the Count means that glory is best won by dying, whether in battle or barracks matters not at all, for glory purchased thus means money in his purse. And if nothing so degrades as the love of money, how are we to judge the Count himself? The Count then explains that he is standing ready to return to Hesse for replacements. "It is true, grown men are becoming scarce there, but I will send you boys. Besides, the scarcer the commodity the higher the price." Is this simply a lesson in economics, that the law of supply and demand will be met, or does the Count mean that with Hesse's manpower reserves badly depleted by the demands of the American war, boys will now be sent who can command a higher price than men did formerly? The longer one ponders the ironic tensions

---

in Feb.–Mar., 1777; first ascribed to Franklin by John Bigelow (*The Complete Works of Benjamin Franklin* [New York, 1887–1889], VII, 191–196); reprinted in Smyth, VII, 27–29.

[59] Martin Price, *Swift's Rhetorical Art* (New Haven, 1953), pp. 24–25.

set in motion by such passages as these, the more powerful the force of the satire is seen to be.

There was much to lure German mercenaries across the Atlantic and, once in America, much to tempt them to desert. Congress offered them land and livestock and promised them the same religious and political freedom as Americans then enjoyed. In spite of such temptations the incidence of desertion was lower among German troops than among American and British, though after the war many of them decided to stay in America.[60] What happened to Peter is the story, in caricature, of many German "volunteers." At a public house in Hesse the British recruiting officer, Colonel Faucit, plies him with beer, bread, sausage, and guineas, and holds out the prospect of his returning home next spring if he signs up now. Faucit further insinuates that like his cousin George, who is serving in America, Peter can have an American wife: "You shall take for wife her who shall seem the prettiest, or who shall bring you the best manor. Her father and brother shall be your valets; and while you shall pass your time in drinking, eating, playing at nine pins, getting children, or sleeping, they will work on your fields; and if they are negligent, you will give them the cowskin." Faucit dismisses the Americans as being "so weak, that one Hessian would kill twenty with his fist, before they could load a musket." He reminds Peter, "if you were obliged to stay here, you would scarcely get a crown a month, labouring like a Bohemian, and you would be lashed for the least fault; they would put irons on you; they would oblige you to work on the highways, in the parks, in the mines, at the bridges, at the palace, at the fortifications." Peter signs up and, except that he is drunk, would set off for America at once.[61] Newly arrived at New York, Peter, who suffered during the passage ("we were all jam'd together like pickled her-

[60] Miller, *Triumph*, p. 15; Max Von Eelking, *The German Allied Troops in the North American War of Independence*, trans. J. G. Rosengarten (Albany, 1893), p. 257.

[61] "PETER in HESSE," *Pennsylvania Journal*, Jan. 31, 1781, pp. 1–2. Colonel William Faucit was the English commissioner and plenipotentiary to the German states.

rings in a barrel"), encounters his cousin standing sentry at the wharf. "Do not you see," asks George, "that I am a poor soldier, half-starved, half-naked; and that I have no hope to be recompensed at the end of the war for my fatigues, and the dangers I have run?" My face is "all murdered with strokes which I received yesterday because my Musket was not as bright as the knocker on the door of a Quaker." Their conversation is interrupted by a sergeant, who gives both of them *"blows with his Cane to make them learn the Hessian discipline."* [62]

Early in the war the British government openly acknowledged the practice of employing Indian auxiliaries. "With a full knowledge of what was to be expected from such allies," writes Andrew Davis, "the English employed them upon expeditions where the opportunity was afforded them of displaying in full force the most revolting features of their barbarous methods of warfare." They justified this policy by pointing out that if they did not gain the advantage the Americans would, and in fairness it must be said that the Americans for their part used Indians whenever they could.[63]

Early in 1782 Franklin published another of his hoaxes, the "Supplement to the Boston *Independent Chronicle*," which was widely circulated in Europe.[64] The "Supplement" contains an extract of a letter from Captain Gerrish of the "New England Militia," which in turn quotes an intercepted letter from one James Crauford to Colonel Haldimand, governor of Canada. "At the request of the Senneka Chiefs," writes Crauford, "I send herewith to your Excellency, under the Care of James Boyd, eight Packs of Scalps, cured, dried, hooped, and painted, with all the Indian triumphal Marks, of which the following is Invoice and Explanation": "No. 1. Containing 43 Scalps of Congress Soldiers, killed in different Skirmishes," also 62 of farmers

---

[62] "Peter at New-York," *Pennsylvania Journal*, Feb. 5, 1781, p. 1.

[63] Andrew M. Davis, *Eng. Hist. Rev.*, II (1887), 728; Lecky, *American Revolution*, p. 221.

[64] Miller, *Triumph*, p. 168.

killed in their houses, "being surprised in the Night"; 98 of farmers who died fighting for their lives and families; 97 of farmers killed in their fields; 102 of farmers, "only 18 marked with a little yellow Flame, to denote their being of Prisoners burnt alive, after being scalped, their Nails pulled out by the Roots, and other Torments"; "No. 5. Containing 88 Scalps of Women; hair long, braided in the Indian Fashion, to shew they were Mothers; Hoops blue; Skin yellow Ground, with little red Tadpoles, to represent, by way of Triumph, the Tears of Grief occasioned to their Relations; a black scalping-Knife or Hatchet at the Bottom, to mark their being killed with those Instruments. 17 others, Hair very grey; black Hoops; plain brown Colour; no Mark, but the short Club or *Casse-tête*, to shew they were knocked down dead, or had their Brains beat out"; 193 boys' scalps; 211 girls' scalps; "No. 8. This Package is a Mixture of all the Varieties above-mentioned; to the number of 122; with a Box of Birch Bark, containing 29 little Infants' Scalps of various Sizes; small white Hoops; white Ground; no Tears; and only a little black Knife in the Middle, to shew they were ript out of their Mothers' Bellies." Captain Gerrish explains that a certain Lieutenant Fitzgerald has offered to take these scalps to England and "hang them all up in some dark Night on the Trees in St. James's Park, where they could be seen from the King and Queen's Palaces in the Morning." The *Chronicle*, in a paragraph dated eight days later, notes that Fitzgerald's wagon with the scalps has reached Boston.

Thousands of People are flocking to see them this Morning, and all Mouths are full of Execrations. Fixing them to the Trees is not approved. It is now proposed to make them up in decent little Packets, seal and direct them; one to the King, containing a Sample of every Sort for his Museum; one to the Queen, with some of Women and little Children; the Rest to be distributed among both Houses of Parliament; a double Quantity to the Bishops.[65]

[65] "Supplement to the Boston *Independent Chronicle*," printed on Franklin's private press at Passy; on Feb. 28, 1782, according to Clarence

In this hoax, as bitter and mordant a work as Franklin ever penned, Captain Gerrish, horror-struck by the contents of these intercepted packages and anxious only to do his duty, is the innocent, well-meaning vehicle for Franklin's attack on "the English barbarities in America, particularly those committed by the savages at their instigation." [66] But because the pathetic part threatens to swallow up the rational, the situational mask is less successful in this instance than in "The Sale of the Hessians."

Most of the satires included in this chapter are highly personal: high-ranking officers in the enemy camp offered an easy target, all the easier when their strategy was unimaginative. It counted as nothing that they were charged with executing plans drawn up in London; for the majority of Americans they were the immediate symbol of a colonial system long since outmoded. As it happened, few of the major battles in which the British suffered humiliation or outright defeat provoked genuine satire; Bunker Hill, for example, called forth much crude invective but little that could be called satirical. As for the policy of engaging German mercenaries and Indian allies, it so outraged American patriots that Franklin was almost the only writer capable of viewing it rationally, this partly because he was living in France at the time far distant from the field of battle. It is fair to say that in the British military establishment patriots and antiministerial writers discovered variety and abundance of objects for satire and that their opponents were unable to retaliate in kind.

Brigham, *History and Bibliography of American Newspapers, 1690–1820* (Worcester, 1947), I, 308; reprinted in Smyth, VIII, 437–442.

[66] Franklin to Charles W. F. Dumas, May 3, 1782, Smyth, VIII, 448.

CHAPTER VIII

The Continental Army

WHEREAS the British military establishment drew heavier satirical fire than the civil, the American military drew less. The rag, tag, and bobtail in the field gave a better account of themselves than the delegates at Philadelphia assembled; or so it seemed to loyalist and ministerial writers, who found the military establishment less vulnerable than the civil. They directed their sporadic bursts at the general condition of this motley of continentals and militiamen, at the officers, and at the military and naval action.

On April 8, 1775, the Massachusetts Provincial Congress resolved to raise an army of 13,600 and asked the other New England colonies to furnish quotas, totaling an additional 30,000, for the general defense. Even though war broke out eleven days later, these quotas were not filled by the end of May. On June 14 the Continental Congress directed that "six companies of expert riflemen, be immediately raised in Pennsylvania, two in Maryland, and two in Virginia" to "join the army near Boston" and on the following day unanimously appointed George Washington "to command all the continental forces, raised, or to be raised, for the defence of American liberties." By the summer's end both King and Congress had proclaimed that a state of war existed.[1]

[1] Charles K. Bolton, *The Private Soldier under Washington* (New

Early in 1776, at a time when the Canadian campaign was going disastrously for the Americans, "Yorick" asked the colonists what they quixotically hoped to oppose to the mighty fleets and armies of Great Britain: "Is it a defenceless coast without a navy, a country without manufactures, a treasury without money, an army without cloathing, arms, ammunition or discipline, and lastly councils without unanimity, in which defection from the cause must be the inevitable consequence of usurpation, folly and rashness?"

I know no past age or period that could be favourable to such wild chimerical projects as the Americans aim at at present, but about the end of the 16th and beginning of the 17th century, when upon application they might have a powerful ally in the renowned Knight of La Mancha, who would undertake their cause without those mean interested motives which influence the actions of men in those later times. Not less has it been thy misfortune most valorous Knight, thou mirror of truth, cream of urbanity, prince of chivalry and apparition of bravery, that this age and this grand theatre, is not reserved for your great atchievements. The Giant NORTH you would deliver bound at the feet of America, as you have done the giant Caraculiambro lord of the island of Malindrania, at the feet of the once peerless empress of your heart the fair del Toboso.—The ministerial conjurers, would feel the weight of your blows, and the keen edge of your sword as did the unfortunate puppets of Melisandra.—With your single arm you would overthrow their armies, as you did the flock of sheep, when you thought you encountered the host of the proud Alisanfaron. Heavens have mercy upon us! How you would lay about you, kick and cuff, slash and hack, helter skelter, cut and thrust, backstroke and forestroke, single and double.[2]

I

The militia and continentals who composed the army were for the most part men of humble background. An overwhelming

---

York, 1902), pp. 9, 15; *Journals*, II, 89, 91, 128–157 (Declaration on Taking Arms).

[2] *Virginia Gazette* (Norfolk), Feb. 3. 1776, p. 35.

majority came from the laboring classes, from the trades and
the farm, the frontier and the sea. "Arch-rebels, bare-footed tatterdemalions," one writer called them, "So dirty their backs, and
so wretched their show, / That carrion-crow follows wherever
they go."

> With loud peals of laughter, your sides, sirs, would crack,
> To see General Convict and Colonel Shoe-black,
>   With their hunting-shirts, and rifle-guns.
> See cobblers and quacks, rebel priests and the like,
> Pettifoggers and barbers, with sword and with pike,
> All strutting, the standard of Satan beside,
> And honest names using, their black deeds to hide.
>   With their hunting-shirts, and rifle-guns.[3]

"The Army in general is not only very badly accoutered," reported a loyalist spy at Cambridge,

> but most wretchedly cloathed—and as dirty a set of mortals as
> ever disgraced the name of a Soldier. . . . They have no Women
> in the Camp to do the washing for the men, and they in general
> not being used to doing things of this sort, and thinking it rather
> a disparagement to them, choose rather to let their linen &c. rot
> upon their backs than to be at the trouble of cleaning 'em them-
> selves.

The food was as bad as the clothing and often just as scarce;
during the winter of 1779–1780, for example, the men sometimes
went for a week at a time without bread and just as long without meat.[4] Despite congressional efforts to maintain adequate
standards, living conditions were sometimes indescribable until
after Yorktown. The often impoverished condition of the Continental Army prompted "A DESERTER from the rebel army,
who came into New York this morning," to report

---

[3] "The Rebels," *Pennsylvania Ledger*, Jan. 7, 1778, p. 3; reprinted in
Moore's *Songs*, pp. 196–197, where it is ascribed to Captain Smyth, an
officer in Simcoe's Queen's Rangers.

[4] Benjamin Thompson to Lord Germain, Nov., 1775, *Lexington to
Fallen Timbers*, ed. R. G. Adams and H. H. Peckham (Ann Arbor,
1943), p. 7; Bolton, *Private Soldier*, p. 84.

that the Congress troops are suffering extremely for food and rum; that there is not a whole pair of breeches in the Army, and that the last news from Mr. Washington's camp was, that he had to tie his up with strings, having parted with the buttons to buy the necessaries of life. . . . At a frugal dinner lately given by the under officers in Heath's command, (supposed to be in honor of his *demand* at Fort Independence,) but seven were able to attend; some for the want of clean linen, but the most of them from having none other than breeches past recovery.[5]

All but those of independent means, common soldiers and officers alike, quickly discovered that military duty meant possible bankruptcy. Not only was the pay scale fixed by Congress on July 29, 1775, too low, starting at six and five-sixths dollars a month for privates, it was paid irregularly and in paper instead of specie.[6] Soon desertions and short-term enlistments were common, and in 1780 there was even mutiny in the Pennsylvania Line. In this dark year before the final turn of fortune Congress reluctantly issued an emergency order that "the officers who shall continue in the service to the end of the war, shall . . . be entitled to half pay during life, to commence from the time of their reduction."[7] "Our Delegates in Congress Assembled," a continental irreverently parodied,

Revered be your Characters, your power increased, your will be done in the civil as it is in the Military Line, Give us Month by Month our Monthly pay, Pay us our debts as we wish to Satisfy our Creditors, And lead us not into poverty but deliver us the evils of desbandation, for yours is the right, the power, and the Generous intention of rewarding us with half pay throughout our Lives Amen [.] [8]

[5] Entered in Captain Smythe's "Diary," p. 51; printed in Moore's *Diary*, I, 399–400, for Mar. 1, 1777. In Jan., 1777, Major-General William Heath led 4,000 militia against the poorly defended Fort Independence on the Hudson and, after firing a few shots, demanded that the fort surrender. The British garrison refused, whereupon Heath retired with only some loyalist property to show for his "attack."

[6] *Journals*, II, 220–223.   [7] Oct. 21, 1780, *Journals*, XVIII, 958.

[8] "The Army's Prayer [to Congress for its pay; a parody of the Lord's

At the war's end a divided Congress, envisioning the rise of a professional military class, commuted half pay for life to "five years' full pay." [9] Though there was general opposition in the country to pay in any form, the officers themselves construed the new order as a breach of faith and told Congress so.[10] "A True Massachusettensian" was reminded of the rats who, hearing a cat cry for help from the brewer's vat she had fallen into, scurry to see the sport.

> The cat desir'd them, in all love,
> To help her out, and swore by Jove,
> That if they'd ease her present pain,
> She'd never worry rats again.
> The rats consent, and, puff'd with hopes,
> They hoist her out with little ropes;
> When, wo to them! with glaring eyes,
> All on the wretched throng she flies:
> The speaker rat was first her prey;
> And as he in her talons lay,
> Most humbly su'd for promis'd grace,
> And prov'd the treaty to her face;
> Which so enrag'd and anger'd puss,
> She grip'd him close, and answer'd thus:
> How now, ye vagrants! do ye think
> I'll keep a promise made in drink? [11]

II

Of the officers who commanded this army, themselves in some cases rough-mannered and of humble stock, a sufficient number

---

prayer; 177–?]," MS in Washington's library, Boston Athenaeum; transcribed by John Sherman of the Continental Army, who may have been the author.

[9] Mar. 22, 1783, *Journals*, XXIV, 207.

[10] Merrill Jensen, *The New Nation* (New York, 1950), p. 261.

[11] *Salem Gazette*, July 10, 1783, p. 2. Another fable, entitled "The Lion, the Mastives, and other Beasts," implied that Congress had no intention of honoring "That *vile commute—the five day's pension*" either, *Pennsylvania Journal*, Sept. 24, 1783, p. 2.

possessed the loyalty and integrity necessary to ensure eventual victory.[12] But no greater respect was shown to them by satirists than to the rank and file. Before independence had been won a British officer held the number thirteen up to ridicule:

A party of naval prisoners lately returned from Jersey, say, that the rations among the rebels are thirteen dried clams per day; that the titular Lord Stirling takes thirteen glasses of grog every morning, has thirteen enormous rumbunches on his nose, and that (when duly impregnated) he always makes thirteen attempts before he can walk; that Mr. Washington has thirteen toes on his feet, (the extra ones having grown since the Declaration of Independence,) and the same number of teeth in each jaw; that the Sachem Schuyler has a top-knot of thirteen stiff hairs, which erect themselves on the crown of his head when he grows mad; that Old Putnam had thirteen pounds of his posteriors bit off in an encounter with a Connecticut bear, (It was then he lost the *balance* of his mind;) . . . that Polly Wayne was just thirteen hours in subduing Stony Point; and as many seconds in leaving it.[13]

From the moment he was made commander in chief George Washington was a favorite target. A song to the tune of "Yankee Doodle" celebrated his arrival at Cambridge on July 2, 1775, to assume command of the army.

> Away from camp, 'bout three miles off,
>   From Lily he dismounted,
> His sergeant brush'd his sun-burnt wig
>   While he the specie counted.
>
> All prinked up in *full* bag-wig;
>   The shaking notwithstanding,
> In leathers tight, oh! glorious sight!
>   He reach'd the Yankee landing.
>
>   .   .   .   .   .

[12] Bolton, *Private Soldier*, p. 40; Allen Bowman, *The Morale of the American Revolutionary Army* (Washington, D.C., 1943), p. 104.

[13] Smythe's "Diary," p. 98; printed in Moore's *Diary*, II, 250, for Jan. 1, 1780.

Old mother Hancock with a pan
   All crowded full of butter,
Unto the lovely Georgius ran,
   And added to the splutter.

Says she, "Our brindle has just calved,
   And John is wondrous happy.
He sent this present to you, dear,
   As you're the 'country's papa.' "

     · · · · ·

Full many a child went into camp,
   All dressed in homespun kersey,
To see the greatest rebel scamp
   That ever cross'd o'er Jersey.

     · · · · ·

Upon a stump, he placed (himself,)
   Great Washington did he,
And through the nose of lawyer Close
   Proclaimed great Liberty.[14]

He, too, like Burgoyne was soon heralded as a proclamation maker, even though he was not bombastic. One writer insinuated that his order forbidding "ALL Officers and Soldiers, playing at cards, dice, or at any games, except those of EXERCISE, for diversion," [15] was a bid for the support of "the parsons and other old women stronger in the cause of rebellion."

Old De Heister used to say, "Isht dakes de veek to fool der Deutsche, isht dakes de day to fool de Anglees, isht dakes der tyfel to fool de rebel, but *all* together couldn't fool de Lord." So it is with Mr. Washington:—However easily he may bait old Witherspoon, Billy Livingston, Jacky Jay, and some of the other pious ones, who are hanging on the rear of his *moral* forces; when the time comes, he'll

---

[14] "Adam's Fall," [1775?], n. p.; printed in Moore's *Songs*, pp. 99–102. Lawyer "Close" is probably a reference to Major-General Charles Lee, who accompanied Washington on his journey north from Philadelphia.

[15] May 8, 1777, *The Writings of George Washington*, ed. J. C. Fitzpatrick (Washington, D.C., 1931–1944), VIII, 28–29.

find he can't "fool the Lord" with pretended piety or Presbyterian general orders.[16]

In the dead of the hard winter at Valley Forge, Washington recommended that the inhabitants of New Jersey, Pennsylvania, Maryland, and Virginia "put up and feed immediately as many of their Stock Cattle, as they can spare, so as that they may be driven to this Army . . . for the use of the Army during the Months of May, June and July . . . at the opening of the next campaign." [17] Whereupon a grateful British light infantryman asked:

> And was this order issued for *our* sakes,
> To treat us with roast beef and savory stakes?
> Or was it for thy rebel train intended?
> Give 'em the *hides,* and let their *shoes* be mended;
> Though shoes are what they seldom wear of late;
> 'Twou'd load their *nimble feet* with *too much weight!*

Then, addressing the "honest Whigs" whose livestock Washington so eagerly sought:

> We, to reward you for your care and pains,
> Will visit soon your crowded stalls and plains;
> And for your pamper'd cattle write, at large,
> With bloody bayonets, a full discharge.
>
> . . . . .
>
> Obey your chief's command; and then, 'tis plain,
> We cannot want for *beef* the next campaign! [18]

On July 29, 1779, Washington wrote Joseph Reed, "I have a pleasure in acknowledging the receipt of your obliging favor of the 15th. Instt., and in finding by it, that the author of the quoeries 'Political and Military' has had no great cause to exult

[16] Captain Israel Carver's "Letters," p. 113; printed in Moore's *Diary,* I, 444–445, for June 2, 1777.

[17] Feb. 18, 1778, *Writings of Washington,* X, 480–481.

[18] *Pennsylvania Ledger,* Mar. 25, 1778, p. 3; reprinted in Moore's *Diary,* II, 118.

in the favourable reception of them by the public." Then he added, "Without a clue, I should have been at no great loss to trace the malevolent writer," meaning General Charles Lee.[19] Piqued by Washington's reprimand for his behavior at Monmouth and by his temporary suspension from command as a result of a court-martial he himself had demanded, Lee had prepared some queries. Herein he tried to denigrate Washington's conduct and defend his own during the three years just passed. In the ninth query, for example, he asks, "Whether it is salutary or dangerous, consistent with, or abhorrent from, the principles and spirit of liberty and republicanism, to inculcate and encourage in the people, an idea, that their welfare, safety, and glory, depend on one man?" Other queries followed.

12th. Whether the armies under Gates and Arnold, and the detachment under Starke, to the Northward, or that immediately under his Excellency, in Pennsylvania, gave the decisive turn to the fortune of war? . . .

20th. Whether, in the defeat of Brandewine, General Sullivan was really the person who ought to have been censured? . . .

22d. Whether our position at Valley Forge was not such, that if General Howe, or afterwards General Clinton, had been well informed of its circumstances, defeats, and vices, they might not at the head of ten, or even of eight thousand men, have reduced the American army to the same fatal necessity as the Americans did General Burgoyne? . . .

24th. Whether if the Generals Schuyler and St. Clair, had been tried by the same Court-Martial as General Lee was, and instead of Congress, General Washington had been the prosecutor, those gentlemen (unexceptionable as their conduct was) would not have stood a very ugly chance of being condemned? And whether, if instead of General Washington, Congress has been the prosecutors, General Lee would not probably have been acquitted with the highest honour?

25th. Whether it must not appear to every man who has read General Washington's letter to Congress, on the affair at Mon-

[19] *Writings of Washington*, XVI, 7–8.

mouth, and the proceedings of the Court-Martial, by which General
Lee was tried, that if the contents of the former are facts, not only
General Lee's defence must be a tissue of the most abominable audacious lies, but that the whole string of evidences, both on the part of
the prosecution and prosecuted, must be guilty of rank perjury, as
the testimonies of those gentlemen, near forty in number, delivered on oath, scarcely in one article coincide with the detail given
in his Excellency's letter? [20]

Occasionally generals other than Washington were a topic for
satire. Philip Schuyler, for instance, who held an independent
command in upper New York province until relieved by Gates
in the summer of 1777, led an expedition early in 1776 against
loyalist settlements in Tryon County which was greeted with
heavy sarcasm:

> Hark, hark! the valiant Hero comes!
> With screaming Fifes, and roaring Drums,
>   To search the Vallies through!
> With clamorous Din, in eager chace,
> The well-train'd Pack, from place to place,
>   The destin'd Game pursue.
>
> Their gallant Leader, though of late
> From martial Deeds restrain'd by Fate,
>   Now feels his Courage high;
> With thirst of fame his Bosom burns,
> Before his face where'er he turns,
>   Affrighted Tories fly!
>
>   .   .   .   .   .
>
> Like Caesar brave, in Arms to shine,
> Like Caesar learn'd, the Palm is thine,

[20] "Some Queries, Political and Military," *Maryland Journal*, July 6,
1779, p. 1; reprinted in the *Memoirs of Charles Lee*, pp. 119–122. Taken
into custody by a mob at Baltimore, the printer William Goddard re-
vealed that Lee was the author; on being released, he apologized for this
defamation of Washington in the July 9 issue of the *Journal*, then re-
tracted the apology as extracted by force (John Richard Alden, *General
Charles Lee* [Baton Rouge, 1951], p. 282).

The Laurel and the Bays:
O matchless Champion! skill'd in fight,
And skill'd thy own Exploits to write,
Accept my feeble Praise! [21]

Israel Putnam was a man of great personal courage but seems clearly to have lacked the tactical genius necessary for high, independent command. After the American rout at Long Island, in which as it happened he had acquitted himself well, there appeared an advertisement in the English press:

LOST, an old black dog, of the American breed; answers to the name of PUTNAM:—had on a yellow collar with the following inscription, "*Ubi libertas ibi patriâ*, 1776. Long Island:" is an old domestic animal,—barks very much at the name of N[ort]h, and has a remarkable howl at that of Howe. Was seen in Long Island some time ago, but is supposed to have been alarmed at some British troops who were exercising there, and ran off towards Hellgate. As he was a great favorite of the Washington family, they are fearful some accident has happened to him.[22]

Horatio Gates, after the American rout at Camden, South Carolina, on August 16, 1780, retreated to Hillsborough, North Carolina. "One hundred and eighty miles in three days and a half," wrote Hamilton. "It does admirable credit to the activity of a man at his time of life. But it disgraces the general and the soldier." Although Nathaniel Greene, who had opportunity to study "the disposition and order of battle" after the action at Camden, later assured Gates, "you was unfortunate but not blameable," the impression left by Hamilton's much-publicized letter was not easily dispelled.[23] In a poetic dialogue, which ap-

[21] "The Tory Hunt, or A March into Tryon County," [1776?], in "Loyalist Rhapsodies," pp. 5–6. A loyalist account of this expedition is to be found in Thomas Jones, *History of New York during the Revolutionary War*, ed. E. F. de Lancey (New York, 1879), I, 72–74.

[22] *Middlesex Journal*, Dec. 3, 1776; reprinted in Moore's *Diary*, I, 330.

[23] Letter to James Duane, Sept. 6, 1780, *The Works of Alexander Hamilton* (New York and London, 1904), IX, 205, quoted in Lynn Montross, *Rag, Tag and Bobtail* (New York, 1952), p. 380; George Washington

peared soon after the battle, Jonathan tells Isaac that "Gates, our gallant general, / Has made a new convention." He laments,

> A thousand slaughter'd friends we've lost;
> A thousand more are taken:
> Horatio's steed, which gallop'd post,
> Has sav'd his rider's bacon.

Jonathan and Isaac conclude in tender duet,

> Now mourn, with sack-cloth cover'd o'er,
> Our Israel forsaken!
> So many slain, while such a Boar
> As Gates should save his bacon.[24]

III

As in the case of the British Army though scarcely in proportion to the reverses suffered, military maneuvers on the part of the Continental Army were an object for satire. In the spring of 1776, Sir William Howe's army evacuated Boston, only to reappear at New York that summer. In a protracted campaign Howe succeeded in dislodging the Americans from Long Island, Manhattan, and finally from the mainland immediately to the north. A writer at New York relates how George III, realizing that the rebels continue to defy him, dispatches Howe to chastise them. When British artillery is leveled against the Americans,

> A'ghast they cry out, "Sure Old Harry is here;
> "What thunders, what earthquakes burst full on my ear? Fa la,
> &c.
> "Are these British regulars? 'Zounds I'll away;
> "They shoot at our muns; I'll be damn'd if I stay."

Nimbly the rebels skulk to the woods, "brave Washington" at their head, while Howe advances.

Greene, *The Life of Nathanael Greene* (New York, 1867–1871), III, 54, quoted in Montross, p. 381.

[24] "A Pastoral Elegy," *Royal Gazette*, Sept. 27, 1780, p. 3; reprinted in *Loyalist Poetry*, pp. 119–120.

The impregnable fortress, Long-Island, is taken,
And York and Kingsbridge are forever forsaken. Fa la, &c.
Now where will the Yankies retreat in their flight?
To JEMIMA, be sure; better bundle than fight.[25]

Howe's rout of Washington on Long Island during the final days of August is the subject of an anonymous farce, *The Battle of Brooklyn* (1776), which satirizes the commanding officers in their personal as well as their military character. As the curtain goes up, Lord Stirling is shown groggily at noon on the day before the battle, concerned less with "spitting, and roasting, and pickling these red coat fellows" than with replenishing his canteens. In an aside his insolent servant Joe King confides, "If he has credit enough with the Commissary, to get his canteens filled with rum, he will belch it out of his stomach in the damn'-dest lies, that ever disqualified a man for the character of a gentleman." In the action which ensues the scene shifts frequently. Lady Gates's servant Betty thinks Washington "the sweetest, meekest, melancholy fighting Gentleman," even though he could afford her but a thirty-dollar bill after taking his pleasure. Lady Gates, though, belittles his conduct of the Boston siege ("he did no more than that old fool Putnam would have done") and deplores her husband's involvement in the war: "O Horatio! that you should sully your laurels in the abominable cause of republican Tyrants, and Smugglers in power: to be runnagate for such miscreants, almost distracts me." On the point of battle Washington confides to Sullivan what it is he really fears: "My apprehensions from the King's troops believe me are trifling, compared with the risque we run, from the people of America at large. The tyranny, that our accursed usurpation has made necessary, which they now feel, and feeling, I fear, will soon make them see through the disguise. Their rage no doubt will be heightened by the slaughter that will probably ensue; and we, as members of the Congress fall the first victims of it."

[25] "*A new* SONG, *Composed by a Prisoner in* Boston Goal," *Royal American Gazette*, Jan. 16, 1777, p. 2.

Putnam, who had bragged in council of throwing up a breast-
work across the Bedford road between two three-foot walls and
who has for some time been profiteering in horse smuggling,
now lusts to confiscate the property of loyalists: "As the best
estates in America belong to them, it is but cooking up some new
fangled oath, which their squeamish consciences wont let them
swallow; then, whip go their estates, like a juggler's ninepence,
and themselves to prison, to be hanged as traitors to the commonwealth." So ends the first act. The second, which is set on
the day of battle, finds the Americans on the point of being
routed. A retreating Pennsylvanian tells Sullivan, "by my soul,
honey, you have brought old Ireland about your ears, at last;
and we can find the way to eat iron without asking such vermin
as you for victuals." Learning that their retreat has been cut off,
Sullivan announces that his troops may do just as they please:
"every man is now his own General, so Gentlemen farewel." The
closing scene finds Joe King and Sullivan's servant Noah alone
in a room at Brooklyn Ferry, where the Americans are crossing
over to Manhattan. Just thinking about the Congress infuriates
Noah: "From the first meeting of that *Hydra* at Philadelphia, its
sixty-four mouths, have all been open to devour two strangers!
. . . Power! and Riches!" After this harangue both reaffirm
their loyalty to King George.[26]

While this farce, in the first act especially, darts from scene
to scene with little regard for unity of action, the rapid succession of episodes affords the reader close-ups of the officers and
their retinue in ludicrous postures. A farcical subplot, though
not immediately to the purpose, pictures two colonels, one a
shoemaker the other a rum retailer in civilian life, engaged in
rounding up cattle for transport to loyalists in Connecticut, taking care all the while to shirk their military duties lest they come

[26] *The Battle of Brooklyn, a Farce of Two Acts* (New York, 1776);
reprinted as Long Island Publication No. 1 (Brooklyn, 1873), pp. 9–45,
which edition I consulted. In actual fact William Alexander, better known
as Lord Stirling, displayed great courage during the battle in the face
of overwhelming odds.

within firing range of the British. Such carefully drawn indigenous types are the play's principal strength.

In August, 1778, Comte d'Estaing brought his fleet to Rhode
Island, where he was to co-operate with Sullivan, commanding
American land forces, in an attack on Newport. Admiral Howe's
arrival at the last moment with a smaller British fleet prompted
D'Estaing to re-embark; a storm so crippled the French fleet that
D'Estaing decided to sail to Boston for refitting, whereupon
Sullivan had to retire.[27] In a satirical ballad Jonathan (Sullivan),
encouraged by the prospect of support from the French, vows to
lead his forces against Rhode Island.

> In dread array their tatter'd crew,
>   Advanc'd with colors spread, sir,
> Their fifes played Yankee doodle, doo,
>   King Hancock at their head, sir.
>
> What numbers bravely cross'd the seas,
>   I cannot well determine,
> A swarm of rebels and of fleas,
>   And every other vermin.
>
>   .   .   .   .   .
>
> They swore they'd make bold Pigot squeak,
>   So did their good ally, sir,
> And take him pris'ner in a week,
>   But that was all my eye, sir.
>
> As Jonathan so much desir'd
>   To shine in martial story,
> D'Estaing with politesse retir'd,
>   To leave him all the glory.[28]

[27] Wallace, *Appeal to Arms*, pp. 193–194; Montross, *Rag, Tag*, pp. 291–
297 *passim*.

[28] "Yankee Doodle's Expedition to Rhode Island," *Royal Gazette*, Oct.
3, 1778, p. 3; reprinted in Moore's *Songs*, pp. 231–234. John Hancock took
command of the Second Massachusetts Line. Sir Robert Pigot commanded
the British forces in Rhode Island.

The Marquis de Lafayette was angered by Sullivan's contention that the operation had failed because French naval forces had not co-operated with his land forces.[29] The New York press carried a report burlesquing Lafayette's sense of outrage. "Don Quixotto, Drawcansiro de Fayetto," highly offended by Sullivan's refusal to give him satisfaction, posts to Congress in high dudgeon.

A challenge was accordingly delivered to each member, but as none of these gentlemen had ever worn a sword, and as those who receive a challenge have the right to choose their weapon, there were warm debates and great diversity of opinions concerning the instrument of death most proper to be used; some declared for needles, some for bodkins, some for ploughshares, some for gray goose quills, and some for clyster pipes.

While three members attempt to resolve the matter with the French minister Gérard, Lafayette "amused himself before the glass, taking snuff, and now and then cutting a little caper." Gérard decides that "the Marquis must fight the Yankees in their own way."

Our young hero, violently offended with such indignity, and resolutely determined to support the honor of his king by some signal exploit, set out instantly for Boston, and on the road, in imitation of the Spanish knight, resolutely encountered a flock of sheep and a windmill. What limbs were lost in this engagement, our correspondent does not mention, but the young Quixote swears, par blue, that Franklin, the Congress, their Generals, &c., are all a pack of jean f[out]res.[30]

At the end of December, 1778, the British captured Savannah. On October 9, 1779, a Franco-American attempt to recapture the town, led by Benjamin Lincoln and D'Estaing, failed. Jona-

[29] James B. Perkins, *France in the American Revolution* (Boston and New York, 1911), pp. 269–270.

[30] *Royal Gazette*, Oct. 21, 1778, p. 3; reprinted in Moore's *Diary*, II, 93–94n. In Buckingham's farce, *The Rehearsal*, Drawcansir is a caricature of the heroic character type.

than Odell, treating the affair with a mixture of invective and heavy-handed irony, pictures D'Estaing's forces setting sail from St. Domingo. "To catch the British napping was their thought; / Now, by my faith, a Tartar have they caught." When the British refuse to surrender, D'Estaing lays siege to the town: "The Gallic Chief, his batteries complete, / Conceives the British humbled at his feet." Thinking to strike terror in them, the French begin a cannonade.

> What, no slain warriors tumbled in the trench?
> Yes, by the Mass:—abundance of the French!
> No cannon yet dismounted can you see?
> Oh yes—a number marked with *Fleurs de Lys.*

The order for assault is given, but "Such desperate efforts the battalions thin. / Disorder and dismay and rout begin." At this point Lincoln's continentals go berserk:

> Deuce take the fools, they level at their friends!
> Some angry Demon sure their sense misleads;
> See, the French tremble, and their General bleeds.
> By rebel hands (Lo! Providence is just)
> The rebels' patron wounded bites the dust.

In terror the allies flee the field. "D'Estaing betakes him to his ship," and Lincoln leaves 1,500 dead and wounded "weltering on the bloody plain." Odell concludes, "What, both o'erthrown, America and France, / By one small splinter of the British Lance!" [31]

On July 20, 1780, Washington sent Anthony Wayne to storm the British blockhouse at Bull's Ferry four miles below Fort Lee on the Hudson and drive the cattle in the neighborhood within the American lines. Wayne returned to camp with a large number of cattle, but the cavalry sent against the blockhouse were repulsed with heavy losses. John André in a parody on "Chevy Chase" celebrated the sally. Early one summer's morn Wayne informs his men of Washington's order:

[31] "The Feu de Joie," *Royal Gazette,* Nov. 24, 1779, p. 2; reprinted in *Loyal Verses,* pp. 52–57.

"Their fort and block-houses we'll level,
　　And deal a horrid slaughter;
We'll drive the scoundrels to the devil,
　　And ravish wife and daughter.

"I, under cover of attack,
　　Whilst you are all at blows,
From English neighb'rhood and Nyack
　　Will drive away the cows;

"For well you know the latter is
　　The serious operation,
And fighting with the refugees
　　Is only demonstration."

At noon the men, now "drunk as pison," prepare for the assault.

The sounds confus'd of boasting oaths,
　　Re-echo'd through the wood;
Some vow'd to sleep in dead men's clothes,
　　And some to swim in blood.

At Irving's nod 'twas fine to see,
　　The left prepare to fight;
The while, the drovers, Wayne and Lee,
　　Drew off upon the right.

At the blockhouse the "loyal heroes" stand firm against Irving.

Now, as the fight was further fought,
　　And balls began to thicken,
The fray assum'd, the generals thought,
　　The color of a lickin'.

Yet undismay'd the chiefs command,
　　And to redeem the day;
Cry, Soldiers, charge! they hear, they stand,
　　They turn and run away.

While Lee is busy driving off the cattle, Wayne is quite willing
to be distracted.

For now a prey to female charms,
　　His soul took more delight in

> A lovely hamadryad's arms,
>   Than cow-driving or fighting.

She takes him by the "bridle of his jade" and convinces him that he should give over the expedition.

> The hamadryad had but half
>   Receiv'd address from Wayne,
> When drums and colors, cow and calf,
>   Came down the road amain.
>
> And in a cloud of dust was seen
>   The sheep, the horse, the goat,
> The gentle heifer, ass obscene,
>   The yearling and the shoat.
>
> And pack-horses with fowls came by,
>   Befeather'd on each side;
> Like Pegasus, the horse that I
>   And other poets ride.
>
> Sublime upon his stirrups rose
>   The mighty Lee behind,
> And drove the terror-smitten cows
>   Like chaff before the wind.

Suddenly this drove encounters another. It is the fleeing cavalry, "Irving and terror in the van."

> As when two kennels in the street,
>   Swell'd with a recent rain,
> In gushing streams together meet,
>   And seek the neighboring drain;
>
> So met these dung-born tribes in one,
>   As swift in their career,
> And so to Newbridge they ran on—
>   But all the cows got clear.

At this juncture a frantic parson prophesies brighter days ahead. His words console all save Wayne, who has lost his horse—

> His horse that carried all his prog,
>   His military speeches;
> His corn-stock whiskey for his grog,
>   Blue stockings and brown breeches.
>
> And now I've clos'd my epic strain,
>   I tremble as I show it,
> Lest this same warrior-drover, Wayne,
>   Should ever catch the poet.[32]

André has substituted for the bloody border warfare, which ended only with the death of the Earls Percy and Douglas on the third day of battle, General Wayne's humiliating defeat in the course of a raid on nothing more consequential than a British blockhouse. His elevated manner of treating this matter creates the incongruity which makes this ballad successful high burlesque.

Although its military strategy was frequently amateurish, the shortage of matériel acute, and the soldiers themselves unable until the latter years of the war to withstand the advance of British regulars, the Continental Army muddled through. Timely foreign aid, the selfless devotion of a few high-ranking officers, and, most significant of all, the simple matter of physiography held the key to final victory. Had victory gone to the British, the satirical record would undoubtedly have been weightier and more often personal. Modest though it is, the record we do possess enlivens the military chronicle.

[32] "The Cow-Chace," *Royal Gazette*, Aug. 16, 30, Sept. 23, 1780; reprinted in Moore's *Songs*, pp. 299–314. "Irving" is Brigadier-General William Irvine, and "Lee," Major Henry ("Lighthorse Harry") Lee.

CHAPTER IX

Patriots

"DOES Parliament possess the right to tax or even legislate for the colonies?" As the prewar decade wore on, it became
steadily clearer that here was the crucial question which would
ultimately rend the American community. In 1763, the Seven
Years' War having come to an end, Britain chose to reassert a
principle she had always reserved the right to apply, that of
parliamentary sovereignty. The more stringent colonial policy
which followed inclined most Americans in time toward either
the patriot or the loyalist camp; the signing of the Declaration of
Independence simply formalized a rift that had long been de-
veloping.

At the outset of this period the seed from which a patriot party
would grow had been germinating for more than a century.
Those who identified themselves with this party reasoned that
by virtue of rights set down in their charters, in the British Constitution, and finally by the very "Laws of Nature and of Nature's God," they, though British subjects still, had all but
achieved home rule. But the "Revolution was not merely a
question of 'home rule,'" as Carl Becker has so felicitously put
it; "it was also a question of who should rule at home." [1] So it
is that from at least as early as the time of the Stamp Act a dis-

[1] *Am. Hist. Rev.*, XXIX (1924), 345.

tinction must be made between conservative and radical patriots.

The conservatives, who generally represented the property interests within the patriot community, respected law and order at all times. Sharing in the century's fear of democracy, they subscribed to a theory of constitutionalism that embraced the ideas inherent in the social compact.[2] While the compact was sometimes construed to include man's natural rights to revolution and national independence, the conservatives, skirting such implications, envisioned for America dominion status within the British Empire. In the prewar decade the voice of conservatism, drowned out momentarily by the noise of the Stamp Act and the Townshend Act mobs, was dominant, in the press, in assembly and town meeting, in the home. In fact, until the time of the tea demonstrations the conservatives were, in the words of Charles M. Andrews, "in the saddle, able to control the movement and hold the radicals in check."[3] A typical conservative of these years is John Dickinson, the "Pennsylvania Farmer," whose arguments for home rule were so logically couched as to win wide acceptance at home and abroad. It is not without significance that at a later date he would absent himself from Congress rather than place his signature on the document declaring the colonies free and independent states.

Except in Massachusetts and Virginia the voice of radicalism sounded feebly until 1774. Not that the radicals lacked numerical strength—frontiersmen, farmers, town laborers swelled the ranks—but it was only in the 1770's that their cause attracted a sufficient number of intellectual leaders to become an articulate and dynamic movement. As the balance of power shifted in favor of the radicals, the vision of dominion status was gradually replaced by another more revolutionary still: national independence. Proponents of the new vision, Thomas Paine for one, found it expedient to ground their arguments less in charter and constitutional rights and more in natural rights.

[2] Max Savelle, *Seeds of Liberty* (New York, 1948), p. 291.
[3] *Colonial Background*, p. 148.

I

Early in the Revolutionary period the phrase "Sons of Liberty" became a synonym for American radicals. Originally, the phrase was applied to those who opposed the Stamp Act and, opposing, organized themselves at the local level to effect a repeal; but when gangs bent on violence borrowed the name, it "came to have a distinctly bad odor." [4] Many conservative and loyal-minded Americans would have regarded the local Sons of Liberty as deserving of the invective heaped on the "Whig" of this poem written in the late sixties.

> He's a rebel by nature, a villain in grain,
> A saint by profession, who never had grace.
> Cheating and lying are puny things;
> Rapine and plundering venial sins;
> His great occupation is ruining nations,
> Subverting of Crowns, and murdering Kings.
>
> To show that he came from a wight of worth,
> 'Twas Lucifer's pride that first gave him birth:
> 'Twas bloody Barbarity bore the elf:
> Ambition the midwife that brought him forth.
> Old Judas was tutor, until he grew big;
> Hypocrisy taught him to care not a fig
> For all that is sacred,—and thus was created
> And brought in the world, what we call a Whig.
>
> Spew'd up among mortals by hellish jaws,
> To strike he begins at religion and laws;

[4] Miller, *Origins*, p. 145. During the Parliamentary debate on the Stamp Act, Isaac Barré had used the phrase "Sons of Liberty" in a speech defending the right of Americans to greater political freedom. Schlesinger, *Prelude*, pp. 13–14, writes: "The Sons of Liberty ceased to exist as a clearly identifiable group by the early 1770's only to reappear in the guise of so-called mechanics' committees. But the original name continued to be used, as it had earlier in many parts of the South, as a generic designation of uncompromising patriots."

> With pious inventions, and bloody intentions,
> And all for to bring in the good of the cause.[5]

Not until 1774, however, did the emerging loyalist press direct more than occasional fire at the Sons. In the fall of that year a writer at New York, in the course of a list of queries that ranges so widely as never to achieve an over-all unity, asked pointedly:

10. Whether the disorder of the colonies, to speak in language taken from animal bodies, be not of the *feverish* kind, as it is attended with an irregular high pulse, and discovers, in some parts, a dangerous swelling and inflammation; and whether it has not been occasioned, in a great measure, by their own *imprudence* and *intemperance?*

11. Whether *heating doses* do not, in all cases, tend to increase a fever; and whether inflammatory publications and harangues be not so many heating doses, with regard to political bodies? . . .

76. Whether the colonies, in a great measure, have not, for ten years past, been under an iniquitous and tyrannical government, namely, the government of unprincipled *mobs;* and whether experience has not yet convinced us, that this mode of governing a country is most detestable?

77. Whether the *sons of liberty* have ever *willingly* allowed to others the liberty of thinking and acting for themselves; and whether any other liberty than that of doing as *they* shall direct, is to be expected during their administration? . . .

89. Whether the several colonies, by having chosen delegates to represent them at the congress, have not taken the matter in dispute out of the hands of the people; and whether those, who, notwithstanding, still endeavour farther to inflame the passions of the populace, already intoxicated with a few magical sounds, are not to be considered and treated as incendiaries, scattering abroad the firebrands of faction, in order to bring on the conflagration of their country? [6]

[5] "The Origin, Description and Portrait of a Whig. An Old Song," *New York Journal*, May 5, 1768, p. 4; reprinted in *Loyalist Poetry*, pp. 56–57, wherein Sargent conjectures, "The piece seems to smack of an English origin."
[6] *The American Querist* (New York, 1774), pp. 8–9, 43–44, 49–50.

And in *The Americans Roused* (1775) Parson Sharp assures his susceptible tavern audience that the firebrand patriot, when he has encountered the military might of Great Britain, will exclaim with his dying breath:

"What have I done, foolish man that I was—why did I blindly rush upon certain ruin—now that my passions are cooled, and reason, alas! too late, has resumed her seat, all those imaginary grievances disappear—I now die a traitor and rebel by the laws of my country—my estate is forfeited—my affectionate wife and our innocent babes, the sweet pledges of our loves—how have I, who ought to have been their guide and protector—how have I left them friendless, forlorn, destitute of the means of procuring daily bread—to what hardships, dangers and distresses have I abandoned them—O my God, how shall I look up in this hour of torture—take them, O take them under thy protection—for they are innocent of the heavy crime that now weighs down the soul of their unhappy husband and father." [7]

II

"The New Englanders," wrote the English traveler Nicholas Cresswell on October 19, 1774, "by their canting, whining, insinuating tricks have persuaded the rest of the Colonies that the Government is going to make absolute slaves of them. This I believe never was intended, but the Presbyterian rascals have had address sufficient to make the other Colonies come into their Scheme." [8] In the case of Massachusetts at least, there was ample justification for such a charge: for a decade patriots there had been a constant irritant to the British government; now, even as Cresswell was writing, the Massachusetts delegates at Philadelphia were vigorously opposing Joseph Galloway's plan for re-

---

C. H. Vance, *Columbia Univ. Quar.*, XXII (1930), 276, asserts that the Anglican minister Thomas Bradbury Chandler is the author, not Myles Cooper, to whom it has usually been attributed. Evans notes that the book was "so violently in favor of toryism, that it was publicly burned by the Sons of Liberty," *American Bibliography*, V, 19.

[7] *Magazine of History*, XX, 147.

[8] *The Journal of Nicholas Cresswell* (New York, 1924), p. 44.

conciliation with Britain. Long after the Stamp Act had been repealed, Boston Sons of Liberty, unlike most others, continued to urge their cause. When the American Secretary, Hillsborough, denounced the Assembly's Circular Letter challenging the legality of the Townshend Revenue Act, the Sons visited their wrath upon the collectors of customs sent over to help execute it. Anne Hulton, whose brother was one of the commissioners, reports:

Mrs Burch at whose house I was, had frequently been alarm^d with the Sons of Liberty surround^g her house with most hideous howlings as the Indians, when they attack an Enemy, to many insults & outrages. . . . These Sons of Voilence after attacking Houses, break^g Window, beating, Stoning & bruizing several Gentlemen belong^g to the Customs, the Collector mortally, & burning his boat, They consult^d what was to be done next, & it was agreed to retire for the night. . . . This is a Specimen of the Sons of Liberty, of whom no doubt you have heard, & will hear more.[9]

When it was learned that the British government was sending troops to Boston, radicalism there greatly increased.[10] Three days before the troops arrived, a local writer in a parody on the then-popular "Liberty Song" inveighed against the Sons:

Such villains, such rascals, all dangers despise,
And stick not at mobbing when mischief's the prize;
They burst thro' all barriers, and piously keep
Such chattels and goods the vile rascals can sweep.

The Tree, which the wisdom of justice hath rear'd,
Should be stout for their use, and by no means be spar'd:
When fuddled with rum the mad sots to restrain,
Sure Tyburn will sober the wretches again. . . .

Then plunder, my lads, for when red coats appear,
You'll melt like the locust when winter is near.[11]

[9] Letter of June 30, 1768, *Letters of a Loyalist Lady* (Cambridge, Mass., 1927), pp. 11–12.
[10] John C. Miller, *Sam Adams* (Boston, 1936), p. 143.
[11] *Boston Gazette*, Sept. 26, 1768, Supplement Extraordinary, p. 2; re-

In fair political weather and foul the local press continued to attack radicalism down to the outbreak of hostilities. "Patrick McAdam O'Flagharty, Esq.," addressing "the sweet Electors of the Town of Boston," offers his services:

I am told you have some meetings here called *caucasses* do you see, or some such *outlandish* word, where they make all the Representatives and Town-Officers. . . . I will but just hint at my qualifications, with as much prolixity as may be: I can *tar* and *feather* any body with the best of you, ay and *cart* them to the D– – –l and all; In *dear Ireland* . . . I was one of the foremost of our gang, and would rob my own Father to serve the *common cause*, but that does not magnify at all: For I was a great man of note in my sweet *West of Ireland*, an *Excise-Man*, next to the LORD LIEUTENANT, one of the KING's *chief Officers* there. . . . I collected a good round bagfull of money, and what did I do with it? Why by my shoul I spent it. . . . My dear Cousin *O'Connolly*, . . . a sweet *Son of Liberty*, . . . informed me . . . that this was the country for an honest industrious-like Gentleman to get his bread in, and rise in the world. . . . I have got a sweet *shillaly* for all sorts of *Tories*, faith! here's at them. . . .[12]

And a swaggering "Boston Whig-Maker" inadvertently puns:

Jack Wilkes the whig-maker first set up the trade,
And many a whig in his time he has made;
But Whigs now in London being quite out of fashion,
He thought it most prudent to drop the profession.

But I, his Successor, in Boston Well known,
I make all the whigs both in country and town;
Pray send your heads to me, and little or big,
I've blocks of all sizes, I'll make you a whig.

---

printed in the *Scots Magazine*, XXX (Nov., 1768), 599, and again in Moore's *Songs*, pp. 41–43.

[12] *The Censor* (Boston), Feb. 29, 1772, pp. 57–59. This is an early example of the comic use to which the Irishman was to be put in American political satire, anticipating by a generation such memorable figures as Brackenridge's Teague O'Regan in *Modern Chivalry*.

> Tho' many large whigs on the Fort-hill appears,
> There are none to be seen 'mongst the Welch fuzileers;
> Tho' the folks on the Common affect to look big,
> Yet among the whole number there is not one whig.
>
> Tho' to you, my good friends, it may seem uncommon,
> Yet I'll make a whig that shall fit any woman,
> For I've known many ladies who've bottoms as full
> As ever yet sat upon any Numskull.[13]

The attack on the Sons of Liberty at Boston in the prewar years was frequently personal. Their leader in the sixties was James Otis, whom John C. Miller calls "the most formidable enemy of royal government in America" at this time.[14] His very real talents for organization and debate are the subject of a political ballad:

> And Jemmy's a town-meeting-man, and Jemmy makes a speech,
> And Jemmy swears that *Liberty* and *Liberty* he'll preach,
> And Jemmy's in the *Caucas*, and Jemmy's with the *Reps*,
> And all who'd rise as Jemmy rose must tread in Jemmy's steps.
>
> . . . . .
>
> And Jemmy is a sorry jade,—ah! Jemmy hasn't mettle,
> And Jemmy *pleads* his bloody nose when quarrels he shou'd settle!
> And Jemmy is as great a puff as Jemmy's a poltroon,—
> 'Tis Jemmy *blusters* all the morn to *slink* away at noon.[15]

In 1770, Samuel Adams, who had first come into prominence at the time of the Stamp Act, assumed leadership of the Boston revolutionary movement when Otis, never fully recovering from a clubbing he had received in a Boston tavern the year before, passed into a mental decline. One of Adams' most trusted asso-

[13] "The Boston Whig-Maker," bound with Thomas Bolton's *Oration* (Boston, 1775), pp. 8–9. Bolton may have been the author.

[14] *Sam Adams*, p. 88.

[15] "Jemmibullero: INSTEAD of Lillibullero," *Boston Evening Post*, May 13, 1765, p. 2; reprinted in 1766 as a [New York?] broadside. This ballad has been attributed to Samuel Waterhouse (*DAB*, XIV, 103).

ciates was Doctor Thomas Young, who came from Albany to Boston in 1766 with a reputation as a zealous Son of Liberty.[16] Adams and Young were attacked in a letter of 1767 to the Boston press, which explores a low-burlesque situation with considerable success. "It is really very hard," the writer begins, "that people can't walk the streets of your town, without being plagued with a pack of *Cur-Dogs*, that keep continually running between their legs, yelping, babling and barking, as if they really intended to bite; . . . they are apt to throw dirt about them and spatter people as they pass about their business." One of these "untoward puppies" is named "Jet" (Samuel Adams).

This dog is very artful, loves blabbling, especially when he gets into a very large Room; has been taught to run into houses, to pick up money, and run away with it directly to his kennel . . . but it is said his Masters (for he belongs to the whole parish) are determined to find out what he has done with this Money (one would imagine this sagacious cur really knew his Masters intentions (for the moment he sees any of them, he runs to them, fawns, licks their hands and leaps upon them with so much cunning and good humour, that they forget all about the Money, spit in his mouth, clap him on the side; then away goes Jet, wagging his tail, and glad enough you may be assured. . . . Jet the other day stray'd into a Vestry (it happened to be a very large one) and in a moment distinguished the smell and voice of one of his best Friends, who was the head of the meeting—then it was that Jet set up his throat—his Master seemed pleased and encouraged him to proceed—Jet barked the louder—the Master found his account in it; and in short, between Jet's noise and the Master's taking the advantage of it—the Vestry was glad to come into Jet's Master's absurd measures—in consequence of which signal service Jet's Master promises that none of the residue of his Masters shall dog him to find out where he has hid the money. . . . Now the best way to get rid of this artful Cur is, to hold a piece of money between your fore finger and

[16] Miller, *Sam Adams,* pp. 82, 218, 219, 236; Davidson, *Propaganda,* p. 26.

thumb, and shew it him in a laughing way, I'll warrant you away he scampers.

"Here comes a large, frouzy-headed, hard, savage countenanced Mungrel Cur of the Dutch breed; he answers to the name of Doctor." If you call,

he won't come up to you; but rather run some distance from you, and look behind and grin—and seem a little madish, which he is something addicted to, having met with an ugly accident (being formerly very fond of sculking into apothecaries shops, in general pretty hungry) happened to lap up a mixture that lay in a skillet, intended for the use of a Burgo-Master, *a posteriori*—Poor Doctor no sooner found out his mistake, then away he runs yelping, with his tail between his legs, and never stop'd to look behind him, from A————y gate till he arrived in your town; where he now herds with a mixed pack of bablers. . . . The way to get rid of him is to put your hand upon your rump and hiss at him, he'll walk off directly.[17]

Edes and Gill's *Boston Gazette* and, after 1770, Isaiah Thomas' *Massachusetts Spy* were rallying points for radicalism in Massachusetts. Among those who contributed to their pages and otherwise supported them were Samuel Adams, Samuel Cooper, John Hancock, William Molineux, Josiah Quincy, Jr., Joseph Warren, and Thomas Young—a fact not lost on the government party. Here is a recipe, writes a Hutchinsonian, "to make a *modern* PATRIOT for the *colonies*, especially for the *Massachusetts*, to wit."

Take of impudence, virulence, and groundless abuse, *quantum sufficit*; of flowing periods, *half a drachm*; conscience a *quarter* of a *scruple*; atheism, deism, and libertinism, *ad libitum*; false reports well adapted, and plausible lies, with groundless alarms, *one hundred wt. avoirdupois*; a malignant abuse of Magistracy, a pusillanimous and diabolical contempt of divine revelation and all its abettors *an equal quantity*; honour and integrity not quite an *atom*; fraud, im-

---

[17] *Boston Evening Post*, Nov. 23, 1767, p. 4. Miller identifies "Jet" as Samuel Adams (*Sam Adams*, p. 98).

position, and hypocrisy, any *proportion* that may seem expedient; infuse these in the credulity of the people, *one thousand gallons* as a *menstrum*, stir in the *phrenzy* of the *times*, and at the end of a year or two, this judicious composition will probably bring forth a Y– – – –, an A– – – –, an O– – –, and a M– – – – – – –.[18]

"This day an Oration was delivered by a Dirty Scoundrel from Mrs Cordis' Balcony wherein many Characters were Unfairly Represented & much abused & mine among the Rest," records the Boston merchant John Rowe in his diary for March 15, 1775, alluding to a mock oration by Dr. Thomas Bolton.[19] Bolton, perhaps recalling the Tea Party of recent memory, opens with a metaphor that would have given the work greater coherence and sharper focus had he held to it steadily:

These *sachems*, or *Indian chiefs*, tho' of different titles, all proceeded from one and the same tribe. . . . It was a matter of dispute for some time whether they were of the *Mohawk* kind or not; and this suspicion, I imagine, first arose from the observation of a learned physiognomist, who perceiving their Os *frontis* to be uncommonly flat, burst out into the following exclamation:

> "Your sapsculls are neither square, oval, nor round,
> "A proof that their judgments can never be found:
> "I really believe they are put wrong way on,
> "As they seem to resemble a cobler's lap-stone."

Notwithstanding, these chiefs openly declare "themselves to be neither more or less than plain Narragansets; who scorn'd to scalp any person who would submit to have his private property destroyed, without complaining." The first is Sam Adams, "a sachem of vast elocution; but being extremely poor, retails out syllables, sentences, eulogiums, &c. to draw in the multitude; and it can be attested, that what proceeds from the mouth of

---

[18] *The Censor*, Feb. 8, 1772, p. 48. Copies at the American Antiquarian Society and the Boston Public Library identify the four patriots as Dr. Thomas Young, Samuel Adams, James Otis, and William Molineux.

[19] *Letters and Diary*, p. 290.

A–––Ms is sufficient to fill the mouths of millions in America. But it is prophesied that the time is near at hand, when the frothy food will fail them." Another of "these incomparable *Indians*" is John Rowe, who "having a skull of an uncommon thickness, and the sutures of the *cranium* being closely compacted, . . . has never been able to display any rational faculties, except when he invented the new method of making Tea." Still another is Dr. Joseph Warren,

a man, who by his great skill in chemistry, could *turn water* into *milk*, and sell it for *six coppers* the quart. He was bound apprentice to an apothecary, and turn'd out for a Quack; but thinking this profession too grovelling for so sublime a genius, he has lately changed it for that of *Orator*, and is already so great a proficient in the *sough*, or true *puritanic whine*, and his notes are so remarkably flat and productive of horror, that when he dismisses his hearers, you would swear they were just come out of the cave of Triphonius.

The oration concludes with a Butlerian portrait of Samuel Cooper, who indulges in political as well as religious dissent:

"When gospel trumpter surrounded
"With long-ear'd rout to battle sounded,
"And pulpit, drum ecclesiastic,
"Was beat with fist instead of a stick;"
He, prostituting his religion,
Turns a dispenser of sedition;
And to the greedy, gaping million,
For holy writ, deals out rebellion;
His sacred function quite forsaking,
Smells profit in oration making.[20]

[20] *An Oration Delivered March Fifteenth, 1775 . . . By Dr. Thomas Bolton* (Boston, 1775), pp. 1–8. Pre-eminent among the Dissenting clergy of Boston who espoused the radical cause was Samuel Cooper of the Brattle Street Church, a polished gentleman "particularly hated by the Tories and the British" (Alice M. Baldwin, *The New England Clergy and the American Revolution* [Durham, 1928], p. 93). Joseph Warren was a radical pamphleteer who fell at Bunker Hill. The others satirized in this oration are Hancock, Charles Lee, Molineux, Quincy, and Young.

III

While it was Massachusetts that labored most steadily to keep the fires of revolution stoked in the decade following the Stamp Act, colonies to the south were not altogether idle. New York, for one. Here the line separating radical from conservative was more sharply drawn than in Massachusetts. On the occasion of the Stamp Act, remarks Carl Becker, "the radical leaders, finding themselves in a minority, identified conservative opposition to their policy with royal oppression, and came to regard themselves, therefore, as the only true patriots—as preëminently the *Sons of Liberty.*" This division within the patriot camp was intensified when in 1768 radical leaders like Alexander McDougall and John Lamb insisted on a rigid enforcement of the nonimportation agreement. As a result of his behavior soon after, McDougall was widely acclaimed and vilified as the American John Wilkes. On December 16, 1769, his handbill *To the Betrayed Inhabitants of the City and Colony of New York* was published anonymously, excoriating the provincial assembly for, ignominiously as he thought, voting supplies to maintain the British troops then quartered in the colony. Arrested on a charge of libel when finally his authorship became known, McDougall was sent to prison for refusing to give bail; later he was released without a trial.[21] On February 9, 1770, the morning following his arrest, the betrayed inhabitants were reminded in a broadside that as a boy McDougall had peddled milk.

> SAY, great M'MILKMAN, why so loud,
> And why so pestilent and proud,
> And wherefore all this dismal cry
> For *independent* LIBERTY;

[21] Becker, *Political Parties*, pp. 50, 80, 81; Becker, *Eve*, p. 146; Halsey, *Port Bill*, pp. 218–219.

Say, SAWNEY, say?—For 'tis not long since,
Instead of all this Noise and Nonsense,
We saw thee trudge, as most was meet,
With MILKPAILS two along the Street.

. . . . .

The most *obsequious Servant* THEN,
Of *serving Maids*, and *serving Men*,
But now the TYRANT—more's the Pity—
Of half the FREEMEN in the CITY.

. . . . .

—The Hog that has no Yoke upon't
At will may root, and groan, and grunt:
And SAWNEY now from Bonds hath broke,
And left—like *other Hogs*—his YOKE.[22]

Later that spring Hugh Gaine printed twelve letters to the
press, entitled "The Dougliad," in which the writer (or, as
seems more likely, writers) attacked McDougall and defended
the provincial government's management of the whole affair.
Not to the legislature, the magistracy, or men of rank and property, sneers the first letter, but "to the TRUE sons of liberty only
it belongs, to *speak and act without Controul.*" Catiline, Masani-
ello, Cade, Cromwell, and now McDougall are five such true
sons.

How immensely then are we indebted to our American champion,
for his patriotic and seasonable address, to the betrayed inhabitants
of this city and colony! What an air of noble freedom breaths thro'
every line! How keen! How bold! How insolent! Not even the
pen of a junius could have contrived an essay, better calculated,
to blind and seduce, to distract and disunite, to foment discontent, tumults and sedition; and in short to trample down all legal
authority, and shake the government to the foundation. Hail illustrious M'Dougall! thou constellation of all *Cromwelian* and *Cadean*
graces, hail! thrice honoured be thy most auspicious name! let *men*
admire, *virgins* sing, and matrons *mumble* thy exalted virtues.

[22] "Out-Lines," New York broadside, 1770.

McDougall preferred prison to giving bail, for a

dreary prison is, in his estimation, the paradise of Mahomet, graced
with forty-five black eyed virgins, who are continually caressing him;
while those angels of light, the TRUE sons of liberty, are offering in-
cense at his shrine. Such is their zeal, that he sickens for retirement,
even in a prison, and beseeches his admirers to allow him some little
time, for contemplating the vast projects he has in view, for the
public good.

The second letter innocently declares that since "we are not
confined to *Truth*" in the newspaper, we may here ascribe to
McDougall "*Honour, Sense, Integrity, Virtue, Patriotism,* with
our Friend *Hambden* [a pro-McDougall writer]; and I will add,
Politeness, Modesty, Diligence, Humility, Charity, and good
Humour." Let us therefore "engage the Printers in the different
Colonies, to insert in their Papers, as from themselves, Sentiments
honourable to our Hero, and reproachful to the Government
under which he suffers."

Swear that there is no Distinction between *Freedom* and *Licentious-
ness, Patriotism* and *Faction.* . . . That every Reason which justifies
the Punishment of our Hero, for villifying our *internal Legislature,*
equally prevails against all who have espoused *America* against ministerial Oppressions; that it is as necessary to *demolish* the *former,* as
it was to *oppose* the *latter.*

In another letter "Ironicus," not confining his remarks to Mc-
Dougall, sings the praises of Sons of Liberty throughout the
colony:

Homer wrote of *Frogs,* and acquired Honour by that Work as well
as by his *Iliad. Virgil* drew his Pen to write of *Flies,* for which he
wears the Laurel-Wreath as well as for the *Aeneid;* and the *French*
Author who wrote a Pangyric on the Ague, displayed his Wit more
than if he had chose a promising Subject. Proclaim aloud that we
Whigs and Independents are the only Lovers and Defenders of *true
natural Liberty;*—that Church *Tories* are its Enemies and Betrayers
—are dead to all its Interests; that they are Nusances to this Land of

Liberty, and should be driven off like Locusts or other pernicious Vermin.[23]

March 6, 1775, was the day fixed for the election of deputies to a provincial convention, at which delegates to the Second Continental Congress would be elected.[24] A loyalist writer, outraged at the spectacle of the Sons at New York trying to ensure an outcome favorable to their cause, mingled invective and too-obvious irony in picturing the two processions that converged on the Exchange that morning:

On the morn of that auspicious day, when deputies were chosen for this city, "the sons of freedom met," and their assembly exhibited the most varied scene that ever feasted my enraptured eyes. People of all sizes and of all hues! red skins, yellow-skins, green-skins, grey-skins, bay-skins, black-skins, blue-skins! Glorious prospect! Enchanting variety! My heaven then began—Insatiate of the ravishing prospect, I enjoyed the celestial scene, till the bright effulgence of the sun reflected from so many different complexions, overpowered my sense, and threw me into a trance of delight, from which I waked not till the alarm was given, that the sons of loyalty and order were approaching.—Hateful sight! no variety in their appearance; all of one colour—*white* as the unsullied snow! their conduct uniform throughout—firm, steady, peaceable, and decent. No rags streaming in the air! No menaces to frighten the timid! a hat covered every head, and shoes guarded every foot. Disgustful was their appearance; like the modest dress of a chaste matron, which represses every wanton thought;—while the jocund and noisy sons of liberty, from their variegated hues, like a tarnished rich brocade on a brimstone's back, invited a more intimate acquaintance. How did my heart exult in the superiority of our appearance!

Nor were my emotions of pleasure less, when I contemplated the difference of the leaders. At their head there was *only* the *speaker* of an assembly; while, on the side of inborn freedom, I be-

---

[23] "The Dougliad," *New-York Gazette; and the Weekly Mercury,* Apr. 9, 16, May 7, 1770. The other nine letters, although somewhat satirical, do not warrant inclusion in the present study.

[24] Becker, *Political Parties,* p. 182.

held His Most Excellent Majesty *King Sears*, the Most Mighty Alexander, Prince of Paradise, his Excellence John Duke of Sheepskins, Generalissimo, and Coney-mouth Barclay, Esq; Attorney General.[25]

Before the war conservatism was probably as great a deterrent to the revolutionary cause in Pennsylvania as it was in New York. Perhaps it was this conservative atmosphere that made many loyalists and British soldiers, then and during the war, feel more at home in Philadelphia and New York City than in Boston. But, as the Bridenbaughs have observed, the "blundering policy of Imperial authorities coupled with the internal mistakes of Pennsylvania's ruling classes from 1763 to 1775 finally exasperated the city's great middle class, forcing from the backgrounds of their consciousness to the forefront of their minds the conviction that aristocratic control must be abolished, socially and culturally as well as politically." [26] It was partly owing to such growing sentiment that the province adopted a surprisingly democratic constitution in 1776. Two years earlier John Drinker, a Philadelphia loyalist, here addressing his "Cousin Tom," burlesques the democratic ambitions of the local Sons of Liberty.

> Your Love of Liberty, you tell us,
> Exalts you high above your Fellows;
>
> . . . . .
>
> You rob your Neighbours of their Freedom,
> While with the empty Name you feed 'em;
> And on the Rights of Britons trample,
> With Impudence beyond Example.
> For Right & Wrong, the best Authority,
> Flow from tumultuous Majority.
>
> . . . . .

[25] *The Triumph of the Whigs: or, T'Other Congress Convened* (New York, 1775), pp. 4–5. Isaac Sears, Alexander McDougall, and John Lamb were well-known Sons of Liberty in New York. Mr. James J. Heslin of the New-York Historical Society conjectures that the "Attorney General" was James Duane and that "Coney-mouth Barclay" may have been John Barclay, mayor of Albany.

[26] *Rebels and Gentlemen*, p. 370.

You've with as righteous Zeal paraded,
As that fam'd Patriot, *Jack Cade*, did;
And tis but Justice to assert you
Are Men of equal Public Virtue.
But while I thus proceed, I fear me,
Sir *Typo-Tar-Tub* will besmear me;
For since the Government o' th' City
Hath late devolv'd on a Committe[e]
Whose Sov'reign Right to rule the Nation,
Has *Tar & Feathers* for Foundation;

. . . . .

Fair Reas'ning & fair Trade are hiss'd at,
As het'rageneous to a *free State;*
To cheat the King is Public Spirit,
Republicanus will aver it,
And prove by Syllogistic Juggle,
True social Virtue is to smuggle.[27]

IV

Throughout the spring of 1776 the question of whether to declare independence at once was debated, in assembly and the press, the street and the pulpit. The conservatives "had no wish to rush into democracy," writes John C. Miller; "they doubted whether the American people possessed the qualifications to make democracy work." The radicals, on the other hand, "saw no reason to be bound by traditional forms of government. . . . The veneration felt by many Americans for the British Constitution was to the radicals one of the most regrettable hang-overs from British rule."[28]

During March and April Reverend William Smith, Provost of the College of Philadelphia, spoke out against the growing

[27] "A Card To my Cousin Tom, the Patriot, by D. J. alias J. Drinker," Philadelphia, Feb. 4, 1774, MS, Historical Society of Pennsylvania.

[28] Miller, *Triumph*, pp. 343–345. See Schlesinger, *Prelude*, p. 261, for a still more precise, three-way distinction (disunionist, unionist, fence-sitter) in the patriot debate on the question of independence.

sentiment for independence, in eight letters to the Philadelphia press over the signature "Cato." Immediately he was answered by James Cannon, a member of the college faculty, who signed himself "Cassandra," and by Thomas Paine ("The Forester"). Francis Hopkinson, siding against his former teacher Dr. Smith, composed a Biblical account of this exchange: The king of the islands plants a tree among the new people in a far country. For a time it flourishes; then a *North* wind blasts it. A prophet (Franklin) urges that the tree be removed and a younger planted in its stead.

Then a certain wise man shall arise, and shall call himself Cato; and he shall strive to persuade the people to put their trust in the rotten tree, and not to dig it up, or remove it from its place. And he shall harangue with great vehemence, and shall tell them that a rotten tree is better than a sound one; and that it is for the benefit of the people that the *North* wind should blow upon it, and that the branches thereof should be broken and fall upon and crush them.

And he shall receive from the king of the islands, fetters of gold and chains of silver; and he shall have hopes of great reward if he will fasten them on the necks of the people, and chain them to the trunk of the rotten tree. . . . And shall tell the people, that they are not fetters and chains, but shall be as bracelets of gold on their wrists, and rings of silver on their necks, to ornament and decorate them and their children. And his words shall be sweet in the mouth, but very bitter in the belly.

Moreover, he will threaten them, that if they will not obey his voice, he will whistle with his lips, and *raw-head* and *bloody-bones* shall come out of *France* to devour them and their little ones; and he will blow with his horn, and the wild bull of *Spain* will come and gore them with his horns, and trample upon them with his hoofs, even until they die. . . .

And it shall come to pass that certain other wise men shall also stand up and oppose themselves to *Cato*. . . .

And one of these wise men shall call himself Cassandra, and the other shall call himself The Forester: and they shall fall upon *Cato*, and shall strip him of every disguise, and shew him naked before all the people. And *Cassandra* shall tie him up, and the *Forester* shall scourge him until he shall become exceeding sore. Nevertheless, *Cato* shall not repent, but shall harden his heart, and become very stubborn, and shall be vexed till he die. And when he shall be dead, his funeral oration shall be pronounced. . . .

And *Cato* and his works shall be no more remembered amongst them. For *Cato* shall die, and his works shall follow him.[29]

On the other side of the debate, a conservative writer, thinking about independence and fearful of the mobocracy that could ensue, pictures the Liberty Tree grateful now that the British besieged at Boston are cutting it down:

'Tis true, I flourish'd many a year,
And spread my branches full and fair:
My Body large and hale and plump,
Fair all around from top to stump,
'Till that fierce creature, huge of size,
With hundred heads and saucer eyes,
Christen'd by name of *Liberty*,
Repair'd with boisterous crouds to me,
And for their *god* they chose a tree.

. . . . .

They stifled me with sweat and stench,
And from me did my branches wrench:
A massy pole they then erected,
And with a rebel standard deck'd it
To make the rabble gape and stare,
Fling up their caps, and roar and swear.
The pole it gall'd my body sore.

. . . . .

Thanks to the hand that cuts me down:
Thanks to the ax that lops my crown:
The path of vice I never trod,
I boast, I liv'd *the people's god*.
My trunk, may't be to fuel turn'd,
By Howe, be honor'd to be burn'd,

[29] "A Prophecy," MS [Apr.?], 1776; printed in *Miscellaneous Essays*, I, 92–97.

That I to him may warmth impart,
Who oft himself's warm'd many a heart.[30]

V

The Declaration of Independence, while marking a victory for the radical party, was a fateful step nonetheless: if America should lose the war, the life of many a patriot leader would be forfeit. Many conservatives thereafter were of a mind with the Englishman Nicholas Cresswell that Americans, "like the Dog in the Fable, quit the substance for an empty shadow." [31] In the spring of 1777 a "staunch" Pennsylvanian warned his countrymen of "Furious Whigs" who

injure the cause of liberty as much by their violence as the timid Whigs do by their fears. They think the destruction of HOWE's army of less consequence than the detection and punishment of the most insignificant Tory. They think the common forms of justice should be suspended towards a Tory criminal, and that a man who only *speaks* against our common defence, should be tomahawked, scalped, and roasted alive. Lastly, they are all cowards, and skulk under the cover of an office, or a sickly family, when they are called to oppose the enemy in the field. Woe to that State or Community that is governed by this class of men! [32]

Late in the war John Trumbull, a conservative at heart, attacked the radicals, and with such telling effect that in later times Federalists quoted his sentiments by way of answering Republican opponents.[33] In what is undoubtedly the most effective such passage, M'Fingal, incensed at finding the Whigs gathered

[30] "The Soliloquy of the Boston Tree of Liberty," *Massachusetts Gazette. And Boston Weekly News-Letter*, Feb. 22, 1776, p. 1.
[31] Entry of July 19, 1777, *Journal of Nicholas Cresswell*, p. 259.
[32] *Pennsylvania Packet*, Mar. 18, 1777, p. 1.
[33] See Alexander Cowie, *John Trumbull: Connecticut Wit* (Chapel Hill, 1936), pp. 192–194, and Leon Howard, *The Connecticut Wits* (Chicago, 1943), pp. 76–77, who discuss the political uses to which *M'Fingal* was put in the early national period.

around the Liberty Pole, denounces them for confounding
liberty with license:

> "For Liberty, in your own by-sense,
> Is but for crimes a patent license;
> To break of law th' Egyptian yoke,
> And throw the world in common stock,
> Reduce all grievances and ills
> To Magna Charta of your wills;
>
>   . . . . .
>
> From dunghills deep of blackest hue,
> Your dirt-bred patriots spring to view,
> To wealth and power and honor rise,
> Like new-wing'd maggots changed to flies.
>
>   . . . . .
>
> You've push'd and turn'd the whole world up-
> Side down and got yourselves at top,
> While all the great ones of your state,
> Are crush'd beneath the pop'lar weight.
>
>   . . . . .
>
> Your Commonwealth's a common harlot,
> The property of every varlet,
> Which now in taste, and full employ,
> All sorts admire, as all enjoy;
> But soon a batter'd strumpet grown,
> You'll curse and drum her out of town." [I, 88–94]

After the Declaration of Independence the ministerial press
on both sides of the water, to which the loyalists frequently contributed, continued to attack the radicals. One writer at New
York tells how John Presbyter, Will Democrack, and Nathan
Smuggle wooed "Fair *Liberty,*" who came over to America
through "Britannia's aid."

> *John Presbyter* was first,
>   And, with a rank Grimace
> All Opposition curst
>   Beyond the Help of Grace:

He Bishops pass'd to Hell alive:—
That he on Earth might better thrive.

    Though Honour to the King
       God strictly has enjoin'd;
    John said, 'Twas no such Thing,
       For God had chang'd his Mind:
That now he'd prove it just and right
To kill the King; and, *ergo,* fight.

      · · · · ·

    Will Democrack came next,
       Who swore all Men were ev'n;
    And seem'd to be quite vex't
       That there's a King in Heav'n:
Will curst the hilly Country round,
Because it made—unequal Ground.

    It gave him vast Surprize
       That Beasts, and Birds, and Fishes
    Were not form'd of a Size
       Like Wedgwood's earthen Dishes:
With wise *Alphonso,* he'd have taught
His god t' have made things, "as he ought."

Will's suit rejected as John's had been, Nathan then advances
his. When Liberty rejects him too, "The Rascal turn'd about,
and swore / That Liberty was but a — — — — —."

    He *veaw'd,* a Cask of Rum,
   * Or contraband Molasses,
    Was better worth at home
       Than twenty such nice Lasses.

      · · · · ·

    He therefore told the Town,
       That the pert Minx was free;
    And to each Scoundrel known,
       And ev'ry dirty *He;*
That she *imported* rank Disease
And swarm'd with "Vermin," Bugs, and Fleas.

All three suitors rail at her and change her name to Slavery, whereupon Britannia instructs the Howes to go and show America that *"Liberty* I love." [34] This skillful allegory, inspired perhaps by the Howes's proclamation of November 30, 1776, calling on the Americans to submit, is at once religious, political, and economic in its sweep; it presents Britain's attitude toward the rebellion in America efficiently and dramatically. Another writer at New York, addressing himself to "Whigs of all denominations," "Anabaptists, Presbyterians, / Independents, Oliverians," inveighed:

> Seed of vile fanatic preachers,
> Who appointed you for teachers?
> Sons of gypsies, thieves and shoolers,
> Who the devil made you rulers? [35]

In 1780, Jacob Bailey, then living at Halifax, Nova Scotia, sent the London press a Hudibrastic poem based on recent experience. Refusing to read the Declaration of Independence in church, take the oath of allegiance to Congress, or refrain from praying for the King, he suffered at the hands of local patriots in Pownalborough, Maine, before finally being permitted to sail away into exile. As a monarchist and an Anglican, Bailey burlesques in this portrait of the "factious demagogue" what he chose to regard as implications of the argument from natural rights.

> As for his Religion, he could mix,
> And blend it well with politics,
> For 'twas his favourite opinion
> In mobs was seated all dominion:
> All pow'r and might he understood
> Rose from the sov'reign multitude:
> That right and wrong, that good and ill,

[34] "Liberty's Choice; or, The Rival Suitors," *New-York Gazette, and Weekly Mercury,* Dec. 23, 1776, p. 4; reprinted in *Loyalist Poetry,* pp. 63–69.

[35] *Royal American Gazette,* July 8, 1779, p. 3.

Were nothing but the rabble's will:
Tho' they renounce the truth for fiction,
In nonsense trust, and contradiction;
And tho' they change ten times a day
As fear or int'rest leads the way;
And what this hour is law and reason,
Declare, the next, revolt and treason.

Then, concerned lest the people "in mighty Congress plod /
To set up *Hancock* for a *God*," Bailey disposes of this doctrine
of divine right with a *reductio ad absurdum* on which the poem
closes.

Yea, they have pow'r to godify
An onion, turnip, or a fly:
And some have even understood
To consecrate a pole of wood;

. . . . .

From this we see, 'tis demonstration
There's no Supreme in the creation,
Except that mighty pow'r, the people;
That weather-cock which rides the steeple;
That noisy and licentious rabble,
Which storms e'en Heaven itself with gabble:
Should these give sanction to a lie,
'Tis plain that Heav'n must ratify! [36]

VI

In Pennsylvania, where loyalism continued strong throughout the war, many refused to support a state constitution so
favorable to the plain people and were persecuted for this show
of disaffection. When some Philadelphia patriots stoned the
windows of Quakers and others unsympathetic to the cause of
independence on July 4, 1777, one writer described how the

[36] "The Factious Demagogue," *Royal Gazette*, Oct. 4, 1780 (from a
London paper); reprinted in *Loyalist Poetry*, pp. 129–131.

rebel chiefs "like ancient heroes sally forth" against the "un-arm'd Quakers and the Tories."

> Our true Don Quixotes, by false guessings
>   Direct their calls and lead the van:
> Mistake the Tories for the Hessians,
>   And Quakers for poor Englishmen! [37]

Later that year the Supreme Executive Council of Pennsylvania, acting on the advice of Congress, arrested some forty persons thought to be disaffected. When twenty-three of these, mostly Quakers, protested their arrest and refused to observe their parole if granted liberty, the Council ordered that they be re-moved to Winchester, Virginia, and there secured. It was never proved that they had had any communication with the British, however, and they were finally returned home and received apologies.[38] Outraged by this flagrant denial of habeas corpus, Stansbury inveighed, "We laugh'd at Oppression, not dreaming or fearing / That Men would be banish'd without charge or hearing."

> If they with our Enemies have been partakers,
> Then prove it in God's name, and punish the Quakers:
> But if there is nothing alleged but Suspicion,
> What honest Man's safe from this State-Inquisition?
>
> .   .   .   .   .
>
> When Quakers and Churchmen have suffer'd your pleasure—
> Their Worship and Consciences shap'd to your measure—
> The Catholics then may expect Penal Laws,
> Whereby we shall have one Religion and Cause.[39]

[37] *Pennsylvania Ledger*, Dec. 10, 1777, p. 4; reprinted in *Loyal Verses*, pp. 14–15, and there attributed to R. Chubb or Stansbury.

[38] Rufus M. Jones, *The Quakers in the American Colonies* (London, 1911), pp. 566–567.

[39] "Song," Nov., 1777, "Loyalist Rhapsodies" (probably written after Sept. 9, the day on which the order was invoked); printed in *Loyal Verses*, pp. 16–17.

In Virginia the conservative attitude of the gentry retarded the revolutionary movement.[40] Robert Munford, a member of this class, attacks radicalism in *The Patriots:* Trueman and Meanwell, conservatives both and Munford's spokesmen in the play, are persecuted by the radicals on suspicion of loyalism. Trueman describes Brazen, the father of the girl he loves, as

a violent patriot without knowing the meaning of the word. He understands little or nothing beyond a dice-box and race-field, but thinks he knows every thing; and woe be to him that contradicts him! His political notions are a system of perfect anarchy, but he reigns in his own family with perfect despotism. He is fully resolved that nobody shall tyrannize over him, but very content to tyrannize over others.

When Captain Flash, "the drawcansir of modern times," convinces Brazen that Trueman is indeed a loyalist, Meanwell remarks:

What a pity it is that all heads are not capable of receiving the benign influence of the principles of liberty—some are too weak to bear it, and become thoroughly intoxicated. . . . I hope my zeal against tyranny will not be shewn by bawling against it, . . . [and] persecuting innocent men, only because they differ in opinion with me. . . . Men who aim at power without merit, must conceal the meanness of their souls by noisy and passionate speeches in favour of every thing which is the current opinion of the day.[41]

One patriot whose pamphleteering from 1775 on made him vulnerable in the Philadelphia press was Thomas Paine. A writer there answered his heavily invective *Common Sense* in this manner:

> Tom mounted on his sordid load,
> And bawling, d– –n ye, clear the road;
> His shovel grasp'd firm in his hands,

[40] Jacob Axelrad, *Patrick Henry* (New York, 1947), p. 57n.
[41] *The Patriots* (Philadelphia, [1777?]); reprinted in *A Collection of Plays and Poems*, ed. William Munford (Petersburg, Va., 1798), and again in the *Wm. & Mary Quar.*, ser. 3, VI (1949), 449–450.

Which far and near the street commands,
No hardy mortal dares approach,
Whether on horseback, foot, or coach;
None in his wits the risque would choose,
Who either wears a coat or nose.
　　So – – – – – in pomp, on Billingsgate,
His arms display'd in burlesque state;
Scurrility and impudence,
Bombast and Bedlam eloquence,
Defiance bids—to COMMON SENSE.[42]

Three years later Paine, who had sided with Arthur Lee, resigned as Secretary of the Committee of Foreign Affairs over
his part in the Deane-Lee controversy. Another Philadelphian
inveighed:

HAIL mighty Thomas! In whose works are seen
A mangled Morris and distorted Deane;
Whose splendid periods flash for Lees defence,
Replete with every thing but common sense.

　　　　· · · · ·

Behold around thee, how thy triumphs lie,
Of reputations hosts before thee die;
On envy's altars hecatombs expire,
And Faction fondly lights her pupil's fire.
That pupil most devoted to her will,
Who for the worthless wags his quibbling quill;
And with a true democracy of spirit
Bravely attacks the most exalted merit.
Thou pupil worthy her attentive care,
By Satan granted to her earnest prayer;
When on the brink of fate smooth Adams stood,
And saw his Arthur flound'ring in the flood.

Lee's reputation hanging in the balance, Satan declares, "Since
on mankind to fix my iron reign, / Nor sin, nor death suffice,
I give them *Payne*." The poem concludes with this mock-epic
simile describing the manner of Paine's birth:

[42] *Pennsylvania Evening Post*, Feb. 6, 1776, p. 65.

> For as Minerva, queen of sense uncommon,
> Owed not her birth to goddess or to woman;
> But softly crept from out her father's scull,
> At a small crack in't when the moon was full;
> So you, great Common Sense, did surely come
> From out the crack in grisly Pluto's bum.[43]

Benjamin Franklin was involved in the diplomatic phase of the revolutionary struggle from its inception. Not until 1775, however, a full year after Wedderburn's harangue against him, did he abandon his dream of dominion status for the colonies and espouse the cause of independence. From the first he was undoubtedly ambitious for political fame. Late in the war Jacob Bailey undertook a long Hudibrastic work entitled "Jack Ramble," which was never completed. Ostensibly the memoir of an itinerant preacher, actually the poem ridicules patriot leaders in general and Franklin in particular. At Boston young Jack (Franklin) appears as a freethinker who scoffs at government as well as religion. Nevertheless, in order to curry favor with the Dissenters, he attacks the Church of England. Soon he abandons Massachusetts for Pennsylvania:

> But now, grown weary of the Saints,
> He left them while their loud complaints
> With deadly bitterness abounded,
> And over Heaven and earth resounded.
> He changed their worship for another,
> And soon became a quaking brother;
> For he beheld with reverence
> Their growing power and opulence.
>
> · · · · ·
>
> He in th' assembly silent sat
> Invested with the broad-brimmed hat.

But at Philadelphia Jack cannot conceal for long the fact that he is at heart a freethinker:

---

[43] "An EPISTLE," *ibid.*, July 16, 1779, p. 183. John Adams also sided with Lee.

'Twas far beneath his high condition
To make to God or man submission.
He did by his own wit discover
Himself a great philosopher.
In's element no bird alive
Knew better how to swim and dive.
He like a loon was often found
O'er head and heels in the profound.

So he casts off all pretense and appears as the infidel philosopher
he is. His composure, urbanity, and even temper render him
more pernicious than a demagogue:

He throbbed for lofty elevation
Some miles above his former station.
So bladders grow and swell, we find,
When blown and filled up with the wind.
He with himself, a certain season,
In manner thus began to reason:

. . . . .

Since I am fitter for command
Than those who govern in the land;
And could I once obtain the sway,
The willing people would obey,
And serve with joy and acclamation,
A man of rising reputation.
But first I must with courage stout
Contrive the present powers to rout;
And to secure me from detection,
Must raise a desperate insurrection;
Lead on the people in delusion
Till all is rumpus and confusion.
In this untoward situation
The king perhaps may take occasion
To call me from my native quiet
To soften and compose the riot—

. . . . .

I'll leave the Congress in the lurch,
And pick a quarrel with the Church;

> Accuse them first of disaffection;
> Then beg His Majesty's protection
> 'Gainst such a crew of dangerous wights,
> A sturdy race of Jacobites.

After rambling at home and abroad, in what are little more than a series of amorous intrigues, Jack reinstates himself with the Boston Dissenters by confessing to his delinquencies. Again he sails for Britain where he is successful in preaching independence, but is eventually known for what he is. At the end he summons his own spirit to extricate him from the terrors of the encompassing gloom: "O was I able to command, / Dear Franklin, thy all-powerful wand!" [44]

In spite of its fragmentary nature the poem deserves to stand beside *M'Fingal* and "The Political Balance" in the Hudibrastic tradition of this period. Bailey, whose Anglicanism and loyalism led a friend to describe him as "the Butler of a new struggle between Roundhead and Cavalier," [45] is here defending the *status quo* against what he regards as political and religious insurgency. Jack Ramble, whose Presbyterianism is scarcely true blue, behaves as a mock hero should, though he goes adventuring without the traditional man-at-arms:

> Some peevish critic may inquire
> Why Jack should rove without a squire
> Since ancient heroes had a friend,
> Their various motions to defend,
> Who round the world trudged with their masters,
> And bore a part in their disasters.
>
> . . . . .
>
> Jack had true courage of his own,
> Nor feared to range the world alone;
> Nor counsel wanted, nor defence,
> Save his superior impudence.

[44] Ray Palmer Baker, *New Eng. Quar.*, II (1929), 80–92, who examined the then-extant manuscript, prints passages of "Jack Ramble" and, for the rest, summarizes the narrative.

[45] *New Eng. Quar.*, II, 59.

The poem exploits low-burlesque situations to good advantage. In the following description of his predilection for electrical experiments, for example, Bailey travesties heroic allusion. Jack—

> Stouter and bolder grown, aspires
> To handle the celestial fires;
>
> .   .   .   .   .
>
> To rend the gloomy clouds asunder,
> And rob the Almighty of his thunder.
> So former giants did assay
> To steal the bolts of Jove away.

To the writing of the poem Bailey, like Trumbull and Freneau, brings wit, invention, and a sense of architectonics. That the historical Franklin was vulnerable on several of the counts herein enumerated only enhances the burlesque.

The majority of the satires in this chapter focus on radical patriots, and for an obvious reason. The natural rights argument for revolution and independence, to which they ultimately had recourse, proved an attractive target, not only to loyalist and ministerial writers but to conservatives as well. While the civil strife implicit in the Revolution was in the final analysis a struggle between radical and conservative, it was much more than that. This fact the patriots acknowledged on the numerous occasions they made common cause against three threats at home: trimming, treachery, and loyalism.

CHAPTER X

Trimmers and Traitors

"THIS innocent word *Trimmer*," writes Halifax in 1684, "signifieth no more than this, That if Men are together in a Boat, and one part of the Company would weigh it down on one side, another would make it lean as much to the contrary; it happeneth there is a third Opinion of those, who conceive it would do as well, if the Boat went even, without endangering the Passengers." [1] There were those in Revolutionary America, as on the eve of England's "Glorious Revolution," who, from cause of conscience, timidity, or self-interest, chose to steer a neutral course rather than work for political autonomy or reaffirm their loyalty to King and Parliament. "Conservatives cursed with an ability to see that there are two sides to an issue," Leonard Labaree calls them, "and unable or unwilling to choose finally and irrevocably with which side they will cast their fortunes." [2] Down to the time of the tea demonstrations many Americans steered such a course; but in the political storm that followed, most men found themselves declaring for autonomy or a continuation of dependency. It was the lot of those who trimmed their sails, from whatever motive, to be suspected by the patriot and loyalist communities alike. There are "great numbers of ignorant thoughtless beings," charges a New Jersey patriot,

[1] *The Complete Works of George Savile*, ed. Walter Raleigh (Oxford, 1912), p. 48.
[2] *Conservatism in Early American History* (New York, 1948), p. 158.

who are one day Tories, and the next day Whigs; and the third day nothing at all; who like the pendulum of a clock are perpetually changing sides and strictly speaking [are] as unsteady as the wind. Having no fixed principles at all, and being wholly unacquainted with the nature of Government, the principles of the English constitution, and the rights of Americans, they are easily influenced any way, and therefore, either change their sentiments daily without being able to assign any just reason for so doing, or else hastily espouse the one side or the other, merely out of humour or party spite. These I shall beg leave to distinguish by the significant name of Turn-Coats.[3]

Some it is true did turn coat, but the majority faced the enmity of their neighbors and the constant threat of disenfranchisement or imprisonment with honest courage. Take the case of Henry Melchior Muhlenberg. This aging Lutheran minister, fully aware that "if a preacher wished to be neutral, he found himself between two fires," asked only to live a quiet, retired life in Revolutionary Pennsylvania.[4] One hesitates to say who showed the greater intellectual and moral courage, Pastor Muhlenberg or those Americans who opposed his wishes.

I

The satirist, of course, took pains to mistake such courage for cowardice. Francis Hopkinson relates that when war broke out between the birds (Americans) and the beasts (British),

---

[3] *The Plain-Dealer* (Bridgeton, N.J.), Jan. [1], 1776. Incidental to the point of view in two war-time plays are portraits of trimmers. In *The Motley Assembly* (1779) Turncoat (Daniel Hubbard) advises his loyalist friends at Boston to "tack about, and make fair weather with the other side" just as he is doing, though later he protests that it is his determination "never to take an active part on either side"; and in Munford's *Patriots* (1777?) there appears Tackabout, a loyalist at heart though a pretended patriot, one "who privately condemns, and publicly approves" men and measures.

[4] "Journal," Oct. 22–23, 1784, quoted in Paul A. W. Wallace, *The Muhlenbergs of Pennsylvania* (Philadelphia, 1950), p. 108.

> The *bat*, half bird—half beast, was there,
> Nor would for *this* or *that* declare:
> Waiting 'till conquest should decide,
> Which was the strongest, safest side;
> Depending on his doubtful form,
> To screen him from the impending storm.

At first the birds are victorious, whereupon he squeaks, "With leathern wings I skim the air, / And am a bird, tho' clad in hair." When the beasts rally, he cries, "With teeth and fur— 'twould be absurd, / To call a thing like me, a *bird*." The birds finally carry the day, but when the bat claims a share in the victory he is called "traitor" and ordered from their sight.

> The bat disown'd, in some old shed,
> Now seeks to hide his exil'd head;
>
> . . . . .
>
> In dark retreats, he shuns the light,
> To hid his mongrel form from sight.[5]

In a variation on this fable weasels are substituted for birds and beasts. A heedless bat happening into a weasel's house, the dame mistakes him for a mouse and vows he shall die; but he persuades her he is a bird and is allowed to fly away. Falling foul of a second weasel, this one a hater of birds, he proves himself a mouse by showing that his outside "is nought but leather," and is set free a second time. The moral?

> There's many a one who change their note,
> Just like this Bat, that's in our story;
> Who as times go still turn their coat,
> One day a WHIG, the next a TORY.[6]

As a matter of course satirists wrote in imitation of that popular ballad, "The Vicar of Bray," substituting events of the

[5] "The Birds, the Beasts and the Bat," *Pennsylvania Packet*, May 6, 1778, p. 4; reprinted in *Poems*, pp. 177–180.
[6] *Royal Gazette*, July 7, 1779, p. 3.

American Revolution for those following the Restoration. One American vicar is made to confess:

> When Royal George rul'd o'er this land,
>   And loyalty no harm meant,
> For Church and King I made a stand
>   And so I got preferment.
> I still oppos'd all party tricks
>   For reasons I thought clear ones;
> And swore it was their politics,
>   To make us Presbyterians.

It was my firm intention to uphold the Stamp Act, but when repeal came,

> I quickly join'd the common cry,
>   That we should all be slaves, Sir;
> The House of Commons was a sty;
>   The King and Lords were knaves, Sir.

I laughed at their tax on tea and supposed, when a Congress was called, that it too would be repealed.

> But Britain was not quickly scar'd;
>   She told another story:
> When Independence was declar'd
>   I figur'd as a Tory;
> Declar'd it was Rebellion base
>   To take up arms—I curs'd it.
> For faith it seem'd a settled case
>   That we should soon be worsted.

I took the test act but was much suspected any way; "I felt myself much like the Ass / In Lion's skin detected." I cried down the French alliance and cheered Howe when he paraded through Philadelphia.

> But poor Burgoyne's, announced my fate:
>   The Whigs began to glory:
> I now bewail'd my wretched state
>   That e'er I was a Tory.

By night the British left the shore
  Nor car'd for friends a fig, Sir;
I turn'd the cat in pan once more,
  And so became a Whig, Sir.

I call'd the army butch'ring dogs;
  A bloody tyrant King, Sir;
The Commons, Lords, a set of rogues
  That all deserv'd to swing, Sir;
Since Fate has made us great and free,
  And Providence can't falter;
So Cong. till death my King shall be,
  Unless the times shall alter.[7]

In Virginia, at a time when the counties were making resolves concerning Britain's coercive measures of 1774 against Massachusetts, one patriot attacked the "unmanly" failure of Middlesex County to support the general sentiments of the province:

To manhood he makes a vain pretence,
Who wants both manly force, and sense;
'Tis but the form, and not the matter,
According to the schoolmens clatter;
From such a creature, Heav'n defend her,
Each lady cries, no *neuter gender!*
But when a number of such creatures,
With Womans hearts, and manly features,
Their country's gen'rous schemes perplex,
I own, I hate this MIDDLE-SEX.[8]

It seems likely that during the war Pennsylvania harbored a larger percentage of trimmers than any other state. Chief among these were the Quakers. Long ago they had declared, "The setting up and putting down Kings and governments is God's pe-

---

[7] "The American Vicar of Bray," *Royal Gazette*, June 30, 1779, p. 3; reprinted in *Loyalist Poetry*, pp. 94–98. Another imitation, centering on the war years, appeared in the *Virginia Gazette or the Independent Chronicle* (Richmond), Nov. 22, 1783, p. 4.

[8] *Virginia Gazette* (Rind), Aug. 11, 1774; reprinted in Moore's *Songs*, p. 68n.

culiar prerogative, for causes best known to himself." Now such
of them as offered neither resistance nor aid to either side suffered
great losses "by fines and distraints and foraging parties." [9] In
the fall of 1778, during a lull in the war effort, "Comus" travestied their policy of neutrality. We abhor war, say the Quakers.

> Our quiet principles compel us
> To put no finger to the bellows,
> But mind what our forefathers tell us,
> Which is, To have no hand therein
> Till truth decrees which side shall win.
> Yet as the wisest men may fail
> To judge which shall at last prevail,
> It may most probably occur
> That *Friends* like worldly men may err,
> And humbly thinking to obey,
> The light within, mistake their way.
> But Error, when it's well design'd,
> Is an obedience of the mind,
> And shews, in colours clear and strong,
> *Friends* may be right in doing wrong.
>
> .   .   .   .   .
>
> It doth suffice that we are true
> To any side we join unto,
> So long, and not a moment longer,
> Than truth shall make that side the stronger;
> For as the truth can never fail,
> Or that which is not truth prevail,
> So by the same unerring guide
> The strongest is the rightest side,
> Which we shall serve with all our might,
> Not as the *strongest*—but the *right*—
> And all we wish or want to know
> Is simply this—*which side is so.*[10]

[9] Jones, *Quakers*, pp. 563, 568.
[10] "A MODERN TESTIMONY For the Year 1778," *Pennsylvania Packet*,
Sept. 29, 1778, p. 3.

II

Editors in particular were liable to attack. After all, it is not always easy to distinguish between the editorial practice of the open forum and political trimming. The biased reader can, if he choose, twist the sense of even so clear a statement as Benjamin Franklin's apology for a free press, made while he was editor of the *Pennsylvania Gazette:*

Printers are educated in the Belief, that when Men differ in Opinion, both Sides ought equally to have the Advantage of being heard by the Publick; and that when Truth and Error have fair Play, the former is always an overmatch for the latter: Hence they chearfully serve all contending Writers that pay them well, without regarding on which side they are of the Question in Dispute.[11]

It comes as no surprise, then, that the loyal Jacob Bailey, determined to attack "the extreme caution of our printers who refuse to insert anything which tends to expose the guilt and madness of rebellion," tells the following story of a trimming printer:

> There lived in our new-fangled nation
> A man of wondrous moderation;
> While some were eager for the laws,
> And others fought in Freedom's cause,

he kept himself concealed at home like a mouse in the "belly of a cheese."

> He was to all disputes a stranger,
> And shut his eyes from every danger;
> To Sons of Liberty was civil,
> But shunned a Tory as the D–v–l.
> And yet my authors all relate
> He had for Whigs a mortal hate.

[11] "An Apology for Printers," *Pennsylvania Gazette*, June 10, 1731; reprinted in Smyth, II, 174.

Despised by his friends and suspected by his enemies, this "trimming politician" is haled before a committee of patriots, whose chairman is able to sway the passions of his audience:

> The mob, who heard this condemnation,
> Was seized with sudden inflammation;
> And, gathering round from near to far,
> Rolled him in feathers, pitch, and tar.

He is carted to the gallows and there threatened with death.

> See him in doleful, piteous case:
> Tears, filth, and blood deformed his face;
> Patient and meek these wrongs he bore,
> And neither threatened, raved, or swore.
> All indignation he supprest,
> Yet felt these insults in his breast;
> His agony, regret, and shame
> Burnt in his soul with smothered flame.

At last, in desperation, he is forced to flee to the British to escape hanging as a spy; but even among them he finds it difficult to establish his innocence, if not his loyalty. Bailey concludes his tale,

> Now, neighbors, whether Whig or Tory,
> Learn from this sad and tragic story
> The voice of Conscience to obey,
> And walk as she directs the way.[12]

As editor of the *New-York Gazette and Weekly Mercury* (established in 1752), Hugh Gaine strove throughout the prewar years to keep his paper unbiased. He was so far successful in concealing his loyalist sympathies that the mob who destroyed Rivington's presses and type in November, 1775, did not disturb his. When the Americans abandoned New York the following September, he removed to Newark, where, enjoying the confidence of Governor William Livingston, he printed seven

---

[12] "The Character of a Trimmer," included in a letter of Mar. 10, 1781, to James Dummer Rogers; printed in *New Eng. Quar.*, II (1929), 74-77.

issues of the *Mercury* as a patriot sheet. Back at New York in
November, he took charge of his paper again and allied himself
with the government party there. But the British never fully
trusted him, and when Rivington returned to the city in September, 1777, he, not Gaine, was appointed "Printer to the King's
Most Excellent Majesty." [13]

Earlier that year Livingston, angered by such trimming tactics,
attacked Gaine in "The Impartial Chronicle," a long letter to
the Philadelphia press purporting to be a series of foreign and
New York dispatches "Printed and sold by Hugo Lucre, under
the inspection and by permission of martial authority, in New
York, in Gasconading square, opposite to Rhodomontado alley,
at the sign of the crown against the bible, where all persons may
be supplied with false intelligence for hard money, and with
truth upon no terms whatever." Many of these dispatches convey military intelligence favorable to the British cause. Thus,
his Majesty has declined the Emperor of Indostan's offer of five
hundred elephants for suppressing the American rebellion; the
King of Denmark will furnish 4,000 Laplanders for winter service in America; the Emperor of Persia is to send 3,500 Korazan
archers, who can discharge their arrows "in the ancient Parthian
manner" as they are galloping away from their pursuers ("a
mode of annoying the enemy, which his majesty's light horse
may adopt to great advantage, as the rebels frequently compel
them to fight in that attitude, or not at all"); the Admiralty is
seriously considering a proposal that the British navy be equipped
with wheels and pulleys to pursue the rebels on land ("however
the rebel fortifications might otherwise damage the new-con-
structed vessels, as they passed them in their progress through
the country, it would be impossible for the art of man to sink
them"); the Ministry, aware of the great range of climate in
America, intends to employ 13,000 Moors to fight in the southern colonies and 4,700 Eskimoes in the northern, finally, because

[13] *The Journals of Hugh Gaine*, ed. P. L. Ford (New York, 1902), I,
51–62 *passim*.

the numerous woods and defiles in America make it difficult to guard against ambush, the British commander in chief has applied for 2,000 Hussars, 2,000 Pandours, and 1,500 Croats, "who are instantly to rush upon the enemy without knowing where they be, and cut them down with their sabres without seeing them." It will be impossible, declares a London correspondent, for the rebels to oppose "this terrific and tremendous armament" with an equal force next summer.

Ye poor deluded, misguided, bewildered, cajoled and bamboozled whigs! ye dumfounded, infatuated, backbestridden, nose-led-about priest-ridden, demagogue-beshackled, and congress-becrafted independents, fly, fly, oh fly for protection to the royal standard, or ye will be swept from the face of the earth with the besom of destruction, and cannonaded in a moment, into nullities and non-entities, and no mortal can tell into what other kind of quiddities and quoddities.

The same correspondent reports that the Grand Seignior of the Ottoman Empire, in order to "repair the waste of his majesty's British subjects in this horrible rebellion, to which the common mode of procreation usually practised in England was by no means adequate," has offered "to present each member of the two houses of Parliament, with five Circassian virgins of the most exquisite beauty, and his majesty himself with a score of the like amiable blooming breeders." Near the end of the letter Hugo Lucre offers gratis

The Mirror of Mercy; or, the Primrose of Favour and Clemency; shewing how every loyal American may preserve the full and free possession of his whole estate real and personal, by suffering the British parliament to deprive him of nine-tenths of it; edited by his most gracious plenipotentiaries. Certainly, nothing can more fully demonstrate the infatuation of the rebels, and their woful seduction by a few artful and ambitious demagogues, than their not being universally convinced of their true interest by the unanswerable reasons contained in this precious, and inestimable publication; though to the honour of the wise and loyal, it must be

acknowledged that thousands, being perfectly cured of their ob-
duracy, by this mollifying cordial, daily flock to the royal standard,
and pretend no other impediment against fighting for their sovereign, than their natural and incurable cowardice.[14]

Livingston's "Impartial Chronicle" and Franklin's "Sale of
the Hessians" adopt essentially the same strategy: in both letters
the satirist keeps out of sight and lets the self-developing irony
of the situation speak for itself. But Franklin's is clearly the superior piece. Granted, Livingston employs a rhetorical device
that is wholly credible, the fiction of a series of news dispatches
domestic and foreign. Granted, too—though this point is not
made explicit until the end—he attempts to focus on the fact
that Gaine is ready to supply "false intelligence for hard money,
and . . . truth upon no terms whatsoever." The fact remains
that because the dispatches are set down according to no readily
discernible logic, most contemporary readers would probably
have failed to grasp the situational irony and would have seen
in the letter little more than a general attack on the British cause
in both its civil and its military aspects.

After 1777, as has been intimated, much of Gaine's patronage
was lost to Rivington, who continued the King's Printer at New
York until the end of the war.[15] Early in 1783, less than a year
before Gaine had to discontinue the *Mercury*, Freneau published
a mock autobiography. At the outset of his story Freneau's Gaine
declares he is proud to be Scotch-Irish:

> (I know you love Teagues) and I shall not conceal
> That I came from the kingdom where Phelim O'Neale
> And other brave worthies ate butter and cheese,
> And walk'd in the clover-fields up to their knees.

For a while after I came to this country and set up my press in
New York City, life ran smoothly. Then

> The feuds of the Stamp Act foreboded foul weather,
> And war and vexation all coming together:

[14] "The Impartial Chronicle," *Pennsylvania Packet*, Feb. 18, 1777, p. 1.
[15] Frank Luther Mott, *American Journalism* (New York, 1950), p. 84.

Those days were the days of riots and mobs,
Tar, feathers, and tories, and troublesome jobs—
Priests preaching up war for the good of our souls,
And libels, and lying, and Liberty poles.

. . . . .

Well, as I predicted that matters would be—
To the stamp-act succeeded a tax upon Tea:
What chest-fulls were scattered, and trampled, and drowned,
And yet the whole tax was but threepence per pound!

During the Battle of Long Island I galloped away to Newark.
But rather than submit to a hundred new masters,

I thought it more prudent to hold to the one—
And (after repenting of what I had done,
And cursing my folly and idle pursuits)
Returned to the city, and hung up my boots.

. . . . .

As matters have gone, it was plainly a blunder,
But then I expected the Whigs must knock under,
And I always adhere to the sword that is longest,
And stick to the party that's like to be strongest:
That you have succeeded is merely a chance,
I never once dreamt of the conduct of France!—

Although I then toasted the Vicar of Bray and was returned
to my "printing and place" at New York for swearing allegiance
to the King, each morning I had to "turn in the ranks at the beat
of the drum," to say nothing of guarding an officer's stable six
hours each day. Rivington, meanwhile, stood by and laughed at
me. Now that the loyalists are soon leaving, please let Hugh
Gaine stay behind.

The Crown he will promise to hold in disgrace:
The Bible—allow him to stick in its place.

. . . . .

Those types which have raised George the third to a level
With angels—shall prove him as black as the devil.

. . . . .

Who knows but, in time, I may rise to be great,
And have the good fortune to manage a State?
Great noise among people great changes denotes,
And I shall have money to purchase their votes—
The time is approaching, I venture to say,
When folks worse than me will come into play.[16]

Whereas Gaine turned coat once, Benjamin Towne, editor of
the *Pennsylvania Evening Post*, turned his twice. Early in the
war he espoused the patriot side. (The *Post* was the first paper
to print the Declaration of Independence.) When the British
occupied Philadelphia in 1777, he stayed and changed his politics.
Upon their withdrawal he ingratiated himself sufficiently with
the revolutionary government to be allowed to continue his
paper, though the circulation thereafter declined steadily. When
Towne asked John Witherspoon to renew his contributions to
the *Post*, Witherspoon with tongue in cheek agreed to do so
only on condition that Towne make a public apology for his
recent trimming. Towne consented, asking Witherspoon to prepare such a statement; when later Towne reneged, Witherspoon
published the document in the *New York Packet* anyway.[17] In
Witherspoon's travesty Towne declares that in view of the hostil-
ity he has incurred by turning coat twice, he now offers his
"humble confession, declaration, recantation & apology" in the
hope that it will assuage the wrath of his enemies. "In the first
place," he confesses, "I never was, nor ever pretended to be a
man of Character, Repute or Dignity."

Had a Hancock or an Adams changed sides, I grant you they
would have deserved no quarter, & I believe would have received
none; but to pass the same judgment on the conduct of an obscure
printer is miserable reasoning indeed. . . . [I] shall ask any plain

[16] "Hugh Gaine's Life," *Freeman's Journal*, Jan. 8, 29, Feb. 12, 1783; reprinted in Pattee, II, 201–214.
[17] Mott, *American Journalism*, p. 88; Schlesinger, *Prelude*, p. 293;
Lorenzo Sabine, *Biographical Sketches of Loyalists of the American
Revolution* (Boston, 1864), II, 360; Collins, *Witherspoon*, I, 234.

Quaker in this City what he would say to a man who should wear the same coat in summer as in winter in this climate? . . .

2.dly I do hereby declare & confess, that when I printed for Congress & on the side of liberty, it was not by any means from principle or a desire that the cause of liberty should prevail, but purely & simply from the love of gain. I could have made nothing but tar & feathers by pointing against them as things then stood. . . . I was neither Whig nor Tory, but a printer. . . . It is pretended that I certainly did in my heart incline to the English, because I printed much bigger lies & in greater number for them than for the Congress. This is a most false & unjust insinuation. It was entirely the fault of the Congress themselves, who thought fit (being but a new potentate in the earth) to be much more modest, & keep nearer the truth than their adversaries. Had any of them brought me in a lie as big as a mountain it should have issued from my press. . . .

3.dly I hope the Public will consider that I have been a timorous Man, or, if you will, a Coward, from my youth, so that I cannot fight;— my belly is so big that I cannot run;—& I am so great a lover of eating and drinking that I cannot starve. When these three things are considered I hope they will fully account for my past conduct, and procure me the liberty of going on in the same *uniform* tenor for the future. . . . I am also verily persuaded that if all those who are Cowards as well as myself, but who are better off in other respects, and therefore can and do run whenever danger is near them, would befriend me, I should have no inconsiderable body on my side. . . . Finally, I do hereby recant, draw back, eat in & swallow down every word that I have ever spoken, written or printed to the Prejudice of the United States of America.[18]

---

[18] "The humble Confession, Recantation, and Apology of Benjamin Towne, Printer in Philadelphia," *New York Packet*, Oct. 1, 1778; reprinted in *The Works of John Witherspoon* (Edinburgh, 1804–1805), IX, 192–198. I also consulted a longhand copy inserted between pp. 206–207 of the *Pennsylvania Evening Post*, June 6, 1778, at the American Antiquarian Society. A year later Towne, in an effort to increase his subscriptions, issued a broadside in which his flight from Philadelphia at the time of the British occupation and his timely return to that city are satirized, *Pennsylvania Evening Post*, Jan. 1, 1780.

III

"Treason against the United States," says the Constitution, "shall consist only in levying War against them, or in adhering to their Enemies, giving them Aid and Comfort" (Art. III, Sect. 3). What is remarkable in this statement, when viewed in the light of the long and often shameful history of treason, is that it makes only disloyal action treasonable, not subversive thoughts, dangerous writings, or vague plots.[19] In Revolutionary times, however, such a distinction had not yet been clearly drawn: refusal to submit to a test act or even questioning the validity of the Declaration of Independence might be held treasonable. Whereas some men prudently trimmed their sails, others tacked sharply about and offered aid and comfort to the enemy. The satirists singled out Charles Lee, whose treachery has never been clearly established, and Benedict Arnold.

The British officer Charles Lee, formerly a major general in the Polish army and now disappointed in his neglect at home, arrived in America late in 1773 and began at once to work in the patriot cause. A year later an epigram in the New York press took note of these facts. The Polish hero Lubin (Lee), disgruntled at not obtaining a regiment in Europe, cries,

> "I swear,
> "To America—I strait will repair:
> "I'll head their bold Sons,—and the sound of my Name
> "Shall lead them to Victory, Freedom and Fame."
> *Jack Catch*, who stood by, with significant Leer,
> Cries, "Courage, my Hero, push on, never fear,
> "Your Reward you shan't lose, I'll be d--n'd if you do,
> "See *here!*"—and a Halter presents to his View.
> "Hands off, (bellows *Lubin,*) away with your string:
> "I've done with my Project, faith, rather than swing.

[19] Nathaniel Weyl, *Treason: The Story of Disloyalty and Betrayal in American History* (Washington, D.C., 1950), p. 28.

> "If these are your Tricks, you shan't catch me to *fight*,
> "But in spite of your slip-noose, by G– –, I will *write*." [20]

Lee, now Washington's second in command, was captured by the British in December, 1776, and carried to New York. Acting on motives that are not altogether clear even now, he formulated a plan for bringing America to her knees and offered to pay with his life if the British did not succeed within two months. He proposed that 4,000 men be embarked, one half to proceed up the Potomac to Alexandria, the other half up Chesapeake Bay to Annapolis, with the common objective of severing the middle states from the southern. While the plan could be construed as traitorous to the American cause, it seems more likely that Lee was here trying to mislead the Howes; for even if communications between the two regions had been cut, the Americans would certainly not have capitulated in two months' time.[21] After the Battle of Monmouth, Lee, now back with the Continental Army, was reprimanded by Washington, though time has shown that his behavior on that occasion was not prompted by cowardice but based on sound strategy. On his own demand he was tried, convicted, and suspended from the army for a year, but his conduct in the interim was such—one remembers his defamatory "Queries"—that on January 10, 1780, Congress dismissed him from the army permanently. Shortly after his death in 1782 one writer damned him, though with praise, in the English press:

> Warrior, farewell! eccentrically brave,
> Above all *kings*, and yet of gold the *slave;*
> In words a very *wit*—in deeds *less wise;*
> For ever *restless*, yet would never rise;
> At least no higher, than to meet the ground;

[20] *Rivington's New-York Gazetteer*, Jan. 26, 1775, p. 3; reprinted in *Loyalist Poetry*, pp. 127–128. The last line of this poem refers to Lee's *Strictures on a Friendly Address to all Reasonable Americans* (1774), a reply to Myles Cooper's pamphlet defending loyalism.

[21] George H. Moore, *The Treason of Charles Lee* (New York, 1860), pp. 406–409 *passim;* Alden, *Lee*, pp. 175–176.

If strong the *blow*, the greater the *rebound*.
Of all men *jealous*, yet *afraid* of none;
In *crowds* for ever—ever still *alone*,
At once the pride and bubble of a throng,
Pursuing *right*, and yet forever *wrong;*
By nature form'd to play the *monarch's* part
At *best* a sad republican at heart.
 But to cast up the aggregated sum—
Above all *monarchs*, and below all scum;
Unsettled *virtues*, with great vices mix'd,
Like the wide welkin, where few stars are fix'd,
Rest, *restless* chief! thy sword has taken rust;
Peace to thy *manes*—honour to thy dust.[22]

On May 30, 1778, Benedict Arnold took the oath of allegiance required of all American officers, vowing:

I do acknowledge the United States of America to be Free, Independent and Sovereign States, and declare that the people thereof owe no allegiance or obedience to George the Third, King of Great-Britain; and I renounce, refuse and abjure any allegiance or obedience to him; and I do swear that I will, to the utmost of my power, support, maintain and defend the said United States against the said King George the Third, his heirs and successors, and his or their abettors, assistants and adherents, and will serve the said United States, in the office of Major General which I now hold, with fidelity, according to the best of my skill and understanding.[23]

Within the year, however, he opened secret correspondence with General Clinton at New York. On May 5, 1779, as though

[22] "To the Memory of General Lee," *Freeman's Journal*, July 23, 1783, where it is identified as from the *St. James Chronicle*. Although Philip Foner includes it in *The Complete Writings of Thomas Paine* (New York, 1945), II, 1099–1100, Alden does not think Paine's authorship established (*Lee*, p. 355n.); and A. O. Aldridge, having examined the circumstances of composition and publication, concludes: "This epitaph is almost certainly not by Paine. . . . The author is an Englishman, who condemns Lee for defection," *Penn. Mag. Hist. & Biog.*, LXXIX (1955), 93.

[23] A facsimile of this oath is printed in Willard M. Wallace, *Traitorous Hero* (New York, 1954), p. 162.

experiencing pangs of guilt for the treason on which he had just embarked, Arnold, in his capacity as military commander at Philadelphia, wrote hysterically to Washington concerning the charge of peculation leveled at him by the Pennsylvania civil authorities, "If your Excellency thinks me criminal, for heaven's sake let me be immediately tried and, if found guilty, executed." [24] On August 3, 1780, he was given command of the garrison at West Point, which controlled the upper reaches of the Hudson, and on September 21 held the fateful interview with André. What followed is history. It outraged the patriot community at home and abroad to think that whereas André went to the gallows, Arnold was appointed to a high rank in the British army. This fact helps explain why the satirists in this instance became so emotionally involved in their object that the pathetic part threatens to swallow up the ridiculous.

Occasionally it did not. A few days after André's execution there appeared a letter in the Philadelphia press, in which Beelzebub congratulates Buzrael (Arnold) for having tried to execute his infernal commands.

You remember that before we sent you into the world to prepare the ruin of America, (the worthy object of our indignation being by its situation capable of more virtue than any country in the world,) we ordered you to begin by great exertions of bravery, to gain the affections of the inhabitants, and bestow on yourself their confidence and their friendship. You succeeded very well in this business, and you were even skilful enough to seduce and associate to your operations some powerful citizens of their country, whom we shall reward in time for their great achievements. . . . But we cannot approve of the choice you made of your face, which has something roguish in it, and does not quite inspire all that confidence we expected. We understand, by some savages, both English and Americans, lately arrived in our dominions, that what they call the virtuous citizens of America suspect you very much of being an enemy to their country. . . .

[24] Letter of May 5, 1779, *The Writings of George Washington*, ed. Jared Sparks (Boston, 1839–1840), VI, 523, quoted in Weyl, *Treason*, p. 47.

We expect that you will find some effectual means to deliver us from this powerful enemy [Washington], but particularly to put an end, by a capital stroke, to all the pretensions of that people, and we flatter ourselves that after their subjection they will be in a few years as corrupted, as wicked, as cruel as their mother country. We rely entirely upon your abilities, but at the same time we require a prompt execution of our orders.[25]

And a few weeks later another Philadelphia writer punned:

> ARNOLD! thy name, as heretofore,
> Shall now be Benedict no more;
> Since, instigated by the devil,
> Thy ways are turn'd from good to evil.
>
> 'Tis fit we brand thee with a name,
> To suit thy infamy and shame;
> And since of treason thou'rt convicted,
> Thy name should now be maledicted.
>
> Unless by way of contradiction,
> We style thee Britain's Benediction;
> Such blessings she, with liberal hand,
> Confers on this devoted land.[26]

Late in 1781, Arnold sailed with his family for England. A writer there described with what warmth the ministerial party received him:

> Mild Abingdon shouts out your praise,
> Burgoyne himself will tune his lays,
>   To sing your skill in battle:
> Greater than Hans, who scal'd the Alps,
> Or Indian Chiefs, who brought him scalps
>   Instead of Yankee cattle.
>
> For camp or cabinet you were made,
> A jockey's half a courtier's trade,

[25] *Pennsylvania Packet*, Oct. 7, 1780, p. 2; reprinted in Moore's *Diary*, II, 329–330.

[26] *Pennsylvania Packet*, Oct. 24, 1781, p. 1; reprinted in Moore's *Songs*, pp. 333–334.

And you've instinctive art;
Although your outside's not so drest,
Bid Mansfield dive into your breast,
And then report your heart.[27]

Besides natural opponents, civil war brings forth trimmers and traitors. An historian can usually distinguish between at least the motives of the two, between Gaine and Towne on the one hand, say, and Arnold on the other. Satirists, impatient with distinctions of this sort, here accused both groups equally of acting from self-interest and lack of principle. So high did their feelings run that only rarely did one of them write with the detachment essential to satire of a high order; Livingston, for instance, in "The Impartial Chronicle." Indeed, their sense of outrage at traitors was sometimes too deep for satire: the knowledge that Dr. Benjamin Church, a long-time Boston patriot, had conveyed secret information to General Gage in 1775 produced only angry verse. All of which is to say that trimmers and traitors were neither so clear nor so easy a target as patriots or, what is the topic of the next chapter, loyalists.

[27] "ODE, addressed to GENERAL ARNOLD. By LADY CRAVEN," *Salem Gazette*, Oct. 17, 1782, p. 4 (from an unidentified English publication). Freneau commemorated Arnold's departure for England in a parody on Horace's tenth Epode, substituting Arnold for Mevius, *Freeman's Journal*, July 10, 1782 (reprinted in Pattee, II, 103–104).

CHAPTER XI

Loyalists

WHEN during the decade preceding the Declaration of Independence, the American community steadily divided on the question whether Parliament possessed the right to tax or even legislate for the colonies, patriots answered the question by advancing arguments to justify political autonomy, loyalists by insisting that America was a dependent part of the British Empire. Thomas Hutchinson, for one, was early convinced that the two views were mutually exclusive and told the Massachusetts Assembly so.

I know of no line that can be drawn between the supreme authority of Parliament and the total independence of the colonies: it is impossible there should be two independent Legislatures in one and the same state; for, although there may be but one head, the King, yet two Legislative bodies will make two governments as distinct as the kingdoms of England and Scotland before the union.[1]

Which is not to say that the loyalists, who thought of themselves as Americans first and British subjects afterwards, always saw eye to eye with the British official class. We have seen how indifferent that class showed itself to colonial rights. To the majority of the loyalists, who sought redress from the most oppressive measures of the Grenville, Townshend, and North Min-

[1] Jan. 6, 1773, *Speeches of the Governors of Massachusetts*, p. 340.

istries through legal channels, the welfare of their homeland was of foremost concern.

I

This political division first arose in the controversy over stamped paper. Whereas Americans in 1763 had not yet begun to choose between home rule and colonial dependency, within two years those who favored enforcement of the Stamp Act found themselves suddenly on the defensive. "The Truth is, we are the Children of a most indulgent Parent who has never exerted her authority over us, till we are grown almost to manhood and act accordingly," complained one loyal-minded Bostonian; "but were I to say so here before our Chief Ruler, the Mob, or any of their adherents, I should presently have my house turned inside out." Some of the Crown officers who saw their duty knew whereof he spoke. It was over the Townshend Revenue Act a few years later, however, that press opinion in America first sharply divided.[2] On this occasion the government press, especially at Boston and New York, opposed nonimportation and challenged the activities of local Sons of Liberty. One patriot, hoping to quash this nascent loyalism before it crystallized into action, sneered:

Every fool is not a Tory, but every Tory is a fool. The man who maintains the "divine right of kings to govern wrong" is a fool, and also a genuine Tory. . . . Wonderful it is, after the reigns of William the Third, Anne, George the First and Second, and in the 11th year of the reign of George the Third, to see the same foolish, absurd, blasphemous principles revived and asserted; but you have the solution above, "Though every fool is not a Tory, yet every Tory is a fool."[3]

[2] Savelle, *Seeds of Liberty*, p. 353; James Murray to Dr. John Murray, Nov. 13, 1765, *Letters of James Murray*, ed. N. M. Tiffany (Boston, 1901), p. 154; Mott, *American Journalism*, p. 75.
[3] "*A Description of a* Tory," *Newport Mercury*, Sept. 2, 1771, p. 4.

And Brackenridge, then an undergraduate at politically minded
Princeton, traced the history of the tories:

> In wretched cain the wicked race began
> Who dwelt in Nod & fled the face of man
> The great arch-tory broke thro' nature's laws
> And slew his brother without any cause [.]
>
> . . . . .
>
> Nebuchadnezar was a Tory too.
> And Haman strung by mordecai the Jew
> Thus all along the tory herd appears
> Sprung from the ordure of 5000 years.—
> In England fair encircled by the main
> Long did the power of tory faction reign
> At length the Whigs—oh! hail the generous sound
> Did all their rage & high blown pride confound
> The Whigs at length regain'd the British crown
> And struck the Pope & all the tories down.[4]

From the moment it organized for action in the fall of 1774
the loyalist party was at a disadvantage. Convinced that many
of the measures recently passed in assembly and others now being debated by the Congress were extralegal, many of its members supported the British government because it seemed, as
Leonard Labaree observes, "the only agency that could be relied
on to restore society to its proper foundations."[5] The following
spring a facetious writer at New York prepared a creed requiring tories to affirm "that opposition of state ministers, is the unpardonable sin" and "that the inhabitants of Great Britain and
North-America, are miserable, only because they are free," and
further to endeavor fervently "to banish that baneful harpy,
Liberty, from the face of the earth forever."[6] All those must
be numbered as "*rank Tories*," inveighed another,

---

[4] "The Origin of the Tories," in "Satires against the Tories," 1770,
MSS, Historical Society of Pennsylvania.

[5] *Conservatism*, p. 145.

[6] "The TORIES CREED," *New York Journal*, Mar. 16, 1775, p. 1.

who religiously adhere to the old absurd and wormeaten Jacobite doctrine of passive obedience, and nonresistance, or an absolute submission to the higher powers and a tame obease subjection to the most
unjust and tyrannical impositions for conscience sake or under the
specious pretence of being conscience bound so to do.[7]

Neither the North Ministry nor Howe's army could alleviate
the suffering which loyalists at beleaguered Boston experienced
during the terrible winter of 1775–1776.

Provisions & fuel were scarce & very dear [reports Anne Hulton],
supplies uncertain, Heavy rains, Tempestuous weather, & the Winter
set in very severe, . . . & it was to be feard some Provission Ships
had been taken by the Provincials. . . .

Amidst all these alarms dangers & distresses the Small pox spread
Universaly, which Obliged them to innoculate the Children. . . .

My Bro[r] says that Ships to Boston laden with Provission might
make a prodigious Voyage of it, The articles they want are Beef,
Pork, pease, & Potatoes, Coals, and Oates &c. . . .

When finally Howe embarked for Halifax, he allowed some
nine hundred loyalist refugees to go first.[8]

The Blockheads: or, The Affrighted Officers, a farce which
appeared in the local press three months after the evacuation,
jeered at the recent plight of the loyalists. Surly (Timothy
Ruggles) complains bitterly to his fellows that Hutchinson cajoled them with talk of *"pensions, posts of honor, and profit"*
and then fled the scene:

O curs'd ambition! much better had it been if I had stay'd among my
countrymen, and partook quietly of the produce of my farm.—Why
need I have medled in politicks, or burnt my fingers dabbling in this
sea of fire.

Simple (Benjamin Eaton) tells his wife that he has exhausted
his resources, to which plaint she turns a deaf ear:

[7] *Plain-Dealer,* Jan. [1], 1776.
[8] Letter from Chester, Eng., Jan. 17, 1776, *Letters of a Loyalist Lady,*
pp. 82–83.

You are afraid I shall ask you for a *silk gown,* or a *new cap;* that I shall want to see the *plays,* &c. and that you must have to bring forth some of those *rusty joannes,* which you have pilfer'd from your neighbours, when you was a justice. . . . Do not think I am to lead my life like a *mope,* as when we were *rusty farmers*—we are now *gentle-folks,* and shall expect to do like gentle-folks. . . . [The farm you are afraid of losing] is all *dirty stuff,* only fit for *yankees.* . . . As to your not supplying me, I am in no way concern'd about it; if you won't another will, and you may expect a pair of horns grow out of your head as large as your old bulls.

Simple retorts:

Do, and welcome, but stand clear if you come within reach of them.

Placing no confidence in British generosity, he decides to support himself by pilfering the town while "*pilfering* is in the fashion; the *General* has set us a very pretty example." Meanwhile Meagre (Harrison Gray) laments:

Half famish'd on land, and pent within the garrison for 10 months, [I] am now *oblig'd* to put to sea, to vomet up what *little guts* I have remaining!

In the final scene British soldiers describe the confusion at the time of embarkation:

The poor *yankee refugees,* run backwards and forwards, like a parcel of cats let out of a bag. . . . The beauty of the whole is aboard the ships—the *yankee refugees* with their *wives,* cut a most ridiculous figure—*vomiting, crying, cooking, eating,* all in a heap.—I was ready to burst my sides in laughing, to see the ladies scampering into the vessels, tumbling one over another, showing their legs, &c. . . . They stow like a *litter of pigs,* or like a young brood of *spaniels;* they even *spew* in one another's mouths.[9]

Though not formally outlawed until July 4, 1776, loyalists found themselves in jeopardy and their cause threatened the moment war broke out. Persecution was widespread and constant. Many loyalists were tarred and feathered, others imprisoned, still others forced to recant or flee to avoid the humiliation. Private

[9] Boston, [June 17?,] 1776, pp. 5, 6, 9–10, 11, 15, 19.

coaches were burned or pulled to pieces, merchants' goods attacked and destroyed or stolen. The defeat of 1,600 loyalists at Moore's Creek near Wilmington, North Carolina, on February 27, 1776, seriously weakened their effective strength throughout the South. Well might Judge Samuel Curwen prophesy, "The use of the property I left behind me I fear I shall never be the better for; little did I expect from affluence to be reduced to such rigid economy as prudence now exacts." Like many another who went into exile, he never did recover his property when he returned to his native Salem after the war.[10]

II

Loyalism tended to assert itself in those who were socially and economically well-to-do, though to this rule there were many exceptions on both sides. At the outbreak of the war perhaps a third of America was loyalist in its sympathies, such sentiment being especially strong in New York, Pennsylvania, and parts of the South.[11] The loyalist cause drew its chief support from Crown officers, Anglican clergy, and recent British immigrants, but to these must be added substantial numbers from the other professions and from the mercantile community.

Convinced that it was morally wrong to resist established authority, the Anglican clergy, many of them, declared for loyalism. It is William Sweet's belief that "the proportion of loyalists among colonial Anglicans," who were most numerous in the South and least numerous in New England, "was in inverse ratio to their numbers in the several colonies." In the North their association with the government party scarcely endeared them to Dissenters. "The Episcopalians," declared Ezra Stiles, "confederate themselves with the Crown officers of every

[10] Van Tyne, Loyalists, pp. 46–47; letter to Dr. Charles Russell, June 10, 1776, Journal and Letters of Samuel Curwen, p. 59.
[11] M. C. Tyler, Am. Hist. Rev., I (1895), 29; Lewis Einstein, Divided Loyalties (London, 1933), p. 189.

department, procure ecclesiastical revenues, monopoly of all lucrative and honorary employments." It is not surprising, therefore, that it was mainly these same Episcopalians, men like Samuel Seabury, Thomas Bradbury Chandler, and Myles Cooper, who stated the loyalist position most clearly and fully.[12] Trumbull's bumbling M'Fingal manages to distort their argument:

> "Have not our High-church Clergy made it
> Appear from Scriptures, which ye credit,
> That right divine from heaven was lent
> To kings, that is, the Parliament,
> Their subjects to oppress and teaze,
> And serve the devil when they please?
> Did not they write, and pray, and preach,
> And torture all the parts of speech,
> About rebellion make a pother,
> From one end of the land to th' other?
>
> . . . . .
>
> Have not our Cooper and our Seabury
> Sung hymns, like Barak and old Deborah;
> Proved all intrigues to set you free
> Rebellion 'gainst *the Pow'rs that be;*
>
> . . . . .
>
> Proved every king, ev'n those confest
> Horns of the Apocalyptic beast,
> And sprouting from its noddles seven,
> Ordain'd, as Bishops are, by heaven." [I, 23–25]

Reverend Samuel Peters of Hebron, Connecticut, who several times expressed his abhorrence of Dissenters in letters to friends, was persecuted by the patriots there. A travesty on one of his letters from Boston to Samuel Auchmuty, another "high-church Tory," reads:

[12] Labaree, *Conservatism*, p. 153; W. W. Sweet, *Hunt. Lib. Quar.*, XI (1947), 52; Feb. 27, 1767, Stiles MSS, Yale College Library, quoted in Namier, *England in American Revolution*, p. 300; Becker, *Political Parties*, pp. 158–159.

Riots and mobs did so pursue me,
Made up of ev'ry man that knew me,
It made me think they would undo me;
'Twas therefore hither I withdrew me.
All the good Clergy of Connecticut,
All those I mean that wear the petticoat,
With their true churches soon must feel
The force of puritannick zeal;
Unless the Dragon should be bound,
Or the old Serpent get a wound.

The patriotic zeal of these Puritans must be curbed:

The friends of Stuart must combine,
Or else our cause will soon decline;
As all the children turn their whistles
Into drums, halberts, swords and pistols,
And half the nation play the devil
For sacred liberty and civil.

I have suffered dearly for preaching passive nonresistance:

Because I taught passive obedience,
According to my sober credence;
Forbad their arming for this reason,
Because it would be deem'd high treason,
The sons of liberty have birch
Apply'd t' a member of my church;
And other members in all weathers,
They have dress'd up in tar and feathers;
My windows broke, my cloathing rent,
And even the sacred cassock, sent
By th' company for propagation,
When first in church I took my station;
They impiously did tear, and tore
The parts that were not rent before.

We Anglicans must "Subdue these protestant dissenters." [13] The
following year another writer reported that Peters, having been

[13] *Essex Journal*, Mar. 22, 1775, p. 4. Throughout his rectorship at

turned out of his old job, obtained "his Majesty's leave to pick hops at 9d per day, a penny more than the usual price, as a reward for his past faithful services; and by this lucrative business it is supposed he will soon acquire a fortune equal to that he left behind him." [14] Both attacks, as it happened, were issued after Peters, twice beset by local Sons of Liberty, had sailed for England.

Although a majority of the colonial lawyers were patriots, most of the eminent ones were loyalists.[15] A catechist early in 1768 cited instances of "ill judging pernicious Lawyers in our Days." It was a lawyer, Jared Ingersoll, who "accepted the first Commission for distributing the Stamps, and helping to ruin his Country." Another declared that the Virginia Resolves "was almost high Treason." Lawyers "endeavour'd to obstruct and embarrass the Business" of the Stamp Act Congress, ridiculed it, and called it "an unlawful Assembly." Nor were they ruined by the Stamp Act itself, for "they were sure to have all the Business, when the Courts were open again, that had been suspended, and more,—occasion'd purely by the Stop of Business." In fact, lawyers thrive on the misfortune of others. "They get one Half of our Estates from us for keeping up our Spirits and Resentment, till we have heartily beat and tired one another; and then they demand the other Half, for making us Friends again." [16]

Among loyalist editors James Rivington of the *New-York Gazetteer* (1773–1775) was one of the most outspoken. In 1774 one patriot inveighed:

Hebron (1760–1774), Peters was supported by the Society for the Propagation of the Gospel in Foreign Parts.

[14] *Pennsylvania Evening Post*, Apr. 30, 1776, p. 218; reprinted in the *New Eng. Mag.*, XXX (1904), 371.

[15] John F. Jameson, *The American Revolution Considered as a Social Movement* (Princeton, 1926), p. 14.

[16] "The VOTER's NEW CATECHISM," *New York Journal*, Mar. 3, 1768, p. 5. Peyton Randolph, Edmund Pendleton, Richard Bland, and George Wythe, all lawyers, opposed the heat and virulence of the Virginia Resolves; later they became patriots.

In politics your very self,
An ign'rant, yet a treach'rous elf
  The public now have found;
For, trying metal as they shou'd,
They, judging 'twixt the bad and good,
  Condemn you from your sound.

        .   .   .   .   .

Attempt to shine on rows of shelves,
From *Folio's* large to smallest *Twelves,*
  'Twill *fairer* profit bring
Than turning dirty hireling scribe,
For sake of wretched paltry *Bribe,*
  From Minister or K--g.[17]

A year later, on November 27, 1775, Isaac Sears, who bore Rivington a personal grudge, led a mob of Connecticut and New
York Sons of Liberty to his shop and there destroyed his presses
and scattered his type.[18] Rivington left for England a few months
after this and did not return until Howe's army was safely lodged
in New York City.

In a letter to the New York press about this time Charles Lee
professed to apologize for Rivington's illiteracy: This little performance (the letter begins) is intended "for his vindication"
against the numerous calumniators who "strain their little wits
to throw a ridicule upon his talents, his style, his integrity, and
even his erudition." Being the other night "amongst a set of the
most flaming factious enemies to all order and government," I
heard Rivington described as

a ridiculous, pragmatical, slipslop coxcomb; they said, that he had
not decency enough for the porter of a bawdy-house, learning
enough for a barrack washer-woman, nor imagination sufficient for
a Christmas-bellman:—that at the age of fifteen he was turned out
of the blue-school, where he had been bred, as too incorrigible a
dunce to make a scavenger of; that they had, by way of jocular ex-

[17] "A MIRROR FOR A PRINTER," Boston broadside, 1774; reprinted in the
New-York Journal, Sept. 15, 1774.
[18] Becker, *Political Parties,* p. 246.

periment, for some time tried him in this capacity; but that he always, in windy days, swept the dust up against the wind.

I defended his style as incomprehensibly fine and called him a Latin scholar; at this last "the whole company burst out into a horse-laugh" and said he couldn't "conjugate the verbs *mentior*, nor *vapulo*, though he so generally practised the former, and has so often experienced the latter."

They then proceeded to fall foul upon his English; they said that when he first set up his press, . . . he used always to write musketeers, musk-cat-ears—dragoons, dragons—battalions, battle lions; . . . I hate the story they told of him, . . . that writing to his niece, who was going to be married to an eminent pawnbroker in St. Martin's Lane, he began his letter thus: "My dear Kitty, as you are going to be married, and are so very young a girl, I would advise you by all means, at least, at first, to act with a little *cushion*," meaning it for *caution*. Now I would appeal to all mankind, who are not totally blinded by party and faction, whether it is credible, whether it is possible, that a gentleman, who has from his cradle been in some sort a retainer of the Muses, should be guilty of such gross, such ridiculous blunders.[19]

Lee, announcing that he is "a studier of men and characters," here creates a spectator mask. The spectator's admission that he has never "passed through a regular course of education" immediately casts doubt on the validity of his apology, especially when he boasts that Rivington as "a retainer of the Muses" "was invited into a society of eminent itinerary comedians." Lee, who inveighed against Washington at a later date, here shows a mastery of that subtler satiric pattern, irony.

Of all the loyalists who served as Crown officers in America, Thomas Hutchinson, eminent leader of the government party in Massachusetts, received the heaviest and most sustained fire. On the night of August 26, 1765, during the Stamp Act riots at

[19] "A Breakfast for R********" [1775?]; printed in *Memoirs of Charles Lee*, pp. 84–87. Although Lee addressed this letter to John Holt, editor of the *New York Journal*, it was apparently never printed; Alden concludes, "A thorough search has failed to discover it in any newspaper," *Lee*, p. 321.

Boston, a mob had entered and destroyed his house and "cast into the street, or carried away all his money, plate, and furniture, together with his apparel, books, papers." [20] In this instance more sinned against than sinning, an embittered Hutchinson henceforth put his duty to the Crown before his deep and abiding love for country whenever the two came into conflict. When he became acting governor in the summer of 1769, the satirists sharpened their pens. In the words of one, Bernard advises the Assembly not to rejoice too soon,

> For when I've taken my departure,
> By Jupiter! you'll catch a tartar;
> Lord Paddy, faith, has taken care,
> To place Tom Gr—p—llin in the chair:
> He'll spoil your fun, I won't bely him,
> But he's a crooked dog—as I am.[21]

In 1771, the year Hutchinson was commissioned governor, another writer charged: "A modern provincial Governor's chief end is, to serve the minister, that he may be found worthy to enjoy a pension, or be advanced to a better place through his favour." For the minister—Hillsborough in this case—creates the governor "after his own image, to have no will, no knowledge, no sentiment, no virtue, but according to his pleasure, with dominion under him over the people." "The modern provincial Governor is gratified with a pension. He has also a salary paid him by the minister, by which he is enabled to ridicule and laugh at the menaces of the people, and which makes him a still more necessary wretch to the designs of the minister, as the continuation of it absolutely depends on his being a finished tool, sycophant and traitor." [22] Distressed by the events culminating in the Tea Party, Hutchinson secured a leave of absence and sailed for England on June 1, 1774, the day the Port Bill went into force. War came within the year, and he stayed abroad.

[20] *The Diary and Letters of Thomas Hutchinson* (Boston, 1884), p. 67.
[21] *New-York Gazette*, July 17, 1769, p. 4.
[22] *A Ministerial Catechise*, pp. 4, 5.

In 1779 his estate in America was confiscated, and he was forced to live on royal bounty.[23]

One of the most relentless critics of the Hutchinson faction in Massachusetts was Mercy Warren. During the crucial years 1773–1775 there appeared in the Boston press three plays: *The Adulateur* and *The Group*, known to be her work, and *The Defeat*, attributed to her. *The Adulateur* (1773), the best of the three, is laid in the time of the Boston Massacre; the action is highly episodic. Rapatio (Hutchinson), seen first in soliloquy, rejoices that with the departure of Brundo (Bernard), "Honor, places, pensions" are now his to command. Bitterly he recalls the days of the Stamp Act,

> when ten thousand monsters,
> Wretches who only claim'd mere outward form,
> To give a sanction to humanity
> Broke my retirement—rush'd into my chamber
> And rifled all my secrets—then flung me helpless,
> Naked and destitute, to *beg* protection.

Later he gives Bagshot (Captain Preston) permission to fire on the crowd at Boston should they insult the British troops again. After this massacre he angrily asks his minions:

> What say my friends? shall patriots, grov'ling patriots,
> Thus thwart our schemes? push back the plan of action!
> And make it thus recoil? mistaken wretches!
> Unthinking fools! they work their own destruction.

At this outburst Meagre (Foster Hutchinson) offers his services:

> If thirst of power;
> A spirit haughty, sour, implacable,
> That bears a deadly enmity to freedom,
> But mean and base; who never had a notion
> Of generous and manly; who would stab,
> Stab in the dark, but what he'd get revenge;
> If such a soul is suitable to thy purpose,
> 'Tis here.

[23] Einstein, *Divided Loyalties*, pp. 184–185.

Others follow suit. Rapatio then calls for a vote of confidence:

> 'Tis well—then swear—that in our general meeting
> This was declar'd, that long before that night
> In which we snuff'd the blood of innocence,
> The factious citizens, urg'd on by hell,
> Had *leagu'd* together, to *attack* the soldier;
> Trample on laws; murder the friends of power
> And bury all things in one common ruin.

Although the realization that freedom is expiring pricks him momentarily, he puts the thought out of his mind, preferring to recall how he raised to his present eminence Hazelrod (Peter Oliver), who presides this day at court:

> I from a fribbling, superficial dabler,
> A vain pretender to each learned science,
> A poet, preacher, conjurer and quack—
> Rear'd the obsequious trifler to my purpose,
> Rob'd him in scarlet, dignified the man:
> An hecatomb of incense is my due.

At the end Brutus (James Otis) warns the patriots in their present distress,

> I fear
> The manacles prepar'd by Brundo's hand,
> Cruel Rapatio, with more fatal art,
> Has fix'd, has rivetted beyond redress,

and exhorts them to

> crush, crush these vipers,
> Who singl'd out by a community,
> To guard their rights shall for a grasp of oar [ore],
> Or paltry office sell them to the foe.[24]

---

[24] *The Adulateur* (Boston, 1773); reprinted in the *Magazine of History*, XVI (1918), 225–259. "The Defeat," *Boston Gazette*, May 24, July 19, 1773, p. 3, was occasioned by the publication of the Hutchinson-Oliver letters; it is attributed to Mercy Warren by Maud M. Hutcheson, *Wm. & Mary Quar.*, ser. 3, X (1953), 384. *The Group* (Boston, [Apr. 3?,] 1775) was occasioned by news of the Massachusetts Government Act, which Mercy Warren called "a burlesque on good government" (letter

While these plays hardly constitute a trilogy, they resemble one another in several respects and can properly be considered together. As examples of the closet drama which had become popular in England a generation earlier, all three contain long unnatural soliloquies and sacrifice action to oratory and posturing. All three exhibit many of the melodramatic conventions associated with this subgenre: the too-easy antithesis of villain and hero; pathetic morality (in *The Adulateur* [I.i.] Brutus laments that in this "sweet retreat of freedom," "the sullen ghost of bondage / Stalks full in view"); and, what is most conspicuous of all, emphasis on the spectacular (in *The Defeat* [III.i.] Rapatio, after his forces are overcome, is seen "in deep mourning" beside the scaffold and blocks). While none of these plays can lay claim to greatness, *The Adulateur* is the most successful because the least static. Maud Hutcheson has justly said of them: "Although arranged in acts and scenes, her 'plays' are lacking in plot, love interest, and women characters. They are rabid conversation pieces, propaganda, intended primarily for reading, as witness her directions. A stage manager would have been hard pressed to provide for abrupt changes of scene, great crowds of people, processions of coaches." [25] One could wish for greater formal control and a measure of humor, however small, but it must be allowed that a number of the character delineations— that of Beau Trumps in *The Group*, for example—and the sheer melodramatic power which informs these plays help to offset such weaknesses.

III

The Declaration of Independence made it demonstrably clear that the war must eventuate in national independence or a con-

---

to Hannah Winthrop, Aug., 1774, quoted in *Wm. & Mary Quar.*, X, 387). These two plays introduce other Massachusetts loyalists, notably Proteus (Timothy Ruggles?), Limpit (Andrew Oliver?), and Beau Trumps (Daniel Leonard).

25 *Wm. & Mary Quar.*, X, 383.

tinuation of colonial dependency, though the Carlisle Commission of 1778 would tempt the Congress and the people at large with the prospect of dominion status. Furthermore, the Declaration convinced patriots and loyalists alike that fundamentally this was a civil war. Granted that the spectacle of the Howe brothers in North Atlantic waters preparing for a massive assault on New York evinced how deeply the British government felt committed to restoring the imperial balance, what lay closer still to the hearts of Americans in the summer of 1776 was the realization that this was first of all a war between fellow countrymen which would end disastrously for one side or the other. Loyalists realized that to sign the test acts, even now being drafted by the states, implied a willingness to reject the very beliefs on which many of them grounded their faith—the inviolability of the British Constitution, the sovereignty of Parliament, the benevolence of monarchy.[26] How could men of faith sign and make peace with their conscience? To refuse meant increased persecution, exile, and even disfranchisement. Yet many thousands did refuse, convinced no doubt that they were further justified than those now struggling to achieve independence.

A Congressional committee informed Silas Deane in October that "Tories are now of various kinds and various principles. Some are so from real attachment to *Britain*, some from interested views, many, very many, from fear of the *British* force; some because they are dissatisfied with the general measures of Congress; more because they disapprove of the men in power and the measures in their respective States." [27]

RANK TORIES [inveighed a Pennsylvanian] are advocates for unconditional submission to Great-Britain. They rejoice in every misfortune that befals the United States. They fabricate lies to deceive

[26] See Van Tyne, *Loyalists*, pp. 130–131, regarding the substance of the test acts.

[27] Committee of Secret Correspondence to Silas Deane, Oct. 1, 1776, Peter Force, *American Archives*, Fifth Series (Washington, D.C., 1853), II, 821, quoted in Henry E. Egerton, *The Causes and Character of the American Revolution* (Oxford, 1923), p. 160.

and intimidate the people of America. They prefer money stamped with the mark of the beast; and at the same time they employ their utmost ingenuity to depreciate the money issued by the Congress and by Conventions. They sicken at the names of the Congress, and of General Washington. They esteem no arts too base to injure or betray the friends of America. They are in love with slavery, and have no more relish for the sweets of liberty than they have for the enjoyments of the kingdom of heaven.[28]

Fearing "the *British* force" or not, upwards of 50,000 loyalists served in the British army, as regulars or in the militia. At New York City, where thousands of loyalists took refuge after it fell to the British, many were pressed into service. Within the army they were barely tolerated by either the officers or the men.[29] Freneau imagines how Clinton might have exhorted them to throw up defenses there in 1779:

> Come, gentlemen Tories, firm, loyal, and true,
> Here are axes and shovels, and something to do!
> > For the the sake of our king,
> > Come labour and sing;
> You left all you had for his honour and glory,
> And he will remember the suffering Tory.
>
> . . . . .
>
> Attend at the call of the fifer and drummer,
> The French and the Rebels are coming next summer,
> > And forts we must build
> > Though Tories are kill'd.
> Then courage, my jockies, and work for your king,
> For if you are taken no doubt you will swing—
> > If York we can hold
> > I'll have you enroll'd;
> > And after you're dead
> > Your names shall be read
> As who for their monarch both labour'd and bled,
> And ventur'd their necks for their beef and their bread.[30]

[28] *Pennsylvania Packet*, Mar. 18, 1777, p. 1.
[29] Van Tyne, *Loyalists*, pp. 183, 147, 246.
[30] First issued as a ballad sheet in 1779, according to Frank Moore

The composition of the loyalist community remained much the same after 1776, though with the departure of Crown officers and others its numbers steadily diminished. At Boston and Philadelphia, as well as at the stronghold of New York, it continued to come under satirical attack. *The Motley Assembly* (1779) exposes certain Boston merchants and their families who remained loyal long after Howe had departed. In the opening scene, a representative one, Mrs. Flourish (Mrs. Gilbert DeBlois) curses the French as the cause of all their misery: "This Rebellion would have been crush'd long before this, but for them —We could not have held out much longer, when they stepp'd in; but must have submitted to such terms as our gracious sovereign would have condescended to offer; which all who know his goodness Mr. Runt, are convinced would have been just and merciful." Mr. Runt (Ralph Inman) agrees that the French are "a treacherous crew" but is confident that "Old England will give them a drubbing yet." "But as to us," he adds, "I think we are in a worse box than ever;—out of the frying-pan, into the fire; and all this for a trifling duty on tea." [31]

Hopkinson pictures "Three Tories, in very foul weather, / Assembled in great consternation" at Philadelphia to "settle th' affairs of the Nation."

> The first by profession a Broker,
> Impertinent, noisy and vain,
> Without wit, would be fain thought a Joker,
> And vended hard money for gain.
>
> The second a Printer by trade
> Who dealt in hard words with the Scholars,
> And ev'ry vile Pamphlet he made
> He sold off at *Ten Paper Dollars*.

(*Songs*, p. 259); reprinted as "Sir Harry's Call" in the *Freeman's Journal*, Apr. 17, 1782, and again as "Sir Harry's Invitation" in Pattee, II, 7–8. Leary says, "No copy of the ballad sheet has since been found," *Freneau*, p. 422.

[31] *The Motley Assembly, a Farce* (Boston, 1779), pp. 6–7.

> The third was a Quaker demure,
> Whose Religion was keeping his Hat on;
> He sigh'd and he groan'd, to be sure,
> But his heart was as wicked as Satan.

The Broker (William Smith) expects a royal reward for having invaded the strength of the rebels "with the mighty pow'r of gold" and debased their currency. The Printer (Benjamin Towne?) deplores the fact that military leaders like Howe and Burgoyne, on whom the loyalists had depended, have let them down. Haled before three rebel "sons of Belial" when a secret letter he wrote is intercepted, the Quaker (Samuel Rowland Fisher?) is of the same mind as the Printer:

> Now such disgrace had ne'er been brought
> Our Tory tribes upon,
> Had but friend *Howe* with vigor wrought
> For our sal-va-ti-on.[32]

One of the ablest loyalist leaders at Philadelphia was Joseph Galloway, who tried to persuade the First Continental Congress to undertake a reconciliation with Britain and failed. The course of neutrality which he attempted to steer thereafter won him enemies on both sides. Late in 1776 he went over to the British side and worked actively though ineffectually to cripple the revolutionary movement in Pennsylvania, hoping thereby to end the war.[33] Soon after he went to New York one writer crudely inveighed:

> GALL'WAY has fled, and join'd the venal Howe;
> To prove his baseness, see him cringe & bow;
> A traitor to his country, and its laws,
> A friend to tyrants, and their cursed cause:—

[32] "A Tory Medley," Philadelphia broadside, [1780?]. Actually William Smith was a conservative patriot. The printer has also been identified but with less certainty with Robert Bell of Philadelphia and with Rivington, the Quaker with S. R. Fisk.

[33] Carl Van Doren, *Secret History of the American Revolution* (New York, 1941), pp. 37, 32.

Unhappy wretch! Thy interest must be sold,
For continental, not for polish'd gold;
To sink the money, thou thyself cried down,
And stab'd thy Country, to support the crown.
Go to and *fro*, like Lucifer on earth,
And curse the *Being*, that first gave thee birth;
Away to Scotland, and thyself prepare,
Coal dust and brimstone, is their only fare;
Fit materials, for such *Tory* blood,
Who wrong their country, and deny their God;
There herd with *Bute, Mansfield*, and his brother,
Bite, twist, sting, and poison one another.[34]

As though in answer to this command Galloway, after serving as civil administrator at Philadelphia during the British occupation, sailed for England in 1778, never to return.

IV

The satirical attack on editors was heavier now than before the signing of the Declaration. It centered on James Humphreys of the *Pennsylvania Ledger* (1775–1778) and, especially, James Rivington of the *Royal Gazette* (1777–1783). In the fall of 1776, at a time when William Howe was conducting the New Jersey campaign and Humphreys had just fled the city, Francis Hopkinson, signing himself "A Tory," addressed two letters to the Philadelphia press: I find it my duty (writes the Tory) to aid the British cause in America in whatever way I can. Since "amongst the implements of war, the Pen and the printing Press are not the most insignificant," I am pleased that the Howes have found a printer at Philadelphia subservient to their purposes, "one perfectly disposed to forward their humane designs." When I boasted "in the fulness of my heart, of *The Pennsylvania Ledger*, printed by Mr. *Humphreys*, to a friend whom I supposed to be a tory like myself," it was a shock to hear him say

[34] *Freeman's Journal* (Portsmouth), Mar. 15, 1777, p. 3.

that while he esteemed liberty of the press as highly as anybody, it ought when abused to be silenced.

"I have now in view [the friend explained] *The Pennsylvania Ledger,* a paper manifestly in the interests of the enemy: whether we consider the complexion of the paper itself, or the known political character of the editor. Why should a dangerous lenity protect a man in the abuse of that very lenity which is his only security, and on which he so ungratefully presumes? or why should he, under the sanction of one right, be permitted to aim at the subversion of all the other rights of his country? Would not our council of safety be very justifiable in silencing a press, whose weekly productions insult the feelings of the people, and are so openly inimical to the American cause?"

I was quite justly reprimanded, for having opened my mind so freely to this friend, by our tory society whose rule it is to be circumspect in such matters. "You can hardly imagine what regularity prevails in our board of tories. We are all formed into committees of various denominations, and appointed to various duties." There is, for example,

a *committee of false reports;*—whose duty is to fabricate and publish such articles of intelligence as may tend to alarm and terrify timid whigs, and distract the minds of the people. These are circulated at such times as the situation of public affairs may make them most probable. Sometimes they are thrown out in whispers, in so dark and secret a manner that their origin cannot be traced; and at other times openly, by means of the *Pennsylvania Ledger.* . . .

Some narrow minded people say, that we are doing all we can to ruin our country, and entail a miserable slavery on our unborn posterity. We believe we are doing the best we can for ourselves—and pray what has posterity done for us, that we should run the risk of confiscation and a halter for them? Our fixed opinion is, that the British army must eventually subdue this country—and setting the right or wrong of the thing out of the question, we think we may as well have the reputation and advantage of assisting them in their designs as not. 'Tis true, if the British Generals should succeed in their enterprise we may see our neighbours and friends imprisoned by hundreds, and hanged by dozens; their estates confiscated, and their children turned out to beggary and want; but then we shall ourselves escape, and enjoy in safety our lives and estates—and, perhaps, be even promoted, for our present services, to places of honour and emolument.[35]

In these letters, prophetic in that Humphreys would revive the *Ledger* at Philadelphia during the British occupation, Hopkinson manages the irony with a rhetorical discipline somewhat less successful than that he displayed five years later involving Rivington in a fictitious controversy (quoted below)—less successful only because a good many readers must have glimpsed the author behind the situational mask.

Returning to New York in the fall of 1777, James Rivington was soon appointed King's Printer there. As a consequence the issues from his press, especially the *Royal Gazette*, gave a strong ministerial slant to all war news. For this reason he was then more often an object for satire than at any time before the Declaration. In an ironic letter of 1779 to the Philadelphia press John Witherspoon has Rivington, who is disquieted by the British evacuation of New York City that he says is then in progress, address the Congress:

I have no desire (Rivington begins) "either to be roasted in Florida or frozen to death in Canada, or Nova-Scotia," and if I should go to England, it is not impossible that I "might be accommodated with a lodging in Newgate." I beseech you, therefore, let me live here in peace. In the first place,

I can assure your High Mightinesses, that no danger can arise from me; for I am as great a coward as king James VI. of Scotland, who could never see a naked sword without trembling. . . . Perhaps it will be said, that though no damage is to be apprehended from my deeds, yet I may do harm enough by words and writing. To this I answer, that I have expanded and exhausted my whole faculty of that kind in the service of the English. I have tried falshood and

[35] *Pennsylvania Evening Post*, Nov. 16, 26, 1776, pp. 573, 592; reprinted in *Miscellaneous Essays*, I, 132–141.

misrepresentation in every shape that could be thought of, so that it was like a coat thrice turned, that will not hold a single stitch. . . .

2. Any farther punishment upon me, or any other of the un-happy refugees who shall remain in New-York, will be altogether unnecessary; for they do suffer, and will suffer, from the nature of the thing, as much as a merciful man could wish to impose upon his greatest enemy. By this I mean the dreadful mortification, after our past puffing and vanity, of being under the dominion of the Congress, seeing and hearing the conduct and discourses of the friends of America, and perhaps being put in mind of our own, in former times. . . . You must remember the many sweet names given you in print in England and America,—Rebels—rascals—raggamuffins—tatterdemalions—scoundrels—black-guards—cowards and poltroons. You cannot be ignorant how many complete victories we gained over you, and what a fine figure you made in our narra-tives. We never once made you to *retreat;* seldom even to *fly* as a routed army; but *to run off into the woods; to scamper away through the fields;* and *to take to your heels as usual.* . . .

Now, dear gentlemen, consider what a miserable affair it must be for a man to be obliged to apply, with humility and self-abase-ment, to those whom he hath so treated; nay, even to beg life of them, while his own heart upbraids him with his past conduct, and perhaps his memory is refreshed with the repetition of some of his rhetorical flowers. . . .

3. I beg leave to suggest, that upon being received into favour, I think it would be in my power to serve the United States in many important respects. I believe many of your officers want politeness: they are, like old Cincinnatus, taken from the plough, and there-fore must still have a little roughness in their manners and deport-ment. . . .

I have imported many of the most necessary articles for appear-ance in genteel life. I can give them *savonnettes,* i.e. soap-balls to wash their brown hands clean; perfumed gloves, paint, powder, and pomatum, the use of which will make their whole persons as soft and delicate as my lady the countess's own darling boy, whom a noble gallantry of soul, and *a desire to please the King,* brought out to subdue the American rebels. I can also furnish the New-Eng-land-men with rings, seals, swords, canes, snuff-boxes, tweezer-cases, and many other such *notions,* to carry home to their wives and mistresses, who will be *nation* glad to see them.

If "virtue and severity of manners are necessary to those who would pull an old government down," "luxury, dissipation, and a taste for pleasure are equally necessary to keep up a government already settled. . . . Now I am proud to say, that there is not a man on this continent more able to serve you in this respect, than myself."

Finally, I hope I may be of service to the United States as a writer, publisher, collector, and maker of news. . . . As I have been the ostensible printer of other peoples lies in New-York, what is to hinder me from keeping *incog.* and inventing, or polishing lies, to be issued from the press of another printer in Philadelphia. . . . I can take a truth, and so puff, and swell, and adorn it, still keeping the proportion of its parts, but enlarging their dimensions, that you would hardly know it, and yet all the *stamina vitae* shall remain, to answer for themselves, in case of a strict investigation.[36]

Soon after Yorktown, Hopkinson informed Franklin, "I shall enclose, if I can, an Advertisement I wrote for Rivington, who curses me for doing him this kindness." [37] He was alluding to a facetious advertisement purportedly sent by Rivington to the *Pennsylvania Packet* a short time before, in which the printer, thinking this a convenient time to remove to Europe, gives notice that his remaining stock in trade is to be auctioned. Among his books are—

The Royal Pocket Companion: being a New System of Policy, founded on rules deduced from the nature of man, and proved by experience: whereby a prince may in a short time render himself the abhorrence of his subjects, and the contempt of all good and wise men. . . .

[36] "*The Humble* Representation *and earnest* Supplication *of* JAMES RIVINGTON," *United States Magazine,* I (Jan., 1779), 34–40; reprinted in the *Works of Witherspoon,* IX, 180–191.

[37] Nov. 30, 1781, Bache Papers, Amer. Philos. Soc., quoted in Dixon Wecter, *Am. Lit.,* XII (1940), 206.

A *Geographical, Historical, and Political History* of the Rights and Possessions of the Crown of Great Britain in North America. This valuable Work did consist of thirteen Volumes in Folio: but is now abridged by a royal Author to a single Pocket Duodecimo; for the greater convenience of himself, his successors, and subjects. . . .

Miracles not ceased: or, an instance of the remarkable Interposition of Providence in causing the Moon to delay her setting for more than two hours, to favour the retreat of General *Joshua* and the British Army after the *battle of Monmouth.*

This Rivington lists among his prints "*The Battle of Saratoga,* and *the Surrender at York;* . . . cut in Copper, and dedicated to the King" and "*The Times:* . . . representing the British Lion blind in both Eyes, thirteen of his Teeth drawn, and his Claws pared off; with Lord *North,* in the character of a Farrier, bleeding him in the Tail for his recovery." His philosophical apparatus and patent medicines include:

A curious new invented magic Lanthorn: very useful for these who are at the head of affairs. This Machine was constructed by an able Artist, under *Lord North's* immediate direction, for the amusement of the good people of England. The Spectators are gratified with an *illuminated* view of the fictitious objects presented, but kept totally in the dark with respect to the *real* objects around them.

Multiplying Glasses; whereby the numbers of an Enemy may be greatly encreased to cover the disgrace of a Defeat, or enhance the glory of a Victory.

Microscopes, for magnifying small objects, furnished with a select set ready fitted for use. Amongst these are a variety of real and supposed Successes of the British Generals in America. . . .

Sp. Mend.: Or the genuine spirit of *Lying,* extracted by distillation from many hundreds of the *Royal Gazette of New York.* Other papers have been subjected to the same process, but the success did not answer the Expence and Trouble of the operation, the produce being of an inferior quality—*Therefore beware of Counterfeits.* The Ink and Paper of the *Royal Gazette* can alone furnish this excellent Sp. Mend. in its greatest perfection. By administering due

proportions of this admirable Medicine, Lies may be formed which
will operate for a day, a week, a month or months; near at hand
or at a distance; in America, or in Europe; according to the design
of the party. . . .

Cordial Drops for low spirits, prepared for the special use of the
Honorable *Board of loyal Refugees* at New York.

Anodyne Elixir, for quieting Fears and Apprehensions: very necessary for *Tories* in all parts of America.

"To every Purchaser to the value of five Pounds," he concludes,
"will be delivered *gratis,* One Quire of counterfeit Continental
Currency. Also two Quires of Proclamations, offering Pardon
to *Rebels*." [38]

Ten days later a notice in Rivington's name assured the printer
of the *Packet* "that said advertisement is *in toto* spurious and
fictitious":

Alas! I am but a *poor printer!* subjected by my vocation to the
execrable task of bringing into the world the monstrous concep-
tions of weak and disordered minds. But I am deemed a tory—
malevolent tory—and why? truly because I have published tory
news, tory lies, and tory essays in my gazette. . . . The truth is,
I am a great friend to liberty; and have actually felt the sacred
flame glow in my breast—first, about the time, or rather just after
the affair of *Saratoga;* and now again on the surrender of *Lord
Cornwallis* and his army. And if the brave Americans should pursue
their success, and confirm their independence, of which indeed there
now seems to be little doubt, you may depend upon it, there is not
a flaming patriot in the Thirteen United States that will garrulate
the charms of liberty with more loquacious zeal than myself.

It is the duty of every citizen to serve king and country:

I have already served my king—my sovereign GEORGE III.—God
bless him! to the best of my poor abilities; and now I am ready
to wheel to the right-about and serve my country; for I call this
my country, wherein I have partook of the viands of luxury, and

[38] *Pennsylvania Packet,* Nov. 10, 1781; reprinted in *Miscellaneous Essays,* I, 159–169.

risen to a height of opulent importance, which I had no hopes of attaining in England, that land of debts, creditors, and intolerable oppression.

Your petitioner,

having given unquestionable proofs of his eminent abilities in the art of political deviation from the truth in support of a *bad cause,* humbly conceives that the same talents may be of singular utility in defending a *good one:* and therefore offers himself, with all his rare and superior accomplishments, to the congress of the free and United States of America; only praying such protection and rewards as his future services may justly merit.[39]

In this fictitious controversy, composed in the days following Yorktown, Hopkinson employs the same kind of rhetorical device that Franklin had used many years before in his ironical defense of London news writers against the slanderings of "The Spectator." [40] The facetious advertisement, a convention long identified with the periodical-essay tradition, becomes the more credible by specifying the time of the auction: "The sales to begin at his store on Monday, the 19th instant, and will be continued from day to day (Sundays excepted) from the hours of ten to one in the forenoon, until the whole shall be disposed of"; and Rivington's answer, by the righteous indignation he displays: "The author of this most wicked forgery, whoever he is, hath most nefariously, and with malice aforethought, made use of my name as a vehicle to impose on the judicious public the nugatory productions of his own flimsy brain, as the genuine offspring of my prolific pen." Save perhaps for *A Pretty Story,* this hoax is Hopkinson's finest achievement in satire during the Revolutionary period.

More Juvenalian than these attacks were Freneau's frequent

[39] *Pennsylvania Packet,* Nov. 20, 1781, p. 2; reprinted in *Miscellaneous Essays,* I, 170–177.

[40] *Public Advertiser,* May 15, 22, 1765, p. 1; reprinted in Crane, pp. 30–35.

outbursts against Rivington in the Philadelphia press after the
time of Yorktown. In what is probably the most successful of
these angry poems Rivington is portrayed soliloquizing about his
fears and his duplicity:

> The more I reflect, the more plain it appears,
> If I stay, I must stay at the risque of my ears,
> I have so be-peppered the foes of our throne,
> Be-rebelled, be-deviled, and told them their own,
> That if we give up to these rebels at last,
> 'Tis a chance if my ears will atone for the past.

I don't think Congress would make me leave New York City
should the troops be evacuated.

> For what have I done, when we come to consider,
> But sold my commodities to the best bidder?
> If I offered to lie for the sake of a post,
> Was I to be blamed if the king offered most?
> The King's Royal Printer!—Five hundred a year!
> Between you and me, 'twas a handsome affair.

Others may go to Nova Scotia,

> but I vow and I swear,
> I'll be boil'd into soup before I'll live there:
> Is it thus that our monarch his subjects degrades?—
> Let him go and be damned, with his axes and spades,
> Of all the vile countries that ever were known
> In the frigid, or torrid, or temperate zone,
> (From accounts that I've had) there is not such another;
> It neither belongs to this world or the other.

With the British government "trimming and twisting and shifting about" and dancing a "theatrical jig," "We are going to ruin
the round-about way!"

> The day is approaching as fast as it can
> When Jemmy will be a mere moderate man,
> Will sleep under ground both summer and winter,
> The hulk of a man, and the shell of a printer,

> And care not a farthing for George, or his line,
> What empires start up, or what kingdoms decline.[41]

Actually Rivington himself continued at New York even after the British left the city, but he was soon obliged to discontinue the *Gazette*.

V

Cornwallis' surrender made it evident to both sides that loyalism in America was rapidly approaching a disastrous end. The patriot press, reacting instantly to the news of Yorktown, related how a loyalist at New York, sobered by the thought that Burgoyne and now Cornwallis suffered defeat on the same fatal day in the "rebel month October," decides that his kind might fare better abroad:

> Better it were to quit the shore,
> And go beyond the sea, sir,
> In Britain they will love us more
> Than here we e'er can be, sir.
>
> A gentle prince upon his throne,
> With goodness looking down, sir,
> Will give us each some beef and bone,
> And call us all his own, sir.
>
> There we may, with Galloway Joe,
> Partake of royal bounty,
> And ministry too, for aught we know,
> May give us each a county.
>
> Should we cross the India seas,
> And undertake the job, sir,

[41] "Rivington's Reflections," *Freeman's Journal*, Dec. 4, 25, 1782; reprinted in Pattee, II, 190–196. Other of Freneau's more successful poems attacking Rivington at this time are "Rivington's Confessions," *Freeman's Journal*, Dec. 31, 1783, p. 2 (reprinted in Pattee, II, 229–238), and "Rivington's Last Will and Testament," *Freeman's Journal*, Feb. 27, 1782, p. 3 (reprinted in Pattee, II, 120–123).

> We may return when e'er we please,
> As rich as great Nabob, sir.[42]

From 1774 on loyalists had faced persecution. After the Declaration many had seen their estates and goods confiscated by state order, and now that the war in America was all but over they had little expectation of being compensated for losses, real and personal. But most terrible of all, many were about to leave their homeland forever. Actually this departure into exile, not always undertaken voluntarily, had commenced early in the war. Some went to England, others to the British West Indies, still others to Nova Scotia, where upward of 40,000 refugees eventually settled.[43] "All our golden promises are vanished in smoke," wrote a refugee at Nova Scotia in 1784. "We were taught to believe this place was not barren and foggy as had been represented, but we find it ten times worse. We have nothing but his Majesty's rotten pork and unbaked flour to subsist on. . . . It is the most inhospitable clime that ever mortal set foot on." [44] Small wonder the patriots renamed the place "Nova Scarcity." Such was the bleak prospect that awaited wave after wave of loyalists departing from Savannah, Newport, and New York. One penitent at Newport was made to lament:

> ALAS! brother Tories, now what shall we do,
> A peace is declared, I find certain true.
> The Rebels will hang us if we tarry here,
> Abroad there's no shelter for us I do fear.
> O shocking condition! from all we must part!
> This tears and distresses each nerve in my heart.
> Was ever poor mortals deceiv'd so before;
> Our lands and our houses we shall never see more,

[42] "Another New York Address," *Pennsylvania Packet*, Nov. 20, 1781, p. 1.

[43] Alexander C. Flick, *Loyalism in New York during the American Revolution* (New York, 1901), p. 175.

[44] Henry Onderdonk, *Revolutionary Incidents of Suffolk and Kings Counties* (New York, 1849), p. 256, quoted in Van Tyne, *Loyalists*, pp. 293–294.

We thought of preferment, o'er Rebels to reign;
But now we find nothing but flight and disdain.
O curst be the hour! O curst be the day!
We listen'd to Satan to take the wrong way.
Our King hath deceiv'd us, and left us forlorn;
O! curst be the hour wherein we were born.
O could we but tarry in our native land,
And lovingly take our old friends by the hand,
The meanest employment that mortals e'er had,
We'd cheerfully enter 'twou'd make us feel glad;
But this is deny'd us, all hopes now doth fail,
We're doom'd to destruction, our sins to bewail,
Unto Nova Scotia, a cold barren land,
To live upon shell-fish and dig in the sand.
Then fare ye well Pleasure, come children and wives,
To fighting musketoes the rest of our lives.[45]

John Trumbull's vigorous caricature of a loyalist supplies a
fitting and fortunate summary: Squire M'Fingal employs "his
time, and tools and talents" helping the government party in
Massachusetts "enslave th' Amer'can wildernesses, / And rend
the provinces in pieces." Endowed by his Highland ancestors
with second sight, he foresees the defeat of the rebels:

Gazettes no sooner rose a lie in,
But strait he fell to prophesying;
Made dreadful slaughter in his course,
O'erthrew provincials, foot and horse,
Brought armies o'er, by sudden pressings,
Of Hanoverians, Swiss and Hessians,
Feasted with blood his Scottish clan,
And hang'd all rebels to a man,
Divided their estates and pelf,
And took a goodly share himself.

At the same time, though, he must accommodate himself to the
times. Speaking for his party in town meeting, he tells the patriots quite frankly:

[45] "The penetential TORY'S LAMENTATION," *Newport Mercury*, Aug. 30,
1783, p. 4.

"we're in peril of our souls
From your vile feathers, tar and poles;
And vows extorted are not binding
In law, and so not worth the minding.
For we have in this hurly-burly
Sent off our consciences on furlow;
Thrown our religion o'er in form,
Our ship to lighten in the storm."

Even after a spade-armed patriot discharges "a blow / Tremendous on his rear below" and he is taken into custody at the Liberty Pole, he boasts, "I'll stand the worst; for recompense / I trust King George and Providence." But after being tarred and feathered and carted through the streets, he revises his earlier prophecy, declaring that the "Whigs will win the day."

"My beck'ning Genius gives command,
And bids me fly the fatal land;
Where changing name and constitution,
Rebellion turns to Revolution,
While Loyalty, oppress'd, in tears,
Stands trembling for its neck and ears." [46]

Granting that the texture of *Hudibras* is inimitable, Trumbull's hero resembles Butler's in attitude and behavior. M'Fingal, like Hudibras, frequently weakens his argument in trying to strengthen it: to the principles of Revolutionary America he opposes those set forth in the British Constitution,

That constitution form'd by sages,
The wonder of all modern ages;
Which owns no failure in reality,
Except corruption and venality. [I, 95]

Like Hudibras, M'Fingal is quarrelsome, boastful, stubborn, one who would bully his opponent into submission on the field or in debate but never quite succeeds in doing either.[47]

[46] The quotations occur in Trumbull, I, 6, 7, 38, 107, 112, 118–119. *M'Fingal* "was published for the first time at Hartford between August 20 and September 10, 1782," Cowie, *Trumbull*, p. 167.

[47] Actually the satirical attack on the loyalists continued after the sign-

Loyalists were as conscientiously motivated as patriots but lacked the patriot courage to revolution. Siding with Crown and Parliament, they saw that authority successfully challenged in America and knew finally the horrors of political bankruptcy.

------

ing of the definitive treaties of peace on Sept. 3, 1783, and the final withdrawal of British troops from New York City three months later. See Louie M. Miner, *Our Rude Forefathers: American Political Verse, 1783–1788* (Cedar Rapids, Iowa, 1937), pp. 54—86.

CHAPTER XII

Conclusion

To call the satirist *Censor Morum* becomes meaningful only as one attempts to define the *status quo* he is defending. Take the Hudibrastic tradition as an example. Whereas the British and their American sympathizers thought that the authority of King and Parliament sanctioned their view of empire, patriots in America, who had in fact been exercising a degree of home rule from the time of the earliest colonial settlements and were only now seeing Britain steadily call it into question, felt justified in attacking this view as gross heresy. Because America was not so homogeneous a society as Butler's England and Americans were not solidly united in opposition to the British view of empire, Hudibrastic writers could ridicule personalities, issues, and events on both sides: Bernard and Gage, George III and members of the Ministry, Burgoyne, Clinton, Cornwallis, Howe, and the editor Rivington, on the one hand; and on the other, Franklin and McDougall, the Continental Association of 1774, the Declaration of Independence, the French Alliance, and the depreciation of paper currency. From this example, and it is representative of the genres that appear in this study, one can only conclude that the two communities of satirists each had a clear conception of what the *status quo* meant, and, save when their sensibilities were too deeply outraged to admit of detachment, each warred vigorously on the side of "virtue" against "vice" and "folly."

These writers all sought the widest possible hearing. And indeed a "great public" was present on every occasion—the levying of Grenville's stamp tax, the convening of the Congress, the consummation of Arnold's treachery—ready to turn a sympathetic ear. None knew how to reach this audience better than Franklin. As colonial agent he managed to conceal from the official class what his left hand was doing, and in a continuous stream of pseudonymous letters to the press not only urged the British nation to avert the holocaust of war but (since many of these letters were reprinted in America) strengthened the patriot community in its resolve to resist Parliamentary authority. By 1775, his mission as press agent in England over, he had gained not merely a national but a transatlantic hearing.

Political satirists in every age seek to touch men's hearts rather than fill their heads, hoping thereby to sway and even to change their beliefs. Thus "the grand American rebellion," as one contemporary put it, was "a legitimate moment for satire." In the struggle toward the declaration and finally the fact of independence the American press, which had been unanimous in its opposition to stamped paper, proved as powerful a lever to revolution as did legislative action and party organization. Not only was the satire that flooded the press from 1765 onward a barometer, it helped shape public opinion. Indeed, the satirical record bears dramatic witness to the truth of John Adams' later assertion that "the Revolution was effected before the war commenced. The Revolution was in the hearts and minds of the people."

The age of satire ushered in by the Stamp Act did not end with the coming of peace, nor did satirists of the Revolution stop writing. To be sure, André and Lee were dead, Bailey, Odell, and Stansbury had gone into exile, and Livingston and Witherspoon now devoted all their time to public service. Trumbull, practically deserting poetry for the law after *M'Fingal*, did collaborate briefly with Barlow, Hopkins, and Humphreys in the composition of *The Anarchiad* (1786–1787), an attack on mob-

ocracy. Hopkinson, continuing his contributions to the Philadelphia press, shortly conceived another successful allegory,
"The New Roof" (1787), written in defense of the new Constitution. Brackenridge composed a long Hudibrastic narrative
against demagoguery, "The Modern Chevalier" (1788–1789),
preliminary to undertaking the still longer picaresque novel,
Modern Chivalry. Franklin, now home from France, addressed
one last ironic letter to the press, "On the Slave Trade" (1790),
before he died. And Freneau, though yielding steadily to the pull
of lyricism, returned to the attack in a series of Antifederalist
essays, *Slender's Letters* (1799).

In an age when men's lives and words formed one seamless
garment, mastery of the patterns of rhetoric brought forth, in
Brackenridge's phrase, "some *d–mn'd* good writers." The high
valuation Revolutionary satirists set on writing well saved many
of them from the danger of flat and stereotyped general expression latent in the theory of neoclassicism. Again Franklin is a
case in point. Although he adhered early and late to such neoclassic ideals as perspicuity, propriety, and purity, he prized
"writing well in his Mother Tongue" so highly as to develop a
vigorous and flexible prose. In fact, so many of his younger
contemporaries achieved a comparable mastery of form and matter that for the moment it seemed as if America had declared her
literary independence from Britain, too. *M'Fingal* and "The
Political Balance," "The Cow-Chace," *A Pretty Story* and "The
Impartial Chronicle," "The Sale of the Hessians"—it would be
many a year before Americans would read their equal.

Bibliographical Note

MOST of the satires whose authorship is now established were published in the following later volumes, some of them for the first time: Ray Palmer Baker, "The Poetry of Jacob Bailey," *New Eng. Quar.*, II (1929), 58–92; *Benjamin Franklin's Letters to the Press, 1758–1775*, ed. Verner W. Crane (Chapel Hill, 1950); *The Writings of Benjamin Franklin*, ed. A. H. Smyth (10 vols.; New York, 1905–1907); *The Miscellaneous Works of Mr. Philip Freneau* (New York, 1788); *The Poems of Philip Freneau*, ed. F. L. Pattee (3 vols.; Princeton, 1902); *The Prose of Philip Freneau*, ed. Philip M. Marsh (New Brunswick, N.J., 1955); *The Miscellaneous Essays and Occasional Writings of Francis Hopkinson* (3 vols.; Philadelphia, 1792) (the second half of vol. 3 contains *Poems on Several Subjects*); *Memoirs of the Life of the Late Charles Lee, Esq.* (New York, 1792); *A Collection of Plays and Poems by the late Col. Robert Munford*, ed. William Munford (Petersburg, Va., 1798); *The Complete Writings of Thomas Paine*, ed. Philip S. Foner (2 vols.; New York, 1945); *The Loyal Verses of Joseph Stansbury and Jonathan Odell*, ed. Winthrop Sargent (Albany, 1860); *The Poetical Works of John Trumbull* (2 vols.; Hartford, Conn., 1820); Mercy Warren, *Poems, Dramatic and Miscellaneous* (Boston, 1790); and *The Works of John Witherspoon* (9 vols.; Edinburgh, 1804–1805). Other satires

were reprinted in *American Broadside Verse*, ed. Ola E. Winslow (New Haven, 1930); *Ballads and Poems Relating to the Burgoyne Campaign*, ed. William L. Stone (Albany, 1893); *Diary of the American Revolution*, ed. Frank Moore (2 vols.; New York, 1860); *Illustrated Ballad History of the American Revolution, 1765–1783*, ed. Frank Moore (New York, 1876; never completed); *The Loyalist Poetry of the Revolution*, ed. Winthrop Sargent (Philadelphia, 1857); *Magazine of History* (Tarrytown, N.Y.), volumes between 1905 and 1922; *Representative Plays by American Dramatists, 1765–1819*, ed. Montrose J. Moses (New York, 1918); and *Songs and Ballads of the American Revolution*, ed. Frank Moore (New York, 1856). In quoting from satires first published in English newspapers and from a few which remained in manuscript until after 1783, I have had to depend on the text established in certain of the volumes above.

The most useful bibliographical aids were Clarence S. Brigham's *History and Bibliography of American Newspapers, 1690–1820* (2 vols.; Worcester, 1947); Charles Evans' *American Bibliography: 1639–1820* (12 vols.; Chicago, 1903–1934); W. C. Ford, "Broadsides, Ballads, etc., Printed in Massachusetts, 1639–1800," *Col. Mass. Hist. Soc.*, LXXV (1922); Oscar Handlin's *Harvard Guide to American History* (Cambridge, Mass., 1954); Charles F. Heartman's *Cradle of the United States, 1765–1789* (Metuchen, N.J., 1922–1923), a check list of 1,000 broadsides and pamphlets, some of them first printed in England; Lyon N. Richardson's *History of Early American Magazines, 1741–1789* (New York, 1931); and W. O. Walters, "American Imprints, 1648–1797, in the Huntington Library, supplementing Evans' *American Bibliography*," *Hunt. Lib. Bull.*, No. 3 (1933), pp. 1–95. Especially helpful in supplying literary and journalistic background were Philip Davidson's *Propaganda and the American Revolution* (Chapel Hill, 1941), Frank Luther Mott's *American Journalism* (New York, 1950), and Moses Coit Tyler's *Literary History of the American Revolution* (2 vols.; New York, 1897). And for their discussion of satire, Richmond P. Bond's *English Burlesque Poetry, 1700–1750* (Cambridge, Mass., 1932) and David Worcester's *Art of Satire* (Cambridge, Mass., 1940). Of works which provide valuable historical background a number deserve special mention. For the British background, Lewis B. Namier's *England in the Age of the American Revolution* (London, 1930) and Charles R. Ritcheson's *British Politics and the American Revolution* (Norman, Okla., 1954). For primary source material on the American background, *Documents of American History*, ed. H. S. Commager (New York, 1958); *Journals of the Continental Congress*, ed. W. C. Ford (34 vols.; Washington, D.C., 1904–1937); and *Letters of Members of the Continental Congress*, ed. E. C. Burnett (8 vols.; Washington, D.C., 1921–1936). And among special studies by period and subject, Carl Becker's *History of Political Parties in the Province of New York, 1760–1776* (Madison, Wis., 1909), Edmund Cody Burnett's *Continental Congress* (New York, 1941), Leonard Labaree's *Conservatism in Early American History* (New York, 1948), John C. Miller's *Origins of the American Revolution* (Boston, 1943) and *Triumph of Freedom* (Boston, 1948), Edmund S. and Helen M. Morgan's *Stamp Act Crisis* (Chapel Hill, 1953), Arthur M. Schlesinger's *Colonial Merchants and the American Revolution* (New York, 1918) and *Prelude to Independence: The Newspaper War on Britain, 1764–1776* (New York, 1958), Claude H. Van Tyne's *Loyalists in the American Revolution* (New York, 1902), and Willard M. Wallace's *Appeal to Arms* (New York, 1951).

A complete entry for these and all other primary and secondary sources is given in the footnotes the first time each is cited, as are reprintings of the satires.

Index